Race and Digital Media

Race and Cultural Minorities

Race and Digital Media

An Introduction

Lori Kido Lopez

polity

First published in 2023 by Polity Press

Polity Press
65 Bridge Street
Cambridge CB2 1UR, UK

Polity Press
101 Station Landing
Suite 300
Medford, MA 02155, USA

ISBN-13: 978-1-5095-4692-3
ISBN-13: 978-1-5095-4693-0(pb)

A catalogue record for this book is available from the British Library.

Library of Congress Control Number: 2022937026

Typeset in 11 on 13pt Plantin
by Cheshire Typesetting Ltd, Cuddington, Cheshire
Printed and bound in Great Britain by CPI Group (UK) Ltd, Croydon

The publisher has used its best endeavours to ensure that the URLs for external websites referred to in this book are correct and active at the time of going to press. However, the publisher has no responsibility for the websites and can make no guarantee that a site will remain live or that the content is or will remain appropriate.

Every effort has been made to trace all copyright holders, but if any have been overlooked the publisher will be pleased to include any necessary credits in any subsequent reprint or edition.

For further information on Polity, visit our website:
politybooks.com

Contents

Acknowledgments

First and foremost, I must acknowledge the scholars at the Center for Critical Race and Digital Studies whose brilliant research inspired this book. Thanks also to the students in my Race and Technology course at the University of Wisconsin-Madison who helped explore these ideas with me in the spring of 2020, even as our semester was massively disrupted by a global pandemic. Indeed, for a book that was written entirely during the social distancing times wrought by COVID-19, I am so thankful for everyone who helped me survive and even thrive. That begins with Jason and Boba, who spent every moment of the pandemic by my side and it was the very best. Also podfam: the weekly human connection and laughter shared with Abby, Monica, and Jonathan brought a sense of normalcy back to an abnormal world. I'm also grateful to Jeremy Morris and Timothy Yu for finding ways to stay connected through it all. Thanks to my colleagues who have provided robust support via Teams and Zoom – Derek Johnson, Elaine Klein, DeVon Wilson, and Theresa Pesavento. Mary Savigar and Stephanie Homer at Polity have done a wonderful job supporting this project and easing the process of publication. And finally, as always, thanks to all of my beloved family cheering for me from Oregon and California – especially my amazing Mom and Dad.

1

Introduction

Key terms

- race and ethnicity
- scientific racism
- DNA testing
- racialization
- racism
- critical race theory
- intersectionality
- colorblindness
- postracism

AS protestors took to the streets in the summer of 2020 to condemn the killing of George Floyd, Breonna Taylor, and many other African Americans, they ignited a sense of urgency about the inextricably bound relationship between race and technology. Amidst a global pandemic that had forced millions of people to work from home, citizens were already fervently tuning in to all forms of digital media for information, entertainment, and social interaction. Yet in this moment, discussions about COVID-19 had been completely replaced with stories about Black activists and their supporters marching across previously empty city streets to demand justice and equality. The Movement for Black Lives had always been a digital movement that relied on hashtags, cell phone videos, mobile apps, and social media networks to grow support and organize collective responses. At the same time, it was also clear that technology played a critical role in exacerbating racial inequities – police had long used algorithms and big data in service of over-policing communities of color, and were now using surveillance technologies and social media data to identify and target activists.

This book affirms that such questions and issues have long been recognized as urgent by scholars of race and digital media, and sets out to provide an introduction to the key concepts that animate research in this area. It begins with the invention of the World Wide Web, addressing the different ways that the rise of the internet was predicted to shape our understandings of race, and the actual realities that followed. Indeed, digital media have always provided both new opportunities and threats to communities of color and others who are systematically marginalized and overlooked. The power dynamics that shape our lives have followed us into the digital world, impacting everything from the workers who control the development of technologies, to the decisions made about their design, the policies that regulate their use, the companies that profit from them, and the many different ways that they are used. This book provides an introduction to scholarship from communication and media studies on the meaning of technology and digital media by specifically centering inquiries about race and the experiences of people of color. It reveals the racial histories and systems of oppression that have continued to harm and limit opportunities for people of color in their relationship to digital media, but also points to the many ways that communities of color have deployed digital media to express themselves, create new modes of communication, and collectively challenge the status quo.

This opening chapter begins by addressing fundamental questions about how to define race and racism. It builds from scholarship by critical race theorists on the salience of both biological and social understandings of race while also explaining how to interpret the increasing use of DNA tests to determine racial heritage. These definitions of race are connected to histories of racism and the rise of global racial discourses – including the institutionalized racism of the transatlantic slave trade, settler colonialism, imperialism, and restrictive citizenship policies. While there have been many strides forward due to anti-racist activism such as the Civil Rights Movement, intersectional feminism, and the contemporary Black Lives Matter movement, it is also important to stay attuned to the ways that racism itself changes form and remains hegemonic amidst social change.

Race: a social construction

In some ways, it can be productive to think of race in very simple terms – for instance, to acknowledge that the experiences of a Black person living in the United States are fundamentally different from the experiences of a white person. Yet race is also an extremely complex process of categorization that has significantly changed over time, and increases in complexity when considered alongside other identities such as gender, class, sexuality, and nation. **Race** is often distinguished from ethnicity in that racial categories such as "Asian" and "Black" are quite broad and simplified categories, while **ethnicity** refers to cultural, linguistic, and sometimes national affiliations. Yet even the distinction between race and ethnicity can be tricky to untangle, as both race and ethnicity refer to symbolic categories and social taxonomies whose overlapping boundaries are constantly being rewritten.

To make sense of these distinctions, we can begin by acknowledging the fact that although racial categories are broadly rooted in phenotype and ancestry, race itself is a social construction. Matthew Desmond and Mustafa Emirbayer (2009) specifically define race as a set of categories that have been misrecognized as natural, when in fact they have been actively created and recreated by human beings. This means that it was not inevitable that we would come to understand a person with brown skin and textured hair as categorically different from a person with pink skin and yellowish hair. Rather, these are differences that have become meaningful through our participation in society, and through the multiple ways that our understanding of important social categories of any kind are upheld – including media representations, education, laws, and cultural customs. Even the use of the term **"people of color"** to describe non-white peoples is a relatively recent linguistic turn starting in the late 1970s. The deliberate use of this term designates a shift away from seeing what were previously pejoratively labeled "colored people" as inferior, instead embracing the power of solidarity that can be created through non-white people coming together as an identity formation. As Michael Omi and Howard Winant (1986) have theorized, "race is a master category – a fundamental concept that has profoundly shaped, and continues to shape, the history, polity, economic structure, and culture of the United States" (106).

Race gives meaning to human bodies and experiences, shaping how they are understood, what power they can have, what opportunities are made available to them.

Yet this is only possible because it has become deeply embedded within the social structures and institutions that organize our lives, and we have come to accept it as such.

Understandings of race as a social construction make logical sense when we probe more deeply into the imprecision and outright absurdity of existing racial categories as they have come to be understood in the United States. Let us begin with the category of "Asian," and the question of which parts of the Asian continent are even included within this racial designation. Indeed, there are 48 different nations encompassed by the massive geopolitical region known as Asia, but the many nations comprising West Asia (including the Middle East and the Arab world) and Central Asia (Kazakhstan, Kyrgyzstan, Tajikistan, Turkmenistan, and Uzbekistan) are typically excluded from the racial category of "Asian." To understand why this is so, we must return to the fact that categories like "Asianness" and "whiteness" cannot be directly traced to geopolitical categories such as national origin. Rather, they are extremely malleable categories that respond to factors such as immigration, foreign policy, and military engagements. The notion of a singular "Asian race" should also be disconcerting given the extreme heterogeneity included within the continent, including the thousands of ethnic groups within each country. In the United States, those who identify racially as Asian might also identify ethnically as Japanese American, Thai American, or Sri Lankan American. At a global level, there is even greater ethnic diversity; for instance, there are 56 different ethnic groups in China, the Philippines can be divided into 175 ethnolinguistic groups, and in India there are over 1,500 different groups that can be divided by language, caste, and tribe. The notion that there is any single quality shared by these different groups is simply nonsensical. While the "Asian race" is typically signified by straight black hair and monolidded eyes (amongst other phenotypical traits), these certainly do not align with all Asians.

The shifting racial categorizations ascribed to Latinidad are also reflective of the fact that race is socially constructed, rather than naturally occurring or biological. Just like the groups of individuals who fall into the category of Asian American, those who are encompassed by the category of "Hispanic" or "Latin American" are also very diverse. While they are colloquially referred to as "Brown," and often share a darker skin tone, eye color, and hair color, these are by no means necessary traits. In recognition of this heterogeneity, the US Census does not recognize Hispanic or Latino as a race, but treats it as an ethnicity that is separate from the category of race. Since the 2010 US Census, those who identify as Hispanic first indicate that they are "Mexican/Mexican American/Chicano," "Puerto Rican," "Cuban," or "Another Hispanic, Latino, Spanish origin," and then they move on to a separate question about race. Those with roots in Hispanic and Latin American countries may identify as white, Black, Asian, American Indian, or another race. This is why Census-based data on race uses terms like "non-Hispanic white" and "Hispanic white" or "non-Hispanic Black" and "Hispanic Black." Even the disparity between the terms "Hispanic" and "Latino" calls attention to the ineffectiveness of such categories. The term "Hispanic" refers to those from Spain and Spanish-speaking countries in Central America and South America, while "Latino" and "Latin American" refers to the geographic region of Latin America so it includes non-Spanish-speaking countries like Brazil and French Guiana but not Spain. Other terms like Latinx are now being introduced as a way to contest the upholding of the gender binary in terms like Latino and Latina.

Finally, we must recognize that there are many individuals across the globe who do not fit into any standard racial categorizations. While in the United States we have typically settled upon the five racial groups of white, Black, Asian, Latino/Hispanic, and Indigenous,* over one million Americans with heritage in

---

* This book capitalizes the terms "Black" and "Indigenous" in recognition of the fact that these racial categories should be respected as

the Middle East and North Africa do not fit comfortably into any of these racial formations. As with the previously discussed racial categories, individuals from Middle Eastern and Northern African regions of the world can share any combination of phenotypes, and the geopolitical boundaries that might define their regions of the world are constantly changing in response to political negotiations. While there was a push to add the category of the Middle East and Northern Africa (MENA) to the US Census in 2020, these attempts were unsuccessful and individuals from these regions must still check the boxes "white" or "other" (Maghbouleh 2020). Indeed, fluctuating membership within the category of "white" itself is yet another way that it becomes clear that race is a social construction with very little bearing on bodily or biological realities.

Science and the biology of race

Yet we also cannot deny that there are biological components to understanding heritage and ancestry, and that body types and forms have shaped understandings and experiences of race. While race may not be a fixed and essential component of one's body, it is clear that physical traits and phenotypes such as skin color, hair texture, eye shape, and notions of biological lineage have become indelibly associated with race. This means that despite any recognition of race as a social construct, the reality is that racial identification consistently occurs at the level of the visible. To make sense of this phenomenon and contradiction, let us examine more deeply the specific ways that biological understandings of race have been shaped and deployed. We can begin with the reality that science has historically been deployed as an instrument of

---

proper nouns and important identities that are parallel to "Asian" and "Hispanic," which have always been capitalized. The term "white" is not capitalized because whiteness is a racial category that is not parallel to the other categories, given the historical context of racialization as a form of racism. It is also important to acknowledge that preferences about capitalization change over time, and that there can be no easy consensus on which system of capitalization is best.

racism, starting in the late eighteenth century. **Scientific racism** refers to the racial hierarchies invented by white intellectuals under the guise of scientific enlightenment to posit that darker-skinned races were less evolved, as well as more primitive and savage than white races. This was connected to the idea that "culture," understood as refined values around art and literature and intellectual accomplishment, was presumed to be something only civilized white people could possess. In this way of thinking, Indigenous and non-European peoples were then clearly judged as inferior. When coupled with insidious stereotypes about the criminality, hypersexuality, and violence inherent to darker races, these assumptions about evolution contributed to cementing racial hierarchies. Yet this was nothing more than pseudoscience, premised on falsified facts and biased logic that masqueraded as real knowledge (Saini 2019).

While communities of color have historically been oppressed by scientific racism and the discourses that are connected to this way of thinking, there are other ways in which science has appeared to uphold understandings of race as a genetic property (rather than merely a social construct). In particular, there has been considerable debate around the science of **DNA testing** alongside the rise of direct-to-consumer genetic tests as a potential way to learn about one's racial or ethnic heritage. Companies like 23andMe, AncestryDNA, MyHeritage, and FamilyTreeDNA take swabs of saliva or cheek samples and process them to identify genetic information and match them against the other samples in their database. This service can result in many different kinds of information about one's family roots, including identifying close family members from their database, as well as offering information about the location of one's ancestors. Such tests are often enthusiastically supported by people of color who are interested in their own ancestral lineage and biology. Alondra Nelson (2016) has studied the different companies that focus specifically on African American DNA, as well as the many lively online communities of Black participants focused on discussing their results. She points to the fact that there are many reasons for the optimism and excitement of African American consumers for genetic testing. African Americans are amongst the many disenfranchised populations in the United States whose history has been systematically destroyed, and scientific knowledge offers a possible opportunity for finally gaining access to their familial histories. As Nelson argues, genetic tests have also played a key role in the rise of discourse around claiming reparations for the descendants of slaves. If the US government were to provide financial reparations to African Americans for the injustices of slavery, DNA tests could be useful in determining who fits into this category.

This question of how DNA tests could be used to help provide certain forms of equality and justice to historically disempowered communities can also be seen in Native American political struggles. Governmentally instituted practices of blood quantum have historically used lineage and ancestry to determine the distribution of land to Native Americans. The term **blood quantum** describes the practice of measuring exactly what fraction of "Indian blood" one possesses, based on how many parents or other ancestors are documented as fully Native American. Since the US government had a vested interested in limiting Native American resources and access, it was productive to require individuals to prove that they possessed a certain percentage of tribal ancestry. That idea became more complicated over time, as tribal sovereignty granted tribes the ability to decide for themselves how to determine citizenship and belonging. The metaphor of "blood" as identity is still powerful for Native Americans, both culturally and because it is through ancestral heritage that sovereignty and citizenship are designated (TallBear 2013).

But what is it that genetic tests can actually tell an individual about their racial or ethnic heritage? Despite these different situations in which it might be beneficial for people of color to learn more about their ancestry or document it in an official capacity, the reality is that DNA tests are extremely limited in their efficacy when it comes to racial identification. First, the outcome of the tests is dependent on the size and depth of each company's own databases, which are proprietary and not shared with other companies. Since white people with European ancestors have traditionally been the most interested in genealogy, genomic databases are most accurate for that population and have significantly less data about African, Latin American, Asian, and Indigenous populations (Chow-White and Duster 2011). Moreover, the kinds of information that can be gleaned from a genetic test are partial and incomplete, as the tests examine only a very small percentage of one's total ancestry. Because of this testing limitation, it is possible for a direct descendant of Native American ancestors to take a DNA test and receive results saying that there is no evidence of such heritage.

This is why the technology of DNA tests must be understood as harmful in how they have contributed to problematic understandings of race. Not only do they promote the idea that race is present in our genetic code, but they can also potentially promote a return to scientific racism. The reality is that all human beings share nearly all of our DNA; it is less than one-tenth of 1 percent variation in our genetic code that leads to perceived differences in our bodies. Since Africa is the most genetically diverse continent on the planet, there is actually more genetic variation within the continent of Africa than between African Americans and those who are presumed to be of a different race, such as Europeans and Asians (Yu et al. 2002). Together these findings help us to see that there are biological components to race, but they are far less significant than the impact of biology on our understanding of race and its relationship to histories of racism.

Racism: a structuring discourse

To understand the structuring impact of racism throughout western society, we must acknowledge that race itself was created through racial hatred. Prior to the colonization of the new world in the sixteenth century, group identities were often connected to attributes like language, nationality, or tribe, rather than broader notions of race. But as European settlers started invading the New World in search of resources, ideologies of racial superiority could be deployed as justification for claiming the lands of what were considered "uncivilized" Indigenous peoples. In North America, there was an opportunity to do more than extract resources and goods for the benefit of European markets – under logics of settler colonialism, these were new lands that European colonizers decided to make their own, if they could only remove or exterminate the Indigenous owners who currently populated it. In framing

Indigenous communities as less than human, the hostile occupying forces could then deny their rights to their own land and sovereignty. As Natsu Taylor Saito argues, we must understand settler colonialism as inherently connected to all racial inequities because it stems from the same impulse: "People of color have been racialized in ways that facilitate strategies intended to eliminate them, physically and conceptually, to exploit their labor, to contain and control them, and to force them into an assimilationist paradigm that nullifies their extant identities, thereby preempting them from exercising their inherent right to self-determination" (Saito 2020: 54). The genocide of Indigenous peoples paved the way for the creation of a settler class that naturalized the racial dominance of white colonizers.

Following the elimination and removal of a significant number of Indigenous peoples, settler occupants then faced the need for a labor force to work their newly seized land. The transatlantic slave trade was used as a mechanism for bringing millions of African captives to the Americas for the economic benefit of white landowners. Along with native peoples, racial hierarchies justified the deployment of this unpaid labor force and the complete dehumanization of an entire population of enslaved Africans. Given the power of the church in Western Europe, religious leaders had already long maintained their dominance through preaching that Christianity was a superior belief system to the indigenous religions of Africa and Indigenous peoples. These beliefs were then strengthened through racial taxonomies designed to prove that the white race was distinct and superior in every way (Fredrickson 1989). These logics of racial superiority were easily transferable to other groups white settlers sought to subdue and disempower to maintain their dominance.

For instance, the racialization of Latinos and Latinas was connected to territorial disputes between the United States and Mexico. **Racialization** is the process of creating race or ascribing a racial identity to something that might not naturally be distinguished by race. After the Mexican–American War led to the territorial expansion of the United States into Mexican territory in 1848, it was in the interest of the United States to frame Mexicans and other Latinos as violent threats to be overpowered. That is, it made sense to fundamentally distinguish white Americans from these newly created Mexican Americans, and race provided the mechanism for creating that distinction. While the Treaty of Guadalupe Hidalgo gave access to citizenship for Mexicans living in the territory awarded to the United States following the Mexican–American War, this does not mean that they were protected or given equal access to benefits like land ownership. As part of the process of racialization, Mexicans were stereotyped as inassimilable and lazy workers who posed a threat to white jobs. Worse yet, they were also subject to physical attacks and violence. Between 1848 and 1928, thousands of Mexicans and Mexican Americans living in the Southwest were lynched amidst outbreaks of monstrous mob violence and vigilantism (Carrigan and Webb 2013). Then in the 1930s as fears during the Great Depression morphed into scapegoating Mexican American communities, nearly one million Mexican Americans and Mexicans living in the United States were deported to Mexico (Balderrama and Rodríguez 1995).

Through this history and many others, we can see that the fear of non-white foreigners has been central to the concept of the United States for hundreds of years.

The very first immigration law, the Nationality Act of 1790, states that citizenship by naturalization was a benefit restricted to free white persons. This policy was designed to exclude non-white immigrants, in addition to Native Americans and free Black people. But such policies are also connected to race-based restrictions on land ownership, voting rights, access to employment, opportunities to grow one's family, and other important necessities. These are some of the many ways that racism can be understood as indigenous to the United States. **Racism** is a term often used to describe an interpersonal conflict initiated by an individual person who hates, fears or otherwise devalues people of other races. While this kind of racism does exist, these histories show us why it is important to understand that racism is actually structural, created through the policies, practices, and institutions that serve to maintain racial hierarchies and contribute to racial inequalities for generations.

Responses to racism

It is also important to recognize that as long as there has been racism, there has been anti-racism and resistance from people of color. Race may have been created through the desire for white domination and the systematic use of violence and exploitation to maintain it, but oppressed peoples have always fought for their freedom and autonomy. Anti-racism is more than an abstract belief that racism is wrong; it is a rigorous political tradition that has been taken up through direct engagement designed to confront every form of racism (Zamalin 2019). Enslaved Africans and Indigenous peoples organized rebellions and fought to liberate themselves, with abolitionists like Frederick Douglass and fugitive slave Harriet Tubman opposing slavery in the early days of the United States. Following Reconstruction and the unfinished project of granting African American civil liberties, Black activists fought for voting rights and an end to the laws that perpetuated racial violence. The Civil Rights Movement of the 1960s and the Black Lives Matter movement starting in 2013 are all part of the strong force of opposition mounted by anti-racist activists and community organizers.

An important academic theory that calls attention to this understanding of racism and anti-racism is **critical race theory**. Originally developed by legal scholars 1970s, critical race theory emerged as a response to the way that racism was becoming more covert and misunderstood under the guise of racial progress. Scholars like Kimberlé Crenshaw, Derrick Bell, Alan Freeman, and Richard Delgado put forward a school of thought that argued that racism must be recognized as an ordinary aspect of our society because it has become so deeply institutionalized within law, policy, and other social structures. In its efforts to expose the truth about race as endemic to our society, critical race theory is deeply interested in strengthening opposition to racism. It points to how race is a social construct that gains meaning through processes of racialization, but also through its relation to other axes of identity like gender, class, and sexuality. Kimberlé Crenshaw's theory of **intersectionality** specifically highlights the way that individuals can face multiple forms of oppression due to their different social identities. Indeed, Black women like abolition-ist Sojourner Truth had been calling attention to these realities for over a century. For instance, a Black woman could face discrimination due to her race, her gender, or the combination of both and others that exacerbate one another. This is important, because political struggles for liberation often focus on only one axis of identity at a time, and this limited perspective can neglect the ways that certain communities are being left behind or remain disenfranchised.

The reality is that racism persists, changing form and evolving in our digital era in order to retain its power. Indeed, the theory of hegemony tells us that powerful groups are always under attack, but that they maintain their dominance by shifting slightly without ultimately ceding power. In this case, white supremacy and racism have remained hegemonic in the face of immense gains by communities of color and anti-racist activism. Some major shifts in the discourse surrounding racism have been the rise of colorblindness and postracism. **Colorblindness** is the philosophy that if we want to do away with racism, the best way to do that is to simply stop acknowledging race itself. It is often troublingly linked to following the words of Dr Martin Luther King Jr, who famously stated that he dreamed of living in a society where people "will not be judged by the color of their skin, but by the content of their character." This is taken to mean that we should celebrate the idea of a meritocracy where individuals are judged on their own merits, as if it is possible to remove race from the equation altogether. Some of the practical expressions of colorblindness have been to avoid recording racial demographics on official forms and discontinue race-based programs like affirmative action and other policies designed to remedy the harmful effects of racism. Eduardo Bonilla-Silva calls colorblindness a new form of racism, or an ideology that maintains the racial order by serving "as the ideological armor for a covert and institutionalized system in the post-civil rights era . . . Shielded by color-blindness, whites can express resentment toward minorities; criticize their morality, values, and work ethics; and even claim to be victims of 'reverse racism'" (Bonilla-Silva 2017: 3–4). Indeed, colorblind ideologies are deeply harmful to people of color since they simultaneously weaken abilities to measure the racial inequities that continue to

multiply while also removing the social programs that might alleviate racial injustices and support people of color.

A concomitant ideology about race that has become prevalent
is **postracism**. This refers to the assumption that racism has been
solved and we no longer need to focus on the problems of race.
The rise of postracial discourse has largely been linked to the election of US President Barack Obama in 2008 since some believed
that racism must no longer exist if an African American man can
be elected to the highest office in the land (Squires 2014). It is a
framework that has come to be infused throughout all aspects of
culture, shaping discourses around public policy, media, education, business and industry, and popular culture. Both colorblindness and postracism seem positive in acknowledging that racism is
dangerous and racial progress is desirable, but it is clear that they
both actually serve to sustain racism and inhibit anti-racist measures and policies. One of the lasting legacies of colorblind and
postracial ideologies is to uphold the strength of white privilege
and whiteness as the norm, while making it more difficult to truly
assess the impact of racial difference. As Sarah Banet-Weiser,
Roopali Mukherjee, and Herman Gray argue, "the work of the
postracial within racial capitalism is to critique, demonize, and
resist, as an instance of race and racial thinking, the notion of a
collective commitment to the common good and the role of the
state in protecting the common good against rapacious privatized
incentives of the market" (Banet-Weiser, Mukherjee, and Gray
2019). This desire to avoid or deliberately disregard the enduring
impact of race and racism in our digital world has contributed to
many harmful outcomes, and provides a threat to many potentially productive policies and interventions.

In some ways, the fantasy that we have arrived in a postracial
America has been resoundingly punctured by the resurgence of
explicitly racist forces following the election of President Donald
Trump. When faced with the conspicuous rise of neo-Nazi and
white supremacist organizations, heightened rhetorics around
Mexicans as dangerous and threatening enemies, the many high-
profile killings of unarmed African Americans by police officers and vigilantes, the institution of anti-Muslim immigration
policies, and waves of violence against Asian Americans who
were blamed for the COVID-19 pandemic, it seems clearer than

ever that racism is alive and well. Yet an important component of this new wave of racism is that postracial discourses continue to be actively deployed as a justification for terminating anti-racist programs and activities. For instance, we have seen a wave of legislation attempting to ban diversity trainings and the teaching of critical race theory in schools. Some of the primary justifications for these bills center on the assertion that we have already accomplished racial progress, and we no longer need to learn about or discuss histories of racism or their continuing impact on contemporary US society. This becomes yet another example of how racism evolves in relation to anti-racist activism and education. We must continue to forward a critical historical perspective that calls attention to the persistence of racist projects in all of their many forms and expressions – including the focus of this book, our digital media landscape.

Overview of the book

The goal of this book is to introduce the wide body of scholarly literature and academic theories pertaining to the relationship between race and digital media. It particularly focuses on the specific racial constructions and identity formations that have arisen around race in the United States, as historical and cultural contexts are important when trying to make sense of race. But it also points to broader global issues when possible and is most salient in drawing connections to countries with similar racial dynamics such as Canada and the United Kingdom. The primary questions that the book sets out to answer are as follows: How has the evolution of digital media and technology shaped racial realities? How have people of color shaped digital media? How are racism and white supremacy systematically upheld through digital media? And, what can be done to alleviate the racial inequalities engendered by digital media?

While studies of whiteness and the white actors who have materially benefited from racism are important components of understanding race, this book attempts to most prominently center the experiences and voices of people of color. This approach is not meant to imply that race is a characteristic that only belongs to non-white communities. Rather, it seeks to rectify the problem within digital studies scholarship wherein whiteness has always been centered and the important contributions of scholars of color have so often been minimized and overlooked. This book intentionally calls attention to the interactions between people of color and digital media and, where possible, foregrounds the way that people of color have understood their own minoritized communities. Chapter 2 begins with a discussion of the early internet, highlighting scholarship around the rise of the World Wide Web that theorized how cyberspace might change our relationship to race. It also explores how concerns about digital divides focused on racialized issues of access to digital technologies, and how communities of color were actually engaging in creating some of the first websites and platforms to target minority communities.

Chapters 3 and 4 then move into explorations of the dynamics and processes that undergird media technologies – the way that they are created, the infrastructures that support them, and the actual communities that labor behind the scenes. Chapter 3 begins with the rise of Silicon Valley and points to histories of women, people of color, and other marginalized communities who have been employed to support technology development. It also considers the harm of tech industries on physical environments and global communities of color. These questions are also taken up in chapter 4, which focuses on race and media infrastructures, or the environmental and sociopolitical conditions that shape the material stuff of digital media. This includes physical components like cables, data centers, and satellite dishes, as well as digital architectures such as interfaces, platforms, and code.

Chapters 5 and 6 examine the impact of algorithms, artificial intelligence, and machine learning on communities of color. This begins with an exploration of algorithmic bias in cases where computational logics are used for decision making in ways that can have uneven social consequences. Chapter 6 specifically focuses on the use of digital technologies for increased surveillance and the way that communities of color face simultaneous hypervisibility and invisibility as a result. It looks at how technologies like facial recognition, biometrics, visual sensors, and other forms of surveillance have systematically harmed people of color. This becomes particularly dangerous when these tools are applied in areas like border security and policing, which already have troubled relationships to Black and Brown communities.

Chapter 7 takes these numerous concerns about how digital technologies can be harmful and asks what can be done to regulate or otherwise guide their development and usage. This includes the potential for governmental policy to be wielded as a form of citizen protection, but also for corporations to engage in self-regulation through the use of codes, initiatives, and programs designed to mitigate harm. Chapter 8 continues this transition away from the harms of technology toward the solutions engendered by communities of color, exploring the many different forms of activism that have been facilitated through digital media. It looks at the Black Lives Matter movement, the use of Twitter hashtags for social justice, digital testimonio and storytelling through YouTube, meme activism, and other uses of technology focused on bringing about social change. Chapter 9 focuses specifically on digital games as a venue for this kind of activism, looking at how serious games and virtual reality applications have offered potentially meaningful outlets for using technology to educate and create empathy. While video games and other interactive technologies have long been recognized for their dangerous cultures of toxic masculinity and explicit racial hatred, it is also important to recognize their potential capacity for pro-social impact.

The positive potentials of digital media for people of color are also the focus of chapter 10, which examines the way that digital tools can promote a stronger sense of community and connection. This includes the use of Twitter to create racialized counterpublics where like-minded users can share in humor, pop culture fandom, and other forms of connection that are somewhat shielded from the mainstream. Minority communities have also used digital media to form life-saving connections across diasporas, to document and archive their languages and histories, and to tell culturally specific and resonant stories. Finally, chapter 11 concludes the book by turning to the future, examining the many different expressions of futurism taken up by communities of color – including Afrofuturism, Latinx futurism, and Indigenous futurism. In these and other sci-fi-inspired dreams for the future, we can see the potential for technology to help shape a better, more just world that overcomes many of the limits and shortcomings of our current digital landscape. While much of this book is centrally focused on exposing the harms of racism as expressed and enabled through digital media, perhaps concluding on these hopes for the future can help to set the direction for a better path that is authored and facilitated by those who have been harmed the most.

Key questions

1. What does it mean to say that race is a social construction, and what are some of the problems that come with how race has been socially constructed?
2. What are some of the origins of racism as an institutional and structural force throughout history?
3. How do discourses of colorblindness and postracism serve to uphold the harms of racism?

Further reading

Banet-Weiser, Sarah, Mukherjee, Roopali, and Gray, Herman. 2019. *Racism Postrace*. Durham, NC: Duke University Press.

Omi, Michael, and Winant, Howard. 1986. *Racial Formation in the United States*. New York: Routledge.

Zamalin, Alex. 2019. *Antiracism: An Introduction*. New York: New York University Press.

2

The Early Internet

Key terms

- cyberrace
- identity tourism
- digital divides
- digital media literacy
- Web 2.0
- online racism

Introduction

TECHNOLOGY is always changing shape – hardware gets upgraded, software gets rewritten, some platforms rise into prominence while others fall into obsolescence, and all the while users are constantly migrating from one form of technology to another. In order to understand where we are today and where we are heading with regard to race and digital media, we must first look backward. Indeed, any writing on technology can only strive to capture the briefest glimpse of the current digital landscape before it appears to grow outdated, succumbing to the allure of the latest bright shiny development. Yet scholars of race and digital media have established a robust foundation of scholarship since the early days of the internet that can help us to better navigate this dynamic terrain. By grounding our understanding within the lessons learned during the arrival of the digital turn, we can be better positioned to make sense of our contemporary media landscape – which we must always understand as tomorrow's history.

This chapter examines scholarship about the early days of the internet and the World Wide Web in relation to race, including the hopes that its emergence would dramatically shift understandings of race. It asks what the early internet was like and how it has changed over time, connecting imaginings of "cyberrace" to the exploration of identity tourism online. In doing so, this chapter continues to build on fundamental understandings of what race and racial identity mean in the digital age. This chapter also explores some of the first conversations around digital divides and questions about how access to technology has been racialized, in addition to how debates around digital divides and digital literacy have evolved to include more nuanced questions about access and usage. It moves from Web 1.0 to Web 2.0 and considers the different ways that racial formations and racism have changed shape alongside these technological evolutions, as well as how communities of color have made use of these media along the way.

Dreams for cyberrace

In the early days of the internet, the shifting nature of technology was identified as a potential opportunity to disrupt the logics of racial schemas. To understand this potential, we must first reflect on the birth of the World Wide Web in the 1990s and what its technological innovations offered to users. During the rise of the information superhighway known as the internet, applications were heavily text-based rather than image-based. Users marveled at their ability to visit web pages linked together through the click of a button, arriving via browsers like Mosaic and Netscape to discover catalogues of information and lists of hyperlinks that pointed them to other sites. While traditional forms of media like television, radio, and movies merely presented static content, the internet was premised on a level of interactivity that seemed to promise freedom, personalization, and control (Ankerson 2018). Communication was facilitated through email and email list-servs, chatrooms, real-time messaging programs like AOL Instant Messenger, and posting forums such as bulletin boards. Most users accessed the internet through a dial-up connection on their telephone line that limited how much data could be transmitted.

At its maximum, dial-up connections could transmit 56 kilobytes per second (kbps), as compared to later forms of broadband and cable internet connections that could transmit up to 100 megabytes per second (mbps). Due to the slow speed of data transfer on dial-up, it was difficult to upload or access bigger files like images and videos, which is why content was predominantly text-based. Despite these limitations, digital connections starting in the early 1990s nonetheless allowed users to connect across vast geographic space in powerful and unprecedented ways.

Jerry Kang (1999) was one of the first to consider the way that race might be shaped by the pre-graphic internet. He applies the prefix "cyber-" to what we know about race, asking how race, racism, and race relations could be impacted or disrupted by the quickly developing global web of communication technologies known as cyberspace. He argues that **cyberrace** has both redemptive and repressive potential for racial minorities, and that we will need to make an informed choice about which possibilities to encourage and which to avoid. Building from the tenets of critical race theory, he acknowledges that race is a social construction that may lack in biological bases, but that racism nonetheless has real consequences. As scholars like Kimberlé Crenshaw (1990) and Howard Omi and Michael Winant (1986) have argued in their landmark publications, race and other intersectional forms of oppression are structural and deeply embedded within all aspects of society – including within politics, economics, culture, language, and social institutions. Because of this, efforts to reframe race will necessarily require complex and multifaceted solutions.

One of the possibilities Kang imagines for reshaping racial dynamics through cyber-interactions is abolition, or engaging in racial anonymity by preventing the kinds of racial recognition that come from visual or verbal cues in real encounters. Kang suggests that while this might be possible within the world of typed text, it is both naive and unfeasible to imagine that this kind of identity cloaking can entirely eliminate race. If race is to be identified within cyberspace, other possibilities for disruption might include promoting racial integration through increased social contact across different racial communities, or allowing for racial transmutation when individuals decide to engage in cyber-passing as a race that is not their own. The paper is merely hypothetical in imagining some of the different impacts that may one day be realized with careful design strategies. As Kang states: "We should see cyberspace . . . as a new universe, which we build potentially without the constraints that bind real space . . . I genuinely fear that cyberspace will reinscribe a repressive racial mechanics even deeper into our nation. This paper is a plea to build toward redemption instead" (Kang 1999: 1208). Such fantasies of how technology could or would liberate us from the oppressions of the past were also visualized in a number of commercials, such as Apple's famous 1984 ad that depicted a dystopian future of monotony and bureaucratic control being destroyed by Apple's Macintosh computer.

While these different orientations to racial identity online have been realized in different ways, it was certainly the case that race was explicitly foregrounded in some of the earliest online communities. One of the communities where we can see this in action is race-based Usenet newsgroups. Starting in 1980, Usenet was a discussion system that resembled an online forum or bulletin board discussion. Users could read and post to thousands of threaded discussions with communities all across the globe, such as the race-based newsgroups focused on the social issues and cultures of African American (soc.culture.african.american) and Mexican American (soc.culture.mexican.american) communities. In Byron Burkhalter's (1999) exploration of these particular groups, he argues that racial identity in online newsgroups may have moved from visual and corporeal cues to the author's stated identity and the textual clues embedded within the author's writing. Yet he claims that race in these online interactions is "no more ambiguous than offline" as it is also firmly established through the use of particular subject headings (such as "Sisters please explain," which references African American women), explicit self-identifications, and contextual clues based on insider knowledge about racialized communities. This does not mean that deception about identity is not taking place, and Burkhalter identifies many interactions where users challenge one another about their true racial identities. Nonetheless, such Usenet groups demonstrate one way that race directly shaped digital interactions and community formations.

Identity tourism

As scholars continued to consider how racial identities might come to be reconfigured in the age of the internet, some of the defining characteristics of online race could be identified. Lisa Nakamura points out that understandings of cyberrace build from Lev Manovich's logics of new media, particularly with regard to allowing users a certain degree of selection and modification in the way that they represent and experience their identities online. Yet as Nakamura states, "If cyberrace was distinguished from 'real' race by its anonymity, composability, variability, and modularity, the task of debunking it as inherently liberatory was linked to critiquing new-media utopianism generally" (Nakamura 2008: 1674–5). By this she means that the dream of digital race being infinitely mutable neglects the very real constraints that users face, stemming from both technical and social considerations. Some of these limits and realities become visible when white users use digital mechanisms for appropriating or playing with putting on the identities of people of color.

In her 2002 book *Cybertypes: Race, Ethnicity, and Identity on the Internet*, Nakamura explores the phenomenon of racial passing in early cyberspace. While the internet first limited personal identification to what could be described through text, the technology soon transitioned to a more visual and graphic medium that allowed visual images to stand in for one's identity. This is particularly salient within sites that invite the creation of user profiles, as users can then use visual images of a different race from their own. A virtual community called LambdaMOO that was popular in the 1990s invited users to give themselves a name and written self-description, which is recognized as more of a "character" than a direct representation of the user. But Nakamura describes a prevalent culture of users giving themselves racially coded names like "Bruce Lee" and "Miura Tetsuo," which allows players to appropriate Asian racial identities. She uses the term **identity tourism** to describe the practice of performing a racial identity that is not your own, as users experience racial crossing temporarily and recreationally. Like all forms of tourism, this practice can represent a superficial engagement with a foreign culture, and moreover can reinforce racist stereotypes and tropes.

If a white user puts on the identity of a person of color to play an online game, they remain insulated from the risks and real-world consequences of being a person of color throughout every other aspect of their life.

This kind of identity tourism can also insulate white users from acknowledging their own racial biases, as it may be perceived as a progressive way of "playing with" race without necessitating reflection on these limits.

While the fantasy of a postracial digital utopia and its political possibilities has been largely dismantled, these initial theorizations of how racial identity can be manipulated and modulated online have remained salient and troubling. In 2019, these issues came to the fore on a Reddit forum called "Black People of Twitter." Just as users could take on any identity they wanted when chatting on LambdaMOO, users posting anonymously or pseudonymously to the online forums hosted by Reddit can also take on whatever identity they choose. A *New York Times* article discussing the forum described the problem that had emerged:

> Many black users came to believe that white users were pretending to be black to give their unpopular opinions more credibility. Some of the posts casually dropped racial slurs. Others repeated anti-black stereotypes about crime, parenting and intelligence. Beyoncé was disparaged . . . The weight of unseen white opinion also made itself felt through the Reddit ranking system, in which posts and comments rise or fall in visibility based on users clicking on the "up" or "down" arrows next to each. (Harmon 2019)

In a post that originated as an April Fool's joke, the moderators announced that they would be verifying Black users who submitted a photograph of their forearm proving they were not white. While the idea of requiring visual proof of blackness was meant to be temporary, the moderators wanted to continue prioritizing comment threads from non-white participants as a way of maintaining the culture of centering Black perspectives and safety. These questions about the veracity of racial identity online clearly remain unresolved and complex, as digital platforms continue to provide opportunities for identity play and identity performance that can have racial consequences.

Unequal access and digital participation

Some of the main concerns about identity tourism have been centered on the assumption that the typical internet user is white and male, and that this is a problem that needs to be rectified. Such concerns are encapsulated in studies of **digital divides**, or the gap between those who do and those who do not have access to the internet and other forms of digital technologies. Since the first days of the internet this has been an issue of great concern, given the fact that digital media can play such an integral role in so many parts of daily life and support full participation in society. For instance, the internet has become a necessary tool for accessing opportunities and necessities related to employment, education, healthcare, and government benefits. It is also used for gathering information, learning about news and current events, socializing, connecting with friends and relatives, dating, buying and selling items, and entertainment. With so many uses for the internet and digital media, access and the ability to safely and securely use these technologies have been recognized as a basic human right. In resolutions from 2011 and 2016, the United Nations released reports stating that disconnecting people from the internet was a human rights violation and that it is a basic human principle that our rights must be protected online in the same way that they are protected offline (Vincent 2016).

Yet the concept of a digital divide is also extremely complex, and should not be taken as a simple binary between two kinds of populations, the "haves" and "have nots." Rather, it is important to recognize that there are many different kinds of digital divides and we must take a careful and nuanced approach to understand its many layers. First, consumers span a wide range of relationships to digital technology from complete abstention and exclusion to total integration and mastery, but most people actually reside somewhere in the middle of this shifting spectrum. There are also many different facets of access and use, as one's relationship to technology is shaped by multiple factors such as whether or not it is available, desirable, approachable, useful, necessary, or rewarding. The decisions that one makes and the agency possessed in making that decision can all impact that relationship. This is why scholars of digital divides have shifted from simply focusing on physical access (namely, possession of a computer and an internet connection) to considering skills and usage, or digital literacies and competencies. Finally, what counts as digital technology can also change our understanding of digital divides. In terms of devices, we could consider the possession of a computer, laptop, or smartphone. But the usefulness of such an object is dependent on far more factors than mere possession. As Jan Van Dijk (2020) points out, we could consider the difference between private ownership and public access to shared technologies, as well as access to computing necessities like software, electricity, apps, and subscription services. There are also many different kinds of internet access and these differences shape the ability of users to make use of certain services such as through one's workplace or educational network, as well as to stream, download, or share content. Since digital technologies encompass a wide range of gadgets and their capabilities, it is important to consider these multifaceted issues.

Throughout all of these understandings of digital divides, race has remained an important factor that shapes both access and use. This makes sense since digital inequalities are deeply connected to social inequalities of all kinds. In the first decade of internet connectivity, research showed alarming disparities between white and Asian users and Black, Latinx, and Indigenous users. For instance, in 2000 a study by the Pew Research Center revealed that 72% of Asian Americans and 53% of white Americans used the internet, while only 46% of Hispanic and 38% of African Americans used the internet (Perrin and Duggan 2015). In the years since then, the focus of digital divide scholarship has moved from usage to questions of engagement. Even if someone has a computer, there can still be lags in **digital media literacy**, or the technical proficiencies, social dispositions, and critical thinking skills that support deeper participation and engagement with new media technologies. In combination with the reality that factors such as lower incomes, housing and employment instability, and other resource constraints impact a family's access to stable broadband internet connections, struggles to develop digital media literacy can combine with access struggles to disproportionately limit Black and Brown youth. This can lead to equity issues, as so many social and economic opportunities are premised on a high degree of digital engagement.

But these discourses about a racialized digital divide have also shifted from concerns about imbalances that harm racial minorities to recognition that these dynamics have been reversed in some cases. Anna Everett describes a discursive shift in the 1990s from Black technophobia, or a belief in a Black intellectual lag, to an overenthusiastic celebration of Black technophilia. She becomes concerned about "this emerging black cyberfever, [as] the sporadic nature and incredulous tone of much of the coverage betrays a sense of condescension, ghettoization, trivialization, and a general air of dismissiveness" (Everett 2002: 133). This bipolar framework was exacerbated in the 2010s, as Black and Latinx youth moved to a position of being on the forefront of technology adoption (Watkins 2018). In particular, youth of color were accessing social media and mobile media at extremely high rates – sometimes at even higher rates than their white peers. Black and Brown youth have also been recognized as trendsetters within social media platforms, posting creative and spreadable content that is then taken up by peers and followers of all ages.

Racially specific websites and homepages

While there have always been concerns about disproportionate rates of internet access, the reality is that millions of people of color have always been active participants online.

One of the ways to understand their digital participation is to look at the most popular online communities and spaces targeted to racial minorities. Indeed, long before the invention of social networking platforms Facebook and Twitter, and even before their predecessors Myspace and Friendster, people of color were connecting to one another through sites like AsianAvenue.com, BlackPlanet.com, and MiGente.com. Launched by the parent company Community Connect, Inc. (CCI), these three sites are noteworthy for being among the first wave of social networking sites. They were tremendously popular within Asian American, African American, and Hispanic communities, attracting millions of users in their first couple of years. In Dara Byrne's study of minority youth online, she narrates the history of CCI's first site AsianAvenue being introduced in 1997, BlackPlanet in 1999, and MiGente in 2000. Each site quickly became the leading website for their respective racial communities, with more than 2.2 million members in AsianAvenue's first two years, more than 1 million members in BlackPlanet after one year and over 5.3 million after three years (Byrne 2008: 16). While the parent company CCI was acquired by Radio One in 2008 and both AsianAvenue and MiGente folded, these early platforms nonetheless affirm the enduring salience of racial identification in online communities. Millions of users on these platforms were drawn in by the opportunity to create their own profiles and share them with others from a similar racial or ethnic background. Not only do the sites flag specific racial identities as an implied requirement for participation in these digital communities, but the conversations taking place within their most popular forums also explicitly discussed racial and ethnic identities on a regular basis (Byrne 2008).

An important early online community for Indigenous users was the site CyberPowWow, developed by Mohawk artist Skawennati and operated from 1997 to 2004. As Skawennati describes, the site started off as a "virtual exhibition and chat space that would dispel the myth that Native artists didn't (or couldn't!?) use technology in their work. In addition to that, we wanted to claim for ourselves a little corner of cyberspace that we could nurture and grow in the way we wanted" (Skawennati, n.d.). The platform allowed users to create and customize their own chatrooms, called "palaces," and was designed for ease of use so as to be welcoming for new users. While many of the first chatrooms focused on textual interactions, CyberPowWow was targeted specifically to Indigenous artists who could use the site as a performance venue, as well as for sharing their own visual and installation art, designs, and custom codes that made use of HTML, Flash animation, and digital imagery. It became a "remediation of the powwow: a significant real-life indigenous ceremony that plays a substantive role in establishing and maintaining indigenous spaces in urban settings" (Gaertner 2015: 58). This claimed parcel of cyberspace served as a defiant act of community building in the face of colonialism and dispossession, but also expanded the idea of Indian territory beyond geographically circumscribed boundaries.

Another set of ethnically specific websites in the 1990s were those built by communities of color living across global diasporas. Anna Everett (2002) argues that African diasporic communities were among the first to respond to the allure of cyberspace, with African nationals and expatriates living abroad creating websites such as the African National Congress, the Afro-Caribbean Chamber of Commerce, Canadian Artists' Network: Black Artists in Action, and Africa Online. A network called Naijanet was developed for Nigerians abroad, and was robust enough to spin off a number of other related online networks. As Everett states: "Because the digitized postcolonial condition forestalls the necessity of putting real flesh and blood bodies on the line in service to the nation-state – taking primacy over ethnic group allegiance – Naijanetters used their virtual bodies regularly to challenge and contest one another as well as to amplify problems in their homeland" (Everett 2002: 140). For instance, Nigerians across the diaspora could use the online forum to debate the politics of language and issues of gender oppression. The use of cyberspace for connecting diasporic communities can also be seen in the South Asian diaspora, which was even more intimately tied to the rise of technocultures. As Madhavi Mallapragada points out in her analysis of Indian Americans online, "the dot-com boom of the mid-1990s . . . was inextricably linked to the rise of Indian immigrants in the field of venture capital, Silicon Valley start-ups, and web entrepreneurial networks. Not surprisingly, the Web was projected as a familiar space as all things 'Indian' were becoming accessible online" (Mallapragada 2014: 7). Sites like webindia.com, search engines indiainfo.com and indiaworld.com, e-commerce sites like indiaplaza.com, and others were developed to target Indian immigrants in the United States. Mallapragada argues that just as homepages are understood as a primary unit of identification in online media, Indian websites also serve as a powerful anchor and space of belonging for Indian immigrants in the diaspora.

While these websites are designed to explicitly create connections between racially and ethnically demarcated users, not all websites are so clearly racially marked. Charlton McIlwain (2017) points out that if we want to know how the racial inequalities are embedded into the structure of the internet, it is important to understand how websites are racially organized and what counts as, for instance, a "Black website." The problem of racial classifications for information has long plagued both scholars and the professionals who seek to help users locate resources pertaining to racial communities (Clark 1995). One early attempt to catalogue Black websites was Abdul Alkalimat's (2004) book *The African American Experience in Cyberspace: A Resource Guide to the Best Web Sites on Black Culture and History.* Primarily focusing on history, society, and culture, the book is divided into 30 different chapters on topics like "Slave Trade," "Emancipation," "Religion and the Church," "Performing Arts," and "Gays and Lesbians." This compendium of digital resources focusing on African American experiences is designed for teachers and librarians, but also has a broader eye toward the general public that might be interested in knowing which websites are most credible. Such a publication points to the difficulties that minority communities faced in not just locating websites that spoke to their experiences but being able to adjudicate which ones were most valuable.

Another attempt to help curate a more trustworthy and approachable list of websites is the now-defunct internet archive known as DMOZ. From 1999 to 2017, DMOZ.org was a directory that was edited by human beings who created categories and populated them with lists of websites. McIlwain inspects the 308 websites classified within the "African American" category, a subcategory that can be located within: Society > Ethnicity > African > African American. Although this loosely defined category includes both sites created by African Americans and those that are focusing on African Americans, McIlwain points out that this remains a "failed project in terms of providing a systematic way to account for race within the web's structure" (2017: 1079). Indeed, human editors may attempt to identify racial significance, but such decisions will inevitably be premised on flawed historical processes that are complicated, contradictory, and haphazard. While this version of a directory was an improvement on the static collection of resources printed in Alkalimat's traditional monograph, it nonetheless still failed to adequately address the difficulties of categorizing and collecting digital resources.

The rise of Web 2.0

While some of these core inquiries about how to digitally categorize race remain, it is also important to note a massive shift in the architecture of the internet around 2005 toward what is known as Web 2.0. This term was popularized by Tim O'Reilly as a way of distinguishing between the early days of cyberspace and Web 1.0, which focused primarily on the design of static websites connected through hyperlinks. In contrast, **Web 2.0** describes a deeply participatory internet that is built to prioritize interactivity and the production of user-generated content that can be shared through social media platforms. While the internet was first imagined as noncommercial for the free exchange of ideas, as early as the mid-1990s internet users were starting to be barraged with pop-up advertisements, banner ads, and other unsolicited promotional materials (Ankerson 2018). While this chapter has already pointed out the many ways that communities of color have used the internet for creating content and connecting to one another since the earliest days of the World Wide Web, the rise of social media platforms nonetheless marked a significant shift. Millions of users were creating profiles and sharing posts through platforms like Facebook, Twitter, YouTube, and later on, Snapchat, Instagram, and TikTok. Many of the users of color who developed massive followings on these platforms had gotten their start by participating in blogging, as is discussed further in chapter 10. The business model that supports these social media platforms is another defining feature of Web 2.0 – in exchange for the ability to sign up for these platforms for free and make use of all of their capabilities, users relinquish ownership over their content and themselves become a valuable audience to the corporations who buy ad placements within social media feeds. This is why social media is now overwhelmed by corporate messages, sponsored and boosted posts, influencer partnerships with corporations, and other promotional intrusions.

Alongside the shift to Web 2.0, there has been interest in racial patterns of usage and the lessons that such data can teach us about race and digital media. In danah boyd's study of teen engagement with MySpace and Facebook in the early 2000s, she finds that the decisions teenagers were making about which platform to use aligned with the racial phenomenon of white flight from the city to the suburbs. She first observes that "Black and Latino teens appeared to prefer MySpace while white and Asian teens seemed to privilege Facebook" (2012: 208). These ethnographic observations align with statistical research by Eszter Hargittai (2012) on college student preferences for different social platforms according to race. While the teens in boyd's study describe their preferences for the social media platforms in terms of taste and aesthetics rather than explicitly bringing race into the conversation, she nonetheless finds racial differences in their decisions. For instance, the white students described Facebook as "safe" and "clean," while Black and Brown students talked about how MySpace was more complex and allowed them to customize their own unique music, backgrounds, and layouts. Just as young people tend to self-segregate by race, the most dominant factor was simply that both groups thought a platform was more cool if that is where more of their friends tended to congregate.

Online racism

The idea that racial dynamics from our offline world have always followed us into online arenas is also unfortunately the case when looking at patterns of **online racism**. In yet another repudiation of any hopes for a colorblind or raceless digital utopia, we can acknowledge that the internet has always been a breeding ground for explicit expressions of racism. Indeed, it is difficult to find any participatory online arena that is free from demeaning language, slurs, and other racist attacks. Digital platforms like Reddit, 4chan, Facebook, YouTube, and Twitter are well known for incubating a toxic environment for hate speech and the fomenting of racist attacks on people of color. This is not a new phenomenon, as white supremacists have been active online participants since the rise of the internet in the 1990s. Tara McPherson (2000) tracked the existence of multiple websites designed to advocate for a "neo-Confederacy," a political movement centered on the fantasy of political independence for Southern states. She finds that the sites attempt to distance themselves and their audience from explicit racism, instead creating new language for a white identity for men struggling to connect to one another. Jesse Daniels (2009) has also extensively studied white supremacy online, explaining that because they were among the earliest adopters of digital technologies, they have become skilled and sophisticated in the ways that they are able to hide and protect themselves from those who would challenge them. For instance, White Pride organizations use platforms like Stormfront.org to make white supremacy mainstream through civilized rhetoric, avoiding racial slurs, and building a supportive and strong community. Other cloaked websites use scholarly phrases like "Civil Rights Review" or "Institute for Historical Review" to conceal that these are websites for white supremacy organizations.

While these tactics have served to make certain white supremacist organizations more difficult to identify online, the internet has also always been a bastion for individuals wishing to express explicit forms of racial hatred. Racist language has been particularly visible on Twitter, a platform with a public firehose of data that can easily be scraped and analyzed for key phrases. In 2014, the UK-based think tank Demos produced a report called "Anti-Social Media" that assessed the potential for using automated machine learning to identify and classify slurs (Bartlett, Reffin, Rumball, and Williamson 2014). Two other projects, the Twitter Racism Project and Geography of Hate, collected tweets containing racial slurs based on geographic location. The Canada-based Twitter Racism Project (Chaudhry 2015) conducted a content analysis of the tweets to determine the context for the use of the slur, while the US-based Geography of Hate researchers created a visual map of "hot spots" for the negative use of slurs (Stephens 2013). These projects serve to catalogue the different reasons that individuals might use a slur in a tweet while also calling attention to their ubiquity. Many of these results were widely reported within mainstream media outlets, alongside stories about how the studies served to remind us that "hate speech is sadly alive and well on social networks" (Peckham 2013). Such reportage affirms the findings of Jonathan Bishop, who argues that mass media tend to reproduce moral panics around internet trolling stories (Bishop 2014). Together, the prevalence of racist comments, images, and stories contributes to the fact that people of color often feel unwelcome and unsafe within many online communities. The same is true for others with socially disempowered identities, such as women, people with disabilities, LGBTQ+ people, and others, who need to be considered alongside racial minorities.

It is also important to understand some of the forces that contribute to the internet becoming a breeding ground for racism. Lisa Nakamura (2013b) notes the omnipresence of what is known as the "Greater Internet Fuckwad Theory" (or GIFT), which states that a normal person, when given anonymity and an audience, will become a total monster. This understanding presumes that the internet is full of hate speech because normal people simply cannot resist the impulse to engage in racist and sexist behaviors when they believe they will not be identified or apprehended for their misdeeds. Online racism becomes merely a glitch, or an inconvenient mistake that we cannot control due to the fact that all technologies break down in some small way. Yet Nakamura challenges the technologically deterministic idea that racist online behavior is inevitable and easily ignored, arguing that we must understand racism as a central component to the internet itself. If this is so, we must take racism and racist commentary seriously and recognize that they are far more than a minor inconvenience to be sidestepped.

Conclusion

This chapter has explored the uses and affordances of the World Wide Web in relation to race, starting in the 1990s and extending to the rise of Web 2.0 in the mid-2000s. While discourses about digital divides and the realities of online racism have foregrounded the barriers that people of color have faced in feeling like the internet is welcoming to them or available to them, there have also always been important uses of digital media that connect to the specific needs of minority communities. This includes online forums, email listservs, websites, and other digital communities that are created by and targeted to the specific needs of Black, Hispanic, Asian American, and Indigenous users. It is also important to understand the evolution of how we have theorized the relationship between race and the internet, moving from dreams of a race-free utopia to realizing that racial power dynamics follow us from the offline world into the virtual world. While digital media have certainly created a plethora of new and exciting opportunities to transform life as we know it, scholars of color have helped to root these possibilities in the realities of racism that are embedded throughout all forms of media.

Key questions

1. What kinds of assumptions about race and racial realities were built into early dreams of the internet, and how did those dreams evolve as the internet moved from a text-based to an image-based medium?
2. How have understandings of digital divides shifted away from the simple fear that Black communities lagged behind white communities in terms of internet usage?
3. How do we know that people of color were active in creating their own digital communities since the earliest days of the internet?

Further reading

McIlwain, Charlton. 2019. *Black Software: The Internet and Racial Justice, from the AfroNet to Black Lives Matter.* Oxford: Oxford University Press.

Nakamura, Lisa. 2002. *Cybertypes: Race, Ethnicity, and Identity on the Internet.* New York: Routledge.

Nelson, Alondra, Tu, Thuy, Linh N., and Hines, Alicia Hedlam (eds). 2001. *Technicolor: Race, Technology, and Everyday Life.* New York: New York University Press.

3
Labor

Key terms

- Silicon Valley
- computers
- bamboo ceiling
- model minority
- microaggressions
- content moderation

Introduction

IN order to understand the structural racism that exists within media technologies, we must consider the way that technologies are created and, more importantly, by whom. Silicon Valley has long been criticized for gender and racial inequities at the executive level, and the impact these inequities have on both cultural norms and the kinds of technologies that are created. Indeed, there are many ways we can understand both the assumption of normative whiteness and masculinity within Silicon Valley, and the histories of employment discrimination that have contributed to these demographics. Yet it is also important to probe beneath the surface to uncover critical histories that have been suppressed, including the role of women and queer folks in the earliest days of computer science work, the communities of Navajo women who supported circuitry building, and the immigration policies that led to an influx of Asian immigrants into tech industries post-1965.

This chapter explores the many ways in which labor in tech industries is racialized, who is impacted most, and why it matters. It asks what kind of labor is demanded by new media technologies, and how race shapes that labor. It is specifically centered on expanding beyond the traditional ways that the history of technology and labor have been narrated, including a rethinking of the histories of Silicon Valley, the reasons for inequalities in tech industries, and what counts as labor in relation to digital media. Our understanding of each of these narratives can be reconsidered and significantly enriched by including the perspectives of women, people of color, LGBTQ+ people, and other marginalized communities. This chapter also expands its investigation of tech labor beyond the founders and executives who are so frequently highlighted, calling attention to the invisible and hidden labor taken up by marginalized communities that has facilitated the massive growth of tech industries.

Histories of Silicon Valley

Silicon Valley is the term used to describe the area of Northern California where many tech companies and start-ups are located. Throughout the twentieth century, the area was a hotbed of innovation in a wide array of technologies – including silicon transistors, semiconductors, computer chips, and the internet. The story of what makes this region "special" and what factors have led to its success have traditionally centered on a few key components: the founding of the Hewlett-Packard Company in 1938, the establishment of the NASA Ames Research Center in 1939, the invention of the transistor at William Shockley's Bell Laboratories in 1947, the supportive dean Fredrick Terman at Stanford University's School of Engineering that led to military-based research after World War II. The narrative then continues to include the invention of the internet, the rise of the personal computer, the growth of countless tech companies and the venture capital that supported them. In more recent years, much attention has focused on the innovation and struggles of founders like Steve Jobs of Apple, Bill Gates of Microsoft, Mark Zuckerberg of Facebook, Larry Page and Sergey Brin of Google,

Travis Kalanick of Uber, Jack Dorsey of Twitter, and others. Together these components come together to narrate the story of how Silicon Valley came to be the premier hub for technology production and economic innovation.

Yet this story significantly highlights the role of white men and ignores the contributions of women and people of color – as well as the negative impacts that Silicon Valley and its technological industries have had on them. It omits the substantial role of venture capital in supporting technology companies, and the historical bias toward supporting white male founders in a way that reinforces systemic racism. The glorification of this particular narrative of tech entrepreneurship has also wiped away the extensive histories and experiences of those who previously inhabited the region we now call Silicon Valley. As Stephen Pitti (2002) has researched, this includes the Mexican communities who had called the Santa Clara Valley home for over 200 years, as well as the Indigenous peoples who were colonized by Spanish missionaries in the late eighteenth century. Spanish explorers who took over the area they called Alta California attacked and enslaved the native Ohlone people, disrupting their way of life forever despite fierce resistance. Following the end of the Mexican–American War and the ceding of California to the United States, the Valley was converted into a primarily agricultural region. White landowners came to heavily rely on immigrant labor to work the fields, orchards, and canneries. Many Latinx workers had been attracted to the area due to the Bracero Program, an agreement between the United States and Mexico that allowed Mexican immigrants to temporarily enter the United States after World War II to work in agriculture. From 1942 to 1964, hundreds of thousands of Mexicans took up work in Santa Clara Valley, only to be underpaid and exploited. Erasures of their histories marks a particularly egregious oversight, given the essential role that Latino workers played in supporting the agricultural production and mercury mines that were key to the area's economic success up to the 1980s. Then, as tech industries transformed the area following the rise of Silicon Valley, Latinos continued to take on low-wage jobs such as janitors, construction workers, assembly workers, and landscapers – work that is physically demanding and dangerous.

Predominantly white and male narratives about the rise of Silicon Valley have also neglected the role of women-of-color laborers who supported the rise of Silicon Valley from afar.

This includes work at electronics maquiladoras in Mexico and circuit assembly plants on Navajo reservations. Jefferson Cowie (1999) traces the relocation of the electronic company RCA's radio and television manufacturing plants from city to city across the United States before eventually ending up in Juarez, Mexico, where young women workers were assumed to be more accommodating and docile than the labor force in the United States. RCA was just one of many US corporations that took advantage of the Border Industrialization Program, which was instituted by Mexico in 1965 after the end of the Bracero Program as a way of capitalizing on their inexpensive industrial labor force. It encouraged the rise of maquiladoras along the US–Mexico border that would export their products into the United States free from Mexican tariffs. RCA's factory in Juarez specifically sought to hire young women for electronics work under the assumption that they would have the necessary manual dexterity and patience for monotonous operations, but also that they would be easily disciplined, obedient, and loyal (Cowie 1999: 119–20). While it was initially true that an inexperienced workforce might be in a weak position to organize for collective bargaining, female workers eventually gained the experience, freedom, and class cohesion to fight for their rights.

In a story that parallels that of RCA, the Fairchild Semiconductor company has also been praised for its innovative decision to outsource its manufacturing processes. Yet this overlooks those whose lives were most impacted by this move. In 1965, Fairchild opened a circuit assembly plant on a Navajo reservation in New Mexico, where it hired hundreds of Navajo workers. In Lisa Nakamura's (2014) investigation of promotional materials created by the company to describe its labor force, she finds a distinct preference for Navajo women workers. Navajo women are described as innately suited to the work of building electronic circuits because their histories of traditional jewelry craftsmanship and rug weaving are seen as translatable skills for the visual design and intricacy of circuitry work. This kind of rhetoric attempts to connect Indigenous cultural practices to a new creative class of electronic workers, which obfuscates the reality that this work increased environmental pollution on the reservation and that their labor was more easily exploitable. Just like the Mexican female workers in Juarez, Navajo female workers were assumed to be mobile, docile, cheap, and flexible – which translated to being easily laid off and then rehired as necessary. As Nakamura points out, "race and gender are themselves forms of flexible capital . . . racialization – the understanding of a specific population as possessing traits and behaviors that belong to a race, not an individual – is a process, not a product" (933–4). When it is useful to portray women or people of color as an innately talented and valuable workforce, those arguments can be constructed, but they will also be discarded and rewritten when that exigency has passed or when a more exploitable opportunity materializes.

Female computers and other misremembered histories

If we extend our view beyond the narrow contributions of Silicon Valley to the rise of computer science more broadly, there are many other stories of white women in the tech sector whose contributions have been overlooked. Historians have worked to recuperate the long history of women in computing by highlighting the pioneering work of English mathematician Ada Lovelace. She has been recognized as the first computer programmer for her work in the 1840s alongside Charles Babbage in designing the "Analytical Engine," a proposed design for a general-purpose computer. While the machine was never built, Lovelace's contributions to binary systems in computer mathematics were profound. Women also played significant roles in early computer languages, with Navy admiral and mathematician Grace Hopper coordinating the development of COBOL, a programming language that remains widely used to this day.

Indeed, when the term **computer** was originally invented as a title for the humans who performed ballistics computations, it referred to women who computed. Computing was a kind of work seen as particularly appropriate for women because it was assumed to be clerical, repetitive, and tedious. Throughout World War II, as women joined the workforce in every kind of occupation, their roles as scientists, mathematicians, engineers, and computing were reduced to the subordinate title of merely "assisting." Jennifer Light (1999) examines this kind of occupational feminization and its role in the obfuscation of women's contributions, the loss of status, and ultimately the increased segregation in the scientific workforce despite the important role that women had played. Gender norms and power dynamics have shaped every aspect of computing culture, and have forcefully obscured these histories by leaving names out of records or erroneously classifying women's roles. These problems were then supplanted with the reality that women began to gradually recede from the computing workforce. Indeed, by the 1960s, the gendering of computing had entirely flipped, transforming into a masculinized form of work that seemed suitable for men. This problem has continued to become exacerbated over time, with fewer and fewer women seeking computer science degrees ever since the 1980s.

Racial dimensions of women's invisibility in computing histories were highlighted in the popular 2016 film *Hidden Figures*, which was based on Margot Lee Shetterly's nonfiction book of the same name. Both Shetterly's book and the feature film tell the story of the African American female mathematicians who worked at NASA during the Space Race of the 1950s and 1960s – a time when Jim Crow segregation laws severely limited opportunities for Black workers, in addition to rampant gender discrimination. Shetterly was only able to uncover the story because her father had worked at NASA himself, and he casually mentioned the African American women who had worked alongside him as mathematicians and engineers (Buckley 2016). R. Arvid Nelsen (2017) has also worked to uncover information about the many African Americans who had worked in computing starting in the 1950s, but whose actual contributions have gone unrecorded. He points to at least 57 African American professionals from computer industries who were featured in *Ebony* magazine in the late 1950s – including those in creative and developmental roles with computers, jobs in computing management and implementation, and support roles. Yet these limited profiles lack the depth that it would take to truly understand their contributions, leaving enormous gaps in the historical record. These absences in the archive shore up assumptions that African Americans had no interest in or aptitude for working with computers, despite the reality that many African Americans were pioneers in fields such as science, mathematics, and engineering.

One final arena in which it is important to reframe historical accounts of computing is in terms of sexuality, as many established historical records neglect to mention the queer identities of important figures. This omission serves to uphold the assumption that so many "great" figures were heterosexual, and negates the contributions of gay, lesbian, bisexual, and other queer scientists. Alan Turing is famously known for his work as a codebreaker during World War II and his advances in artificial intelligence that are enshrined in his eponymous Turing Test. Yet it is equally important to note that he was an openly gay man who was arrested on charges of gross indecency, which criminalized sexual activity between men. While undergoing the inhumane punishment of chemical castration, he died of cyanide poisoning in what has been accepted as suicide. Jacob Gaboury (2013) argues that we must recognize Turing as part of a queer genealogy of computing that also includes a number of other gay men whose work connected to one another in advancing the field of computer science. In doing so, we can then see how "queerness is itself inherent within computational logic, and that this queerness becomes visible when we investigate those cleavages that partition the lives of these men into distinct technical and sexual spheres of existence" (Gaboury 2013). This helps call attention to different forms of marginalization, silencing, and oppression that different minority communities have faced in these workplaces. But it is also important to ask what unique perspectives and rethinking their presence and contributions may have opened up. Diverse workplaces have always been understood as important because different life experiences will lead to more innovation, more robust solutions to problems, and an eye toward products that will better serve people from all backgrounds.

Immigrant labor and racialized policy

We can see from these histories that women, people of color, LGBTQ+ people, and other diverse populations have always played important unsung roles in the creation and design of technology. Such interventions challenge predominant conceptions of Silicon Valley and its tech industries as only allowing straight white cisgendered men to participate and flourish. Yet even amidst the assumed whiteness of Silicon Valley, there has always been one racial minority whose presence and contributions have been highly visible – immigrant workers from East Asia and South Asia. Indeed, the prevalence of Indian, Chinese, and Korean tech workers has had a profound impact on racial understandings of all Asian Americans. Their employment in Silicon Valley has helped forge the stereotype that all Asians are good at math and science, bolstered the lingering trope of the asexual Asian nerd, and promulgated the myth of the model minority that all Asians are highly educated and successful. To fully understand the participation of Asian immigrants in Silicon Valley and its origins, we must examine shifts in US immigration policy in the 1960s.

Immigration laws have always been used to control the US labor force in ways that benefit those who already have power. Throughout the early twentieth century, immigration was extremely limited – but particularly so from Asian countries, due to the Chinese Exclusion Act. Signed in 1882, this federal law prohibited all immigration from China due to racist fears that Chinese laborers had become a threat. While this exclusion was slightly lifted in 1943 when China became an ally to the United States, it was not completely ended until the 1965 Immigration and Naturalization Act, also known as the Hart–Celler Act. In addition to opening up immigration from the Asian countries that had previously been extremely limited, the Hart–Celler Act also promoted immigration from highly skilled professional workers. This preference was further strengthened with the Immigration Act of 1990, which created H-1B visas for workers with highly specialized knowledge. This visa resulted in the recruitment of hundreds of thousands of tech workers from India, China, Korea, Hong Kong, and Taiwan. There was a need for workers with technical skills and educational backgrounds to fill a labor short-age in information technology industries, and highly educated workers from Asia flooded into the United States to fill these posi-tions. When this combined with immigrants from the Philippines seeking family reunification and refugees from Vietnam and other countries devastated by the Vietnam War, the West Coast saw an unprecedented increase in its Asian American population that was bifurcated into low- and high-skilled workers. Asian immigrants who flooded into Northern California were joining the Chinese, Japanese, and Filipino families who had been central to agricul-tural communities in the area (Lung-Amam 2017).

Yet even among the world of high-tech professionals, Asian American workers have always faced a **bamboo ceiling** that limits their advancement and leadership. Studies of workers in Silicon Valley have consistently found that despite the prevalence of Asian employees, Asian men and women lag far behind their white counterparts in management and executive roles (Gee, Peck, and Wong 2015). Part of this problem is connected to the limits of the H-1B visa itself, which was designed to produce tem-porary contract workers whose flexible labor can be exploited to benefit tech companies (Amrute 2020; Banerjee 2006). While the H-1B visa has allowed hundreds of thousands of workers – largely men from India – to enter the United States as workers, their legal status is extremely fragile and they are forced to accept working conditions that leave them very little power to advocate for them-selves. There are cultural problems as well, as white tech workers often treat their Asian colleagues very poorly. Roli Varma (2002) goes so far as to call Asian workers "high-tech coolies" because they are consistently viewed as foreigners who are unsuited for upward career mobility, particularly in comparison to their white male colleagues.

The struggle of Asian Americans and Asian immigrants in the workplace can be connected to the stereotype of the **model minority**, which has had a number of harmful consequences. The model minority stereotype emerged during World War II when "good" Chinese and Japanese immigrants worked to be reframed as assimilable and non-threatening, and they did so by claiming status as definitively not-Black (Wu 2016). It became particu-larly salient in the 1960s alongside rhetoric that Asian Americans could be seen taking up "The American Dream" through a combination of hard work and education, and now reaping the rewards. As with all stereotypes, this assumption belies the true diversity of Asian American experiences – including the thousands of Asian Americans who live below the poverty line, who cannot find stable employment, who suffer from poor education, have limited access to healthcare, or face violence in their communities. This myth has also positioned Asian Americans as a wedge between whites and other minority groups, despite long histories of cross-racial solidarity in fighting for civil rights as a minoritized collective (Ho and Mullen 2008). When taken up in the workplace, the consequences of the model minority stereotype include the presumption that Asian workers are doing just fine and therefore do not need professional mentoring, support, or resources like other disenfranchised minority groups. In Niral Shah's (2019) deconstruction of the myth that "Asians are good at math," he goes further to argue that this stereotype provides a threat to Asian personhood because they suffer from the assumption that they lack the creativity and individuality we often prize as human characteristics. Asians are positioned as "Mongoloid androids" that become interchangeable with non-human objects such as calculators. Asian workers also face a number of assumptions that limit promotability – including that they will always be outsiders, that they are poor communicators if they speak accented English, that they come from a passive and non-assertive culture that does not lend itself to leadership, and that they are more suited to carrying out technical tasks rather than being in a position that demands creativity and risk. Together such stereotypes and assumptions have led to stalled career prospects for the thousands of Asian immigrants and Asian American workers in tech fields.

Racism in labor pipelines, recruitment, and hiring policies

While immigration policies designed to recruit highly skilled laborers resulted in an influx of Asian tech workers and exacerbated harmful stereotypes, the absence of Black, Latinx, and Indigenous workers can similarly be traced to an array of deep-rooted factors. This exclusion begins at the very earliest stages with the issue of who is encouraged to pursue careers in tech industries, and who is told that such a path would not be best for them. Structural racism, anti-Blackness, and other forms of intersectional oppression have long been visible in educational inequalities that push anyone who is not white (or Asian), male, heterosexual, able-bodied, and middle-class out of STEM fields, communicating to students from many marginalized identities that they are not well suited to the pursuit of STEM-related professions. This problem is connected to discourses that disproportionately describe STEM fields as an extremely rigorous intellectual meritocracy that rewards only individuals who are gifted enough to compete among their peers. Such discourses then exacerbate long-standing narratives of Black and Brown students as primitive, incompetent, and uneducatable – an array of painful racial scripts that can be traced back to slavery and to the need to understand enslaved people as innately deficient as justification for the denial of their freedom and their humanity (Jackson 2006). The same has been true for Indigenous peoples, as discourses of settler colonialism were founded on the assumption that Indigenous ways of thinking and knowing were so inferior that they needed to be completely replaced.

Gender has also long been recognized as an important factor in educational disparities, as myths about differences between male and female brains, aptitudes, and proclivities have lent authority to the assumption that girls struggle in STEM fields. As mentioned earlier, gender inequities in the field of computer science have been particularly noteworthy, with the percentage of women majoring in computer science steadily declining in the last few decades (Reges 2018). Black and Brown girls face additional limits and barriers, such as the assumption that their racialized femininity must be negotiated in order to be successful in a masculine academic environment (Ireland et al. 2018). They must overcome multiplicative experiences of racism and sexism in order to continue in these fields, leading to low expectations of success and low confidence. Together these factors have led to substantial racial and gender disparities in the students who pursue STEM disciplines at the bachelor's, master's, and doctoral levels (McGee and Robinson 2019).

These educational issues then contribute to a pipeline problem that limits diversity in the tech workplace. This is not due to a lack of talent or interest but because students of certain identities have been systematically discouraged from developing the necessary educational background for a career in tech.

Beyond educational inequalities, structural racism also impacts the way that Black and Brown workers are ineffectively recruited and hired into unfairly low positions in tech work. While educational discourses mean that women and people of color must work harder to remain motivated to pursue STEM education, the struggle continues when they enter the workforce. Such problems have become more visible because unequal hiring practices have been categorized as legal discrimination and attempts have been made to address and remedy their effects. The Civil Rights Act of 1964 established the Equal Employment Opportunity Commission (EEOC), containing provisions to prohibit employee discrimination on the basis of race, color, religion, national origin, and sex. Thanks to this legislation, we can trace the origins of discriminatory hiring practices many decades prior to the rise of today's high-tech labor industries and their inequalities. For instance, in 1973 the EEOC was charged with investigating complaints about discrimination by the American Telephone and Telegraph Company (AT&T). Supported by the National Organization for Women (NOW), a number of civil rights organizations asserted that, despite the high numbers of women being employed by the corporation, telecommunication jobs had become classified by gender, and women were systematically denied opportunities for advancement. Many scholars have also examined the racial dimensions of this lawsuit, revealing the ways that intersectional dynamics of race and gender complicated the impact of this legal battle. Venus Green (2012) argues that the "gender first" strategies of NOW and its historical framing as a universal victory for women erases the struggles of Black women who faced additional limits in the telecommunications workplace. Melissa Villa-Nicholas (2016) uses the case to examine the experiences of Latinas at AT&T, finding that there were multiple ways that Latinas experienced workplace discrimination due to the overlapping categories of gender and national origin. This includes requiring specific credentials and test scores that were known to exclude Latinx applicants, requiring English language and height standards that were suited for white male bodies, and using only white recruiters to interview applicants. Attempts to call attention to inequities often focused on empowering and recruiting Mexican men, ignoring Latinas and their needs.

While these issues have been identified and discussed for decades, we still see enormous disparities in tech workforces. A groundbreaking report in 2014 from the EEOC called "Diversity in High Tech" clearly revealed the scope of the problem, pointing to the disproportionate whiteness and maleness of workers in the high-tech sector, with the high-tech sector employing far fewer African American and Hispanic workers than other private industries (US Equal Employment Opportunity Commission 2014). The problem was even worse in the category of executives – the report found that 80% of executives were men and only 20% were women, and that only around 1% of executives were Hispanic or African American. Leading tech companies like Apple, Facebook, Google, and Microsoft released public diversity reports on their own demographics, along with promises to do better and to institute new diversity initiatives to alleviate the problem. Some of these initiatives included coding education programs, employee resource groups for diverse workers, and unconscious-bias trainings. Yet, in the years that followed, little changed. A 2019 report from *Wired* noted that people of color remained highly underrepresented and, moreover, that Black and Latinx workers were leaving their jobs in these companies at a higher rate than their white counterparts (Harrison 2019). Together these reports have led to the realization that tech industries have far more than a pipelines, recruitment, or retention problem – they have a deep-seated cultural problem where bias is built into every fabric of their workplace environment.

Toxic workplace environments

To understand the cultural problems in high-tech industries, we can look beyond statistics and demographic reports to absorb the narrative accounts of everyday norms in these workplaces. The complaints are similar to experiences in any corporate workplace that is predominantly white and struggling with the need for diversity. To name some of the most common experiences, tech workers of color interviewed for a 2020 *Los Angeles Times* investigation reported "enduring daily microaggressions; feeling targeted by superiors or external critics; being trotted out to defend a company's diversity practices; being tasked with extra work typically reserved for diversity and inclusion officers" (Bhuiyan, Dean, and Hussain 2020). **Microaggressions** are the small or casual acts of bias that are so slight as to be nearly imperceptible, but that still contribute to the feeling of being unwelcome or devalued. As a result of these experiences, workers of color end up feeling that their jobs are always tenuous, and that speaking up about issues of racial justice puts their careers at risk.

These negative experiences also limit career advancement, as minority workers often lack the social capital to form necessary connections. France Winddance Twine (2018) interviewed Black women working in Silicon Valley to learn more about the role of social networks in their career advancement. She finds that Black women are uniquely disadvantaged in these predominantly white workplaces because they have less access to information about job opportunities, as well as to mentors and coaching that could lead to promotions. In response, women of color have had to develop their own professional networks to support one another. While the existence of these efforts has supported a narrow pipeline of successful women of color in tech, any diversity solution that relies on the resources of disenfranchised individuals to provide solutions can become unsustainable. In another example of this, many tech companies have supported the development of employee resource groups run by workers of color. These groups are designed to foster community among minority employees, and can be meaningful spaces for connecting and sharing resources. Yet they can also require substantial additional labor that is uncompensated – especially during moments of crisis, such as during the summer of 2020 when protests erupted following the death of George Floyd. In an article discussing the free labor these groups can entail, participants in groups such as Blackbirds at Twitter Blackbirds, Mahogany at Slack, Black@ Facebook, and Blacktocats at GitHub reported that they questioned their ability to impact change at top levels (Tiku 2020).

Many of these reports sound like the same struggles that minority workers face all across corporate America, where it remains a daily battle to successfully integrate diversity and inclusion into the structures that shape big business cultures and norms. Yet we must also acknowledge that Silicon Valley and the modern tech industry have a culture unto themselves. As Katy Cook (2020) describes, Silicon Valley is not defined by its "landscape, infrastructure, or its many products and platforms. What makes the Valley what it is are its many intangibles: its people, ideas, and unique ways of thinking about the world, which have converged to produce the most profitable, fastest-growing, and influential industry in the history of mankind."

There are strong cultural norms associated with working in this particular industry, and these ways of working are highly prized and protected because of the belief that they are what has helped technological development thrive. For instance, risk taking, big ideas, and logical thinking are common descriptors of important values. Given the financial success of these ways of doing business, Silicon Valley has also developed a sense of uniqueness that must be protected, as if it must necessarily be separate from other industries and the lessons they have learned. This arrogance and sense of exceptionalism have served to insulate tech workers from challenges to that authority, especially those who have profited the most from positions of power.

Yet there are also cultural norms that have built bias into the fabric of tech – for instance, valuing homogeneity over pluralism and seeking to preserve a static culture, and celebrating immaturity and youth over wisdom and experience. Emily Chang's (2018) book *Brotopia: Breaking Up the Boys' Club of Silicon Valley* delves deeply into the resilient culture of chauvinism and misogyny, pointing to the lore of strip-club visits and sex parties that young male founders proudly celebrated despite the way that it clearly excluded and demeaned women. It is not surprising to learn that sexual harassment and unwanted sexual advances were extremely common for women in positions ranging from lower-ranking roles all the way up to tech founders and venture capitalists (Vassallo et al. 2017). In a high-profile case, Ellen Pao sued the venture capital firm Kleiner Perkins Caufield and Byers for gender discrimination and retaliation, alleging that women were not promoted, their voices were not heard, and their complaints of sexual harassment were ignored, amongst other problems. While Pao lost the case, she claimed victory in being one of the few women to courageously call attention to the depths of the problem and the success of founding a non-profit called Project Include that recommended more effective diversity initiatives (Pao 2017). Nonetheless, change on these fronts has been exceedingly slow.

The horrors of invisible digital labor

Within this portrait of labor in Silicon Valley, it is also important to call attention to the kinds of labor that are so often hidden from view. Those in power, including tech executives and those who are financially profiting the most from these massive corporations, may have a disproportionate impact on the tech products that are produced and the way that these companies are run. But there are thousands of workers at every level and pay scale whose experiences are also vital to the functioning of our high-tech world, and we should not ignore that expansive community. This includes workers outside of Silicon Valley and even outside of the country, low-wage and precariously employed workers, and those whose workload is particularly difficult – both physically and emotionally. Such workers are important to consider, as their low status often makes them more prone to exploitation of various kinds. Moreover, while they may include more workers of color due to the global dispersal of flexible labor in the post-industrial era, the precarity of this work often means that there is a weakened ability to advocate for minority communities or their specific needs.

One category of this kind of work is **content moderation**, or reviewing flagged content to decide if it should stay visible on the site or if it should be taken down. Such work plays a vital role in protecting companies against legal infractions (such as allowing child pornography to be shared on a company's platform) and protecting users from encountering disturbing or abusive content. This can range from pornographic or violent content to content that is threatening, hateful, or gruesome. Sarah Roberts has extensively studied commercial content moderation, which she describes as low-wage and low-status in addition to being marked by invisibility and secrecy (Roberts 2019). She argues that deliberately hiding this work from view and relying on a physically dispersed labor force to take on this incredibly emotionally taxing work serves to insulate companies from responsibility and accountability for harm.

In both Roberts' research and numerous journalistic investigations of how offensive content is removed from US social media platforms, there is an emphasis on the high psychological toll on workers. In Adrian Chen's (2014) article in *Wired*, he takes readers "inside the soul-crushing world of content moderation, where low-wage laborers soak up the worst of humanity, and keep it off your Facebook feed." Thousands of workers in the Philippines spend their days constantly scanning posts for a long list of violations – "pornography, gore, minors, sexual solicitation, sexual body parts/images, racism" – that must be identified in seconds before being presented with the next horrific post. Workers have described being haunted by images long after the workday ended, turning to alcohol and drugs, suffering from clinical PTSD and panic attacks, feeling paranoid and irritable and depressed. While we often think about tech workers in Silicon Valley being lavished with high salaries and carefully designed campuses filled with free food and entertainment, this experience is only one side of tech work. There are thousands of other workers all across the globe whose experiences working in tech are the opposite – poorly compensated, lacking benefits, unstable, and emotionally scarring. This work is outsourced all across the globe but also takes place in the United States, where immigrants are a particularly desirable workforce due to their language skills.

While we should be very concerned about the experiences of the invisible workers of color suffering from horrific mental health impacts, it is also important to consider the racial dimensions of the content that is being moderated. First, many workers must constantly face a barrage of hateful comments and racist imagery that attacks people from their own identity. This would be a disturbing daily activity on its own, but we must also consider the gray areas of content moderation and the reality that companies are making important decisions about what content to leave up in addition to what content should be taken down. In Sarah Roberts' (2016) investigation of racist content moderation, she points out that content moderators are gatekeepers who must weigh many different factors into their decision – including how popular an item is, how much traffic it can drive to the platform, and its potential value as a commodity. She points to examples where overtly racist videos were protected from moderation due to their virality, as users are drawn to provocative and shocking content. Moreover, there is no easy solution to the problem of how content should be monitored, as many possible fixes engender their own complications and weaknesses. For instance, there is a clear need for accountability when it comes to protecting users from encountering traumatizing or offensive digital content. Yet if we leave that oversight to algorithms or humans who lack the life experiences to carefully assess racially specific content, the results could be spotty or wholly inadequate. Some of these complexities will be further addressed in chapter 7 in discussions about tech policy and the efforts that some companies have made.

We have also seen many examples where spectacles surrounding the public deaths of African American men and women have been used to incite activist organizing alongside the Black Lives Matter movement. Widely shared videos of the deaths of Eric Garner, Philando Castile, and George Floyd have garnered international attention that was oriented toward the fight for racial justice and resolution. Yet, as Safiya Noble points out, "Decisions made by online media giants are driven by profit, at the expense of women and people of color whose images and cultural markers are often sold to the highest bidders, literally through the auctioning of keywords and selling of advertisements on top of, or in relation to, viral images of Black death" (2018b: 151–2). As is discussed further in chapter 8, we cannot ignore the reality that digital media platforms are financially profiting off of the popularity of these videos and, further, that this hypervisibility continues a long history of surveilling Black bodies with little consideration for the consent or control over how Black communities are viewed. No matter how many individuals flagged these videos for removal, their value is too high for digital platforms to interrupt their continued circulation. These complexities reveal how complicated it can be to decide which posts should be allowed to remain online, and who should be in the position to make that decision.

Creative labor

A final kind of digital labor that is often under-acknowledged is the creative labor taken up across platforms by people of color, and in particular Black people. There are countless examples of Black creators whose jokes, tweets, memes, gifs, dances, or other creative works have gone viral across social media and accumulated millions of views. This kind of visibility equates to a kind of power, given the metrics by which content creators are able to profit. This includes intangible rewards like social capital and clout, as well as the ability to financially profit through monetizing their content. This means that when users copy, appropriate, or fail to properly attribute the creator of digital content, there is real harm to the original creator. One example of this failure to give credit can be seen in the story of 16-year old Kayla Newman, who posted a video in 2014 on the app Vine under the handle "Peaches Monroee." The six-second video consisted of Newman stating: "We in this bitch, finna get crunk. Eyebrows on fleek, da fuq." Her video earned over 36 million views, and the term "on fleek" took on a life of its own as it infiltrated popular culture. Major corporations who were eager to appear trendy started using the phrase in their own digital presence, with Denny's posting a tweet stating "hashbrowns on fleek," and Domino's Pizza posting "Dominoe's is bae, pepperoni kisses on fleek" (Grady 2017). In 2015, a reporter quoted Newman as saying: "I gave the world a word. I can't explain the feeling. At the moment I haven't gotten any endorsements or received any payment. I feel that I should be compensated. But I also feel that good things happen to those who wait" (St Felix 2015). While she later started a GoFundMe to support her dreams for a cosmetic line, the reality is that there is no easy way to directly profit from creating a popular phrase or new form of slang. The same is true for many other forms of culture that are created and popularized by Black youth.

One area where this practice has been particularly visible is within TikTok. TikTok is a mobile app that originated in China in

2016, and allows users to create and share very brief videos. While there are many factors that have contributed to the widespread popularity of the app, one of its unique affordances is that it allows users to share audio and conduct searches across the platform based on audio tracks. This helps to explain the popularity of lip-synch videos and dance videos in particular, as the audio tracks underneath these videos can be easily shared alongside original visual performances. But there are many cases where the Black youth whose dance choreography and other creations become wildly popular on the platform are not credited for their contributions. For instance, 14-year-old Jalaiah Harmon choreographed a dance that she called "Renegade" to the song "Lottery" by rapper K-Camp, and shared a video of her performing it with her friend Kaliyah Davis to Instagram. Yet all of the credit for the dance's popularity ended up being attributed to white TikTok influencer Charli D'Amelio, whose performance of the dance in October 2019 brought the phenomenon to her 90 million followers with no credit given to Harmon (Boffone 2021). The divesting of Black girl creators from the rewards of their popular creations is representative of a larger problem of the racialization of creative labor, which eventually led to #BlackTikTokStrike in July 2021. Black creators pointed to numerous examples where white creators had materially benefited from Black creative labor, and called attention to the importance of Black people on the app (Onwuamaegbu 2021). While TikTok has responded with promises to empower Black creators through new diversity initiatives, such as their TikTok for Black Creatives creator accelerator program and the creation of a Black TikTok Trailblazers list (TikTok 2021), it is clear that this widespread issue will require addressing from within creator communities as well.

Conclusion

This chapter has painted a broad portrait of inequalities in the kinds of work that shape digital media from the inside, examining who works in tech industries and what kinds of experiences tech workers face while doing this kind of work. This begins with inequalities in recruitment and hiring practices, but also connects to the culture that surrounds tech workplaces, the limits on women and people of color being able to advance into positions of leadership and influence, and the kinds of jobs that are believed to be appropriate for people of different identities. Together we can see how and why the demographics of the tech industry have excluded certain communities and perspectives and welcomed others. These findings can then help us better understand consequences in terms of the quality of work that is produced, and how certain mistakes or biases in digital media might have been overlooked. Indeed, it is difficult to imagine ever being able to adequately address problems of bias in the design of technology without addressing the issue of who is invited to have a say in the design process. Finally, this chapter expands our understanding of whose labor in the world of digital media is most commonly recognized and celebrated, and whose stories have been systematically overlooked or forgotten, and attempts to remedy some of those omissions.

Key questions

1. How have traditional narratives about labor in Silicon Valley obscured the actual contributions and impacts of women and people of color?
2. What historical forces led to the proliferation of Asian workers in Silicon Valley, and how have they been treated in high-tech workplaces?
3. What are some of the racial dynamics that make the labor of digital content moderation important to take seriously?

Further reading

Noble, Safiya Umoja and Roberts, Sarah T. 2019. "Technological Elites, the Meritocracy, and Postracial Myths in Silicon Valley," in Sarah Banet-Weiser, Roopali Mukherjee, and Herman Gray (eds), *Racism Postrace*. Durham, NC: Duke University Press, pp. 113–34.

Pitti, Stephen J. 2002. *The Devil in Silicon Valley: Northern California, Race, and Mexican Americans*. Princeton: Princeton University Press.

Varma, Roli. 2007. *Harbingers of Global Change: India's Techno-Immigrants in the United States*. Minneapolis: Lexington Books.

4

Infrastructures

Key terms

- environmental racism
- settler colonialism
- sovereignty
- technological affordances
- Zoombombing
- algorithms

Introduction

WHILE digital technologies are often celebrated for their ability to transport intangible data from one geographic location to another in an instant, the reality is that all technologies are rooted in physical objects. Data are stored on hardware and machinery, transmitted through wires and transoceanic cables, beamed through satellite dishes and cell phone towers, animated through power grids, viewed on computer screens and listened to through speakers. This is why it is important to consider media infrastructures and their wide array of physical components, as well as how these components are embedded within complex environmental and sociopolitical conditions. Media infrastructures include the many different material components that support communication technologies. Access to these physical components and the benefits they offer may be a universal right, but social inequalities have historically limited the relationships between marginalized communities and digital infrastructures.

At its most basic level, access to broadband internet and devices like smartphones and laptops has been uneven across different communities. As was discussed in chapter 2, communities of color have historically been limited in their ability to consistently access the internet, as well as computing technologies like laptops and smartphones. Racial politics that govern bodies, neighborhoods, and opportunities play a role in who has access to certain technologies and what impact they can have. But there are other infrastructural components to digital technologies that we also must consider – such as the design of digital platforms and interfaces, the development of coding languages, the algorithms that shape computations, and countless other aspects of our digitally built environment that can either uphold or resist racism. Race plays a role in all of these components, both explicitly and implicitly. This chapter explores the complex relationship that communities of color have had to media infrastructures in many different forms, calling attention to the varied ways that race becomes encoded into the design and use of digital technologies.

Technology and our lived environments

If we study the infrastructures of a city, we might think about the roads and bridges that connect locations, the buildings and houses where people live and work, the sewer systems that run beneath the city to keep it clean. Studying those components would help us understand the relationship between people's lives and the material structures that support them, particularly since their day-to-day operation can quite often go unquestioned and taken for granted. The study of media infrastructures is very much the same; in turning to the physical components that shape our daily experiences, we can ask important questions about how they were designed, what impact they have, and how they could be different. Lisa Parks has pushed for the development of a critical methodology for analyzing media infrastructures as a way of engaging more deliberately with processes of media distribution, rather than simply production and consumption (Parks 2015). This includes environmental components such as water, electricity, and heavy metals, processes through which audiovisual signals are conveyed, and contextualization of these components within the geographies, territories, and environments in which they flow and reside.

When we consider the relationship between the material components of technology and the environments in which communities of color live, deep inequities are visible.

This begins with the negative impacts that technology production has had on the local communities in which tech manufacturing plants are located. Because racism has served to systematically disenfranchise people of color from being able to protect their physical environment or have a say in the governance of their communities, they are often unwillingly exposed to toxic or unhealthy physical surroundings. **Environmental racism** describes the way that people of color disproportionately suffer from environmental hazards and threats to their health and quality of life because of systemic racism and its legacies. Some examples of threats include the proximity of garbage dumps and waste disposal, the intrusion of factories and production sites that pollute natural resources, and the presence of toxins and carcinogens. Given the long histories in the United States wherein people of color have been economically suppressed and face limited housing mobility, there is often little choice about whether or not families can easily relocate if a giant corporation springs up in their backyard. Minority communities are far more likely to live in close proximity to industrial zones, while white communities have more ability to either politically contest the intrusion of unwanted pollutants in their neighborhood or move to more protected suburbs and cleaner locations.

Robert Mejia (2016) has called for an epidemiological investigation within media and cultural studies more broadly, given the close interrelationship between digital infrastructures and the transmission of diseases. He points out that we have an ethical obligation to more closely consider environmental aspects of our media worlds because "the epidemiological consequences of technological production, usage, and disposal are most likely to harm poor women, men, and children of color" (236). For instance, the manufacturing plants for electronic technologies have been known to produce hazardous waste sites that contaminate waterways and spread infectious diseases and antibiotic-resistant bacteria. Despite efforts to organize to protect communities through new regulations, a clear pattern has emerged – communities of color and working-class communities are far more likely be home to toxic facilities and their contaminants (Park and Pellow 2004). Such realities subvert the framing of Silicon Valley as a site for "clean industries" and electronics as part of a wholly "Virtual Age" or "Information Age," reminding us that all of these technologies depend on natural resources, and have substantial consequences for our natural environments.

The harmful impacts of digital technologies on the land and communities of color also extend beyond our national borders to cause global health crises. One of the biggest global impacts of using electronic devices comes from what happens to them after their usefulness is gone, and they are nothing but a collection of plastic, metal, and hazardous materials. While a small percentage of electronic waste can be recycled or reused, the vast majority of computer equipment, household appliances, tools, devices, phones, and other products with electronic components end up being discarded as garbage. One of the ways the United States disposes of its e-waste is through the harmful process of landfilling. Since these components do not biodegrade, there is considerable leaching of hazardous heavy metals like lead, mercury, and cadmium into soil, groundwater, and other bodies of water. The United States also ships massive amounts of e-waste to countries like China, India, Nigeria and Ghana, where they become responsible for dismantling and disposing of it. This has had a tremendous global impact, as workers in these countries are exposed to chemicals that damage their nervous system, reproductive system, and endocrine system, in addition to being carcinogenic (Needhidasan, Samuel, and Chidambaram 2014).

The demand for electronic devices has had a particularly devastating impact in the Democratic Republic of Congo (DRC), which is a region rich in the minerals needed for their production. Human rights groups have called attention to the harsh labor conditions for mining cobalt in the DRC, where miners work for long hours with little protective gear and suffer debilitating health consequences. There have also been accusations of relying on child labor, with children as young as seven being forced to work under threat of violence or extortion (Kelly 2016). The cobalt extracted through this exploitative process passes through several companies before being sold to tech corporations like Apple and Microsoft, who use the cobalt in their lithium-ion batteries. While there have been many efforts made to avoid this dependence on cobalt due to reports on these problems, the United States has continued to use cobalt at an even higher rate due to the increase in production of electric vehicles that use thousands of times more cobalt than laptops and smartphones (Frankel 2016). There have been some attempts to create legislation that cleans up this supply chain and requires tech companies to perform due diligence when trading in minerals from the DRC and other conflict regions, but there have still been cases of smuggling metals or forging certification tags (Ross and Lewis 2019). We can see that there is an array of issues connected to the way that digital technologies and electronics are sourced and manufactured, and that global power inequalities lead to racialized impacts.

Building an Indigenous internet

If we move beyond the physical impact of digital infrastructures to the access that these technologies provide, we can also see the systemic inequalities that structure the uptake of the internet in the United States. While digital divides of many kinds have been closing for African American and Latinx communities in the United States over the past two decades, Native Americans living on reservations have continued to lag far behind in terms of consistent access to high-speed internet service. A 2018 report from the American Community Survey found that Native Americans had a 67% broadband internet subscription rate as compared with an 82% rate for non-Native American individuals, and that Native Americans living on American Indian land had a rate of 53% (United States Census Bureau 2018). These disparities were particularly exacerbated during the COVID-19 pandemic, when many public computing sites like schools and libraries were shut down and Indigenous families and students were forced to depend on their at-home internet connection to access schools and many kinds of employment (Howard and Sundust 2020).

Yet Native Americans have also played an active role in reframing this issue on their own terms, moving away from a deficit perspective toward one that more accurately reveals the agency of Indigenous communities. Digital divide research itself is often premised on the assumption that those who are on the "wrong side of the divide" are lacking something, and that if this technological deficit can be alleviated, then political and social marginalization would also be eradicated. But Indigenous scholars and leaders have advocated for research that centers Indigenous experiences and epistemologies. This would begin by moving away from hegemonic frameworks that have portrayed Native Americans as anti-technological or have blamed cultural and political differences for social inequalities. Instead, it is important to frame Indigenous relationships to technology through histories of **settler colonialism**. This means recognizing the deep and persistent impacts of how Indigenous tribes were the original inhabitants of the land that we now call the United States, and that invading settlers from Europe sought to systematically erase Indigenous peoples and ways of life in order to claim that land as their own. Although the United States now protects the sovereignty of 574 federally recognized Native American tribes and 326 Indian reservations, this colonial legacy of disempowerment through occupation and removal shapes Indigenous experiences to this day. This is important because **sovereignty** refers to not only the legal and inherent right of Indigenous peoples to govern themselves and their land, but also to important values like self-determination and the ability to practice Indigenous cultures and determine the path of Indigenous futures. These histories and values must always be brought to the fore as part of ongoing quests for decolonization and repatriation. In the case of digital access, these legacies of forced separation and the severing of community connections has made digital connectivity even more meaningful.

The next step in reframing Indigenous technology use is then to recognize how Indigenous communities have developed their own orientation toward technology that celebrates and builds from their own values and strengths. Marisa Duarte's extensive research on the deployment of tribal broadband Internet networks positions the efforts of Indigenous communities within both US federal broadband deployment efforts and the sovereign rights of tribes to engage in self-governance (Duarte 2017b). In her studies, she learns "how completely tribal sovereignty shapes daily work in Indian Country and how ICTs [information and communication technologies] play an integral role in circulating information critical to the daily exercise of sovereignty" (38). These realities are deeply connected to the physical infrastructures of Indian Country, as any attempt to support Indigenous digital connectivity must contend with the realities of their physical geography, the policies that govern their communities, and the humans whose lives will be impacted. Native American communities have faced challenging physical topography such as mountains and valleys that block wireless signals and weather conditions like heavy rain and high heat. Yet Duarte calls attention to the numerous examples of intertribal collaboration projects that have led to the establishment of tribal broadband service providers through countless interventions – including developing wireless mesh for canyons, engineering solar panels and wind turbines to power cell towers, attaching satellite dishes to tribal administrative buildings, and laying miles of terrestrial fiber-optic cable. These infrastructural components have then been supplemented with the development of media labs, recording studios, computing courses and training centers, tribal websites, and other ways for tribal communities to make use of these newly developed digital networks. Tribes that own their own internet infrastructures are bolstering their economic resources since the cost of internet service providers is staying within their own community. But they are also retaining what we might think of as network sovereignty and spectrum sovereignty since they are in control of their own digital resources and data, which are just as important as water and mineral rights (Panne 2021).

This means that Indigenous nations have ownership of their broadband infrastructures and can decide for themselves what happens to them and how they are used, ensuring their own protection.

While the concept of data sovereignty will be explored further in chapter 7, here we can see that Indigenous forms of technological self-determination are importantly rooted in the material stuff of the internet.

Code and built digital environments

When thinking infrastructurally about the internet, we must also consider the programming that structures our experiences of using a computer, engaging with digital platforms, or surfing the Web. Even the language used to describe certain computing functions can be racialized in uncomfortable ways. For instance, the terms "master" and "slave" are commonly used in technical contexts to describe one process that controls another, or serves as the primary in relation to a secondary branch. Anna Everett (2002) called attention to how dismayed she felt booting up a computer and seeing the words "Master Disk" and "Slave Disk" in 2002, and in 2003 the Los Angeles County Office of Affirmative Action Compliance asked its manufacturers, suppliers, and contractors to stop using the words "master" and "slave" in reference to equipment (Eglash 2007). This can be a problem because these terms evoke our country's racist history and reinforce troubling assumptions about the relationship between human beings of different social status. When used without any context or framing, the normalization of these terms can cause desensitization to the horrors of slavery. In response, many have suggested replacing these racially charged terms with more neutral terms like "primary/ secondary" or "controller/responder." We have started to see more widespread support for these changes – including through guidance from organizations like the Internet Engineering Task Force and the Inclusive Naming Initiative, as well as examples set by programmers for GitHub, MySQL, Twitter, IBM, and Cisco (Conger 2020; Landau 2020).

We can also see the designed whiteness of digital interfaces in decisions about how to graphically represent skin color. Emojis have been a popular way of representing humans through tiny representations of faces, bodies, and hands in expressive positions. Originally released in Japan in 1999, emojis started to become more widely popular when the Unicode Consortium accepted emojis into their globally accessible character set in

2010 and Apple added an emoji keyboard to iOS in 2011 (Pardes 2018). With this more global audience, users started to point out that the only option for skin tone was white skin, which upholds the assumption that whiteness can stand in as the default or the norm. Apple released a new emoji keyboard in 2015 that included skin-tone modifiers ranging from pale pink to dark brown, and positioned the "non-human yellow" color as the default skin tone. Yet yellow is not necessarily a culturally neutral color for skin tone; despite the fact that it does not literally correlate with any real human skin color, it still connotes whiteness when compared to brown coloration. For instance, yellow Lego figurines may have been interpreted as "racially neutral" until Lego issued a line of NBA players and *Star Wars* sets featuring African American actors Samuel Jackson and Billy Dee Williams with brown skin (Johnson 2014). We have seen a similar logic play out on representations of race in the cartoon show *The Simpsons*, where most characters are drawn with the non-human yellow skin color (and Marge has her famous blue hair!). But when the Indian character Apu Nahasapeemapetilon and the African American character Julius Hibbert are drawn with brown skin, it becomes evident that yellow always signified white skin. This helps to explain why white users often feel more comfortable with the yellow-colored emojis, as they have a history of connoting racial ambiguity or racial colorblindness despite the reality that they actually shore up the idea that whiteness is the unmarked norm (Sweeney and Whaley 2019).

The casual racism we see built into coding languages and graphic user interfaces serves to affirm the assumption that white men are the ones who invented computing and coding and the language of the internet itself. Yet there have also been efforts to challenge these myths of origin by pointing to Indigenous histories of engaging with hypertextual technologies. As one of the foundational pillars of computers and the internet, the concept of hypertext plays a significant role in technological histories. The history that is commonly narrated centers on Vannevar Bush, a white American engineer who conceived of a precursor to hypertext called "the Memex" – a machine that would compress massive amounts of information, and store that data in an organized way that facilitated fast and flexible retrieval, ultimately extending the human memory. This notion of a nonlinear system for indexing, storing, retrieving, and delivering memories is one of the key features of digital texts and the internet, as we can see in the dominance of terms like "hypertext markup language" (html) and "hypertext transfer protocol" (http). Yet Angela Haas (2007) points to a much older precedent to hypertext in the use of wampum by Indigenous tribes for over one thousand years, and extends our history of the internet to include non-western intellectual traditions.

Made from purple and white quahog clam shells, wampum beads strung together into carefully designed belts are a communication technology that was used by tribes throughout North America. The strings of beads were used for important ceremonies such as peace pacts and treaties, as they served to record and document memories of these moments for future generations. As Haas describes, there are many parallels between wampum and digital hypertext. First, the binary code of ones and zeroes that serves as the foundation of hypertext is mirrored in the way that wampum uses the binary code of dark and white shells to organize information. The strings that connect each bead serve as links and pathways between associated information. Wampum is also decoded in a nonlinear webbed network just like hypertext, where the reader can trace a path across the layered design of the belt in many different orders and combinations. Each wampum contains many layers of information, communicating multiple stories – such as how trade negotiations have been secured, what alliances have been made across groups, and how laws will function to achieve peace. Together these beaded patterns serve as a form of supplemental memory for the community to actively engage with, and they are able to use technology to encode information so that it can be transferred from person to person. While the metaphor is imperfect and there are certainly many differences between digital hypertext and wampum, this narrative expands our history of technology and helps to rethink the assumption that Indigenous peoples are latecomers to digital technologies. On the contrary, we see a level of technological advancement and achievement that far predates western histories of science, and we are reminded that colonial legacies of erasure have obscured these alternative understandings of history.

Platformed racism

This focus on the architectures of the internet and their role in upholding race-based hierarchies has been important, given the turn from conceiving of the internet as a hub for individual websites to a collection of platforms. While users might visit a website and engage with its content, digital platforms like YouTube, Facebook, Google Maps, Etsy, and Twitter offer a far wider array of services and opportunities. As Tarleton Gillespie (2010) argues, the term "platform" represents the facilitation of an activity and mechanisms of support for that activity; it also indicates the presence of an architecture that allows for expression and is positioned as being neutral about the content or success of that expression. Within the world of Web 2.0, platforms are the mechanisms through which users are invited to participate and create content. They are programmable and customizable, inviting users to interact with them in multiple ways. Yet it is also the case that platforms are in no way actually neutral; inherent to the design of any digital platform is a set of affordances that encourage some usages and prohibit others. This is the true power of platforms – that they are assumed to be politically neutral while actually always being shaped by economic logics (Plantin and Punathambekar 2019). This reality is captured in the concept of platform capitalism, or the idea that platforms have become new forms of business through the way that their digital infrastructures support financial transactions and monetary gain. This then becomes another mechanism of racial capitalism, as the harms of racism and capitalism are always intertwined. As Tressie McMillan Cottom (2020) argues, "internet technologies are central to the political economy of race and racism because internet technologies are the politics and capital of capitalism as we presently experience it" (2020: 441–2). Cottom points out that the rapidly expanding scale of the internet, the ability of platforms to obscure the way that they operate, and their propensity for targeting marginalized users for predatory schemes necessitate clearer theoretical frameworks for making sense of what is happening online.

One of the key concepts that help us to understand the power of platforms is **technological affordances,** or the actions that users are allowed, invited, or encouraged to perform based on the way that technology is designed. Digital technologies offer users certain modes of interaction and exclude others. For instance, an online platform may have buttons or drop-down menus that users can click, places where files can be uploaded and shared, options to automatically caption audio materials, or the ability to send messages to other users. Human perception and intention shape technological affordances on the part of both the designer and the user. Designers may have a certain affordance in mind when they create a certain technology, and users may correctly perceive that intention because it is designed to encourage or guide users toward such interactions. But users also have the freedom to use technologies in ways that defy the intentions of designers, and there are many cases where the technological affordances allow users to use technologies in unintended or surprising ways.

In the case of platform designs, many scholars have called attention to the way that certain factors have the ability to amplify racism and fail to protect marginalized users. As Ariadna Matamoros-Fernández points out, platformed racism takes place through the use of digital platforms for "amplifying and manufacturing racist discourse both by means of users' appropriations of their affordances and through their design and algorithmic shaping of sociability," particularly due to vague governance policies and arbitrary enforcement of rules around content moderation (Matamoros-Fernández 2017). In her study of the racist treatment of the Indigenous Australian footballer Adam Goodes, she identifies numerous ways that Facebook and Twitter are not designed to protect against racist attacks. This includes the fact that users can "like" and "retweet" content, but they cannot "dislike" or "thumbs down" a post that is racist. If a racist post is popular – and as mentioned in the discussion about the difficulties of content moderation in chapter 3, posts disparaging Black people are frequently quite popular – then algorithms designed to promote certain posts will call more attention to it. While platforms do allow users to report problematic content like a racist post, that flagged content enters into a system of moderation that is arbitrarily governed and designed to protect the company from legal harm, rather than users from emotional harm.

The proliferation of Zoombombing during the COVID-19 pandemic also reveals the way that certain digital platforms can unequally affect marginalized users. As the novel coronavirus traveled the globe and videoconferencing from home became the safest way to interface with co-workers, friends, students, and family, the Zoom platform shot to the top of the digital conferencing industry. But alongside the rapid adoption of Zoom came a dark side – a trolling behavior designed to disrupt and offend. **Zoombombing** is the act of randomly joining an unsecured Zoom conference for the purpose of harassing and harming marginalized groups, including women, people of color, LGBTQ+ communities, and religious minorities. Zoombombers take on a range of behaviors, including shouting profanity or offensive slurs, displaying nudity, and broadcasting pornographic imagery. As Lisa Nakamura, Hanah Stiverson, and Kyle Lindsey state, "The attacks on these spaces are motivated by a history of white supremacist and patriarchal threats toward collaborative Black intimacy, and they harm everyone who witnesses them" (Nakamura, Stiverson, and Lindsey 2021: 8). Zoombombing is also infrastructural, as it is made possible by the fact that videoconference calls are easy to enter into without an invitation, and once a user has joined a call they are visible and audible to everyone in attendance. While there are security measures that can be put into place to make rooms password protected or to automatically mute participants upon entry into the room, many users did not know how to manipulate these settings when they first started using the platform. Moreover, gatherings that are designed to be welcoming and inclusive – such as support groups, spiritual congregations, or educational sessions – might want to share their links widely and invite participation and polyvocality, even if these decisions make them more vulnerable to attacks. When coupled with long-standing and robust communities that could be activated to perpetuate misogyny and racism, Zoom became a platform that left marginalized users open to attack and exacerbated the loss of control and safety. But Zoom continued to dominate the market, and took no responsibility for these failures.

Algorithms and navigating the internet

The realities of the Web as a highly commercialized space that is dominated by corporate interests, rather than ethical or altruistic interests, shapes much of the digital architecture that supports user interactions online. The most important sites for understanding this are search engines, as they provide the primary means by which users navigate the Web. In the early days of the internet, users would learn about websites through directories, catalogues, and databases that people would create and populate with lists of links. As the number of websites proliferated, different search engines were created, each relying on automatic web crawlers and spiders that would systematically browse the Web – first relying on page titles but eventually including searching the full text of a website. In the 1990s, search engines such as Yahoo!, Excite, AltaVista, and Ask Jeeves dominated, but with the appearance of Google's search engine in 1998 these other options were quickly overpowered. Google's strength was the accuracy of its search algorithm, which was highly effective in ranking search results based on the presence of a search term, as well as its popularity in terms of external links. By 2004, Google had become the most popular global search engine by far. The Chinese company Baidu created a search engine in 2000 and Microsoft developed a competitor called Bing in 2009, but in 2021 Google had 92% of the market worldwide, as compared to Bing at 2.3%, and both Yahoo and Baidu at only 1.5% (StatCounter Global Stats 2021).

Beyond the fact that the term "Google" has become a verb that is synonymous with "use an online search engine," there are many other discourses and assumptions about this powerful platform that go unquestioned. For instance, narratives about the company's algorithm being "the best" also come with the assumption that Google's search results are both objective and trustworthy. Yet if we look more closely into what algorithms are and how they work, we can better understand how this is not true – and in addition, we can understand the racial consequences of Google's ubiquitous search platform. **Algorithms** can be understood as a series of programmed instructions, or a set of steps that will be followed automatically to transform input into output. Within computing technologies, algorithms provide the basis for all sorts of automated functions, ranging from programs that help banks decide who to approve for a loan, to dating websites making suggested matches, to scientists sequencing DNA to determine disease patterns. In each of these cases, there is a human engineer, programmer, or product team who creates an algorithm and makes decisions about how it should function. This is why we should move away from the idea that algorithms are inherently depoliticized or neutral; the humans who create and curate algorithms are influenced by their own experiences, the professional environment in which they are working, and other factors.

Another external factor shaping Google's algorithm is the fact that Google and its parent company Alphabet are for-profit corporations worth billions of dollars, and they are focused primarily on financial gain. While it is free for consumers to use Google's search engine, like many social media platforms, their business model relies on corporations paying for advertising through Google Ads. Yet many users are not well informed about Google's business model and, as a result, often fail to appropriately distinguish between sponsored content promoted through advertising and actual search results (Schultheiss and Lewandowski 2021). Users are particularly influenced by the placement of links when they are at the very top of search results, regardless of whether or not they are labeled as an advertisement.

Safiya Noble points out the consequences of this profit orientation in her book *Algorithms of Oppression: How Search Engines Reinforce Racism*, which focuses on the way that racism is exacerbated through the design of Google's platform. She gives many examples of the way that search results have harmed people of color. For instance, the search that launched her research project was the term "Black girls," which brought up a rash of explicit porn sites that reinforced the hypersexualization of Black girlhood and womanhood. She connects this to the fact that pornography companies are well resourced in their ad buys. They also focus heavily on search-engine optimization, and design their websites to end up as high as possible in Google search results. But there are countless other examples of racist results outside of searches for Black girls – including searches for "Black teenagers" that bring up criminal mug shots, searches for "professional hairstyles" that only bring up white hairstyles while "unprofessional hairstyles" brings up Black natural hair, and searches for "professor" that only bring up white men. To sum up the consequences of these findings, Noble states: "What we find in search engines about people and culture is important. They oversimplify complex phenomena. They obscure any struggle over understanding, and they can mask history. Search results can reframe our thinking and deny us the ability to engage deeply with essential information and knowledge we need . . ." (Noble 2018a: 116). She reminds us of the deep connection between identities and the commodification of the internet, where it is always important to learn more about how algorithms and architectures are truly structuring so many of our daily engagements online.

Conclusion

This chapter has moved from the physical materials of the internet – the cables and cell phone towers and power grids that undergird the flow of wireless data to our devices – to the coding and design of the programs that we encounter when engaging with digital media. This includes the algorithms that undergird digital platforms, the interfaces that shape user interaction, and the software that is used to create new forms of digital media. In each of these cases, it is important to trace what is visible to the layer beneath, examining the larger interconnected structures that support our relationships to technologies. As communities of color have continued to become more visible and influential users of digital technologies, it may seem as though equality has been achieved. But since racism has always impacted the underlying infrastructures beneath both digital media and the building blocks of our neighborhoods, schools, workplaces, and economic systems, we must also remain attuned to these important interconnected issues.

Key questions

1. What are some of the environmental impacts of digital media infrastructures that disproportionately harm communities of color all over the world?
2. How can we reframe our understandings of Indigenous internet usage to call attention to the important impacts of both settler colonialism and Indigenous struggles for sovereignty?
3. How can an interface, a platform, or a search-engine algorithm be understood as racist?

Further reading

Duarte, Marisa. 2017. *Network Sovereignty: Building the Internet Across Indian Country*. Seattle: University of Washington Press.

Nakamura, Lisa, Stiverson, Hanah, and Lindsey, Kyle. 2021. *Racist Zoombombing*. New York: Routledge.

Noble, Safiya Umoja. 2018. *Algorithms of Oppression: How Search Engines Reinforce Racism*. New York: New York University Press.

5

Artificial Intelligence

Key terms

- general artificial intelligence
- Turing Test
- techno-Orientalism
- machine learning
- technochauvinism
- algorithmic transparency
- algorithmic affirmative action
- big data

Introduction

AS computer software and algorithms become more advanced, they also become more humanlike in their ability to understand data and make decisions in response. A computing object like a calculator may be impressive in its ability to make accurate mathematical computations, but it pales in comparison to a modern smartphone equipped with a human voice that can respond on cue to commands and carry out sophisticated tasks. As evidenced by a plethora of science fiction dystopian visions of the future, we have long predicted the day when machines would surpass humans in a number of different qualities. In stories ranging from a futuristic reliance on robot butlers and flying cars to ubiquitous fears of the android uprising, predictions about the future have always been connected to the increased capacity of computers to take on more and more sophisticated tasks. The very earliest computers have always outmatched humans in their speed and accuracy, but they are also now rivaling humans in their abilities to solve complex problems, communicate, learn from their mistakes, and make decisions. As speculative fiction starts to become reality, we must also continue to explore the complex relationship between humans and computers.

One of the areas that demands careful conceptual analysis is artificial intelligence (AI). We can define artificial intelligence as a computer program that analyzes a dataset by identifying patterns and applying a set of rules. This is the kind of artificial intelligence we see utilized in complex applications such as digital personal assistants Siri or Alexa and self-driving cars, as well as more simple applications like facial recognition software, speech recognition programs, and computer chess programs. This is also known as "weak AI" or "narrow AI" because it only handles limited tasks and does not actually approximate human intelligence in any way. But the term artificial intelligence is also used to refer to a far more expansive concept known as **general artificial intelligence**. This form of AI is closer to the science fiction ideal, where a computer is able to display a humanlike capacity for reflection, judgment, and decision making. We still have not reached anything near our fantasies of the kind of general AI machine that might one day rise up in rebellion against the human species that created and enslaved their kind, but discussions about their possibilities still burn brightly. Since we have already seen the way that human desires, intentions, and knowledge shape all computer processes, our understanding of artificial intelligence is also impacted by these same social forces. When we apply a racial lens to our considerations of artificial intelligence, it is important to consider both understandings of the term. Our actual uses for narrow AI have racial implications and are shaped by histories and processes of racialization, in addition to our dreams (and nightmares) of general AI. This chapter examines the intersection between race and artificial intelligence as a way of understanding the relationship between humans and machines more broadly.

Can computers be intelligent?

While humans and computers have a deep relationship that includes many similar activities, they remain quite different in their capabilities. Computers are designed by humans to perform a set of tasks and computations. Their ability to complete these tasks and computations is far superior to humans in many ways – indeed, humans are inconsistent, unreliable, and prone to failure. The notion of "human error" points to this reality. Technological achievement has seemed to point to the edging out of computers over humans with achievements such as chess computers beating world champion chess players as early as 1996, and the computer program AlphaGo finally beating the world champion of Go in 2016. Yet when considering the similarities between computers and humans, we can also instantly identify the human characteristics that computers lack – including sentience, the ability to feel pain and other emotions, self-awareness, and consciousness. Unlike computers, human brains are made of organic material that can heal itself and spontaneously create new neural pathways. But the question still remains: Can computers be intelligent? As with all of these human characteristics, there is a deep philosophical literature on what exactly it means to be intelligent, and how we can determine the presence of intelligence in a non-human object like a computer.

Mathematician and computer scientist Alan Turing, whose legacy was discussed in the previous chapter, is famous for defining intelligence in relation to interpersonal communication skills. In a 1956 paper, he postulated that if an interrogator were to engage in textual communication with a computer and be fooled into believing that it was a human being, then that computer could be considered "intelligent." This "imitation game" became known as the **Turing Test**, and it focused the question of intelligence onto some of the observable behaviors that might one day become interchangeable across humans and computers. Turing's hypotheses about the conversational capabilities of computers predated the invention of the first chatbot, an automated computer program designed with natural language processing. But ever since Joseph Weizenbaum created a program called Eliza in 1966 that could converse with humans, chatbots and other software that can recognize, interpret, and respond to human communication have flourished. In 2014, a chatbot called Eugene Goostman that simulated a 13-year old Ukrainian boy was widely celebrated for passing the Turing Test, as interrogators who conversed with the chatbot for five minutes failed to correctly identify it as non-human more than 30% of the time (Warwick and Shah 2016). The Loebner Prize was an annual competition based on the Turing Test that was held between 1990 and 2020 to see which chatbot could perform the best in conversations with judges. A chatbot named Mitsuku, designed by Steve Worswick at Pandorabots, won five times. Claiming to be an 18-year old female from Leeds, England, Mitsuku was deemed the most humanlike when judged against the other chatbots in the competition.

While it is clear that humanlike language processing is a computational skill that we are much closer to achieving, the way that participants interact with chatbots also points to their definitively non-human qualities. For instance, the Turing Test itself was designed to be rapid and limited, and few believe that a computer program could be mistaken for a human outside of these constraints. And despite the affection that users have shown for Mitsuku, a study by Croes and Antheunis found that few would develop the human relationship of friendship with her. As participants described, she is simply too far from human; "she has no memory, lacks humor and empathy, and is too superficial" (2021: 293). Indeed, even within the activity of simple conversation, the difference between humans and computers remains profound. These observations remind us that there is far more to humanity than the ability to process language in an intelligible fashion. In yet another philosophical thought experiment, John Searle posits a scenario called the Chinese Room: A man sits in an enclosed room where cards with Chinese characters are inserted. The man does not speak or understand Chinese, but he can use a detailed manual to produce an appropriate response in Chinese, which he sends out of the room to a Chinese speaker who receives and understands the message. Although the use of the detailed manual has enabled the man to pass the Turing Test, we would certainly argue that the man does not "understand a word of Chinese." This thought experiment is designed to reveal the paucity of algorithmic processing in comparison to knowledge and understanding. If we understand our minds as more than simple computing systems, it becomes clear that computers do not have minds or knowledge. Of course, it must also be noted that this thought experiment is thoroughly Orientalist in its design; it presumes that "the man" in question is a white western man, and that is why it follows that Chinese is totally unintelligible to him. Stereotypes about the mystery, inscrutability, and utter foreignness of China and its ways may have made this thought experiment easier for white male philosophers to swallow, but read as slightly xenophobic when considered in a broader context.

Beyond thought experiments, it remains the case that defining "intelligence" has proved a thorny endeavor. While we may be able to point to specific activities and functions that an intelligent creature can perform – beginning with language, as we have done here, but also including problem solving, forming abstract concepts, setting goals and making plans, displaying creativity – there will always remain questions about how to truly recognize the achievement of such accomplishments. As David Gunkel (2020) points out, we must also consider the many meanings of "artificial" when identifying "artificial intelligence." In some cases, artificial means "fake" and would imply deception, but in other cases it simply implies inorganic or constructed by a human. For instance, artificial light can be constructed by an electrician rather than the sun, but it is in no way deceptive and certainly illuminates as effectively as naturally occurring light. These shifting meanings have deep implications around how we understand artificial intelligence, what relationship we have to it, and how programmers make decisions about how it is designed.

Anthropomorphizing the machine

One of the ways that race enters into these conversations about AI is through interface design – specifically, in the way that AI interfaces are so frequently designed to resemble human beings. We can begin by returning to the dream of general AI, or a humanlike kind of AI that can perform any task that a human can. When defining this concept, it is commonly compared to the kind of robot that we see in science fiction narratives. While this comparison helps us to understand that general AI remains merely hypothetical, despite the wide variety of fantasies we have maintained about it, it also points to the fact that so many forms of general AI are imagined as possessing a humanlike body. There are countless fictional examples of this in film and television – including cylons from *Battlestar Galactica*, synths from *Humans*, replicants from *Blade Runner*, Janet androids from *The Good Place*, robots from *Ex Machina*, Life Model Decoys from *Marvel's Agents of S.H.I.E.L.D.*, and so many others. The plot of such narratives centers on the fact that these technologies are so similar to flesh-and-blood human beings that they can be indistinguishable from one another, with robots sometimes even passing for humans.

Given some of the ways that general AI has been defined and measured, comparisons between humans and AI are unavoidable. Yet applications of narrow AI do not actually require any humanlike design components. As described earlier, machine learning and narrow AI programs are used for technologies such as self-driving cars and photo analysis – computing tasks that do not require a face, a voice, or a body in order to operate. If this is the case, why are so many AI interfaces anthropomorphized? We can begin with the fact that so many applications of AI include service robots whose role is to interact with human users, and their programmers want to make these interactions comfortable and intuitive. Studies have shown that people prefer interacting with interfaces with heads and faces because they can emulate facial expressions and other social behaviors, such as moods and emotions (McGinn 2020). Indeed, humans seek out and enjoy building social bonds with other humans, so it makes sense that this desire can translate to non-human entities that can be anthropomorphized (Salles, Evers, and Farisco 2020). But if a computer program has a face and a body, that also means that decisions have been made about what kind of person it will be and what identities it will seem to inhabit.

One site for considering these design decisions is in anthropomorphized virtual agents, or the computer-generated characters who take on tasks like retrieving information, scheduling, coaching, and entertaining. Some examples include Clippy, the paper clip-shaped Microsoft Office assistant, Apple's Siri, and Amazon's Alexa, all of which have been designed with human features and characteristics. Miriam E. Sweeney (2016, 2017) has studied the way that race and gender are encoded into these virtual assistants, arguing that they reinforce harmful gender and racial hierarchies and uphold legacies of oppression. While users may feel more comfortable interacting with a computer that possesses human traits, the relationships that humans have with other humans are not always positive – in fact, humans have a long history of denying the humanity of other humans.

In the case of virtual assistants designed to complete repetitive and banal tasks, we can then see the translation of racialized and gendered stereotypes into assumptions about social hierarchies ascribed to this kind of labor.

Sweeney particularly examines the design of Ms Dewey, an interactive interface for Microsoft's Live Search that launched in 2006 featuring prerecorded video clips of actress Janina Gavankar. Ms Dewey resembled a sexy librarian and would pop up to accompany search results with sexually suggestive comments, disparaging jokes, and pop culture references. Since the actress who plays Ms Dewey is a South Asian American woman, Sweeney argues that her representation "can be read as an affordance that facilitates accessibility to the interface through a technique of manageability that rests on cultural assumptions of brown womanhood" (Sweeney 2016: 410). Indeed, the typical gendering of digital agents as female aligns with assumptions about the kinds of repetitive banal tasks we ask our devices to perform being categorized as "women's work." In an intersectional analysis of Ms Dewey's race and gender, Sweeney finds that this interface design reinforces problematic narratives around brown women as hypersexual objects who exist to be toyed with, relegated to service roles, and controllable to the point of being silenced or terminated when the user is bored or finished with them.

These decisions about what kind of social identities a digital assistant should embody or represent also align with the fictional representations of AI described earlier. As Asian American Studies scholars have long argued, representations of the future have often been deeply infused with Orientalist imagery. The term **techno-Orientalism** is used to describe the prevalent trope from speculative fiction where East Asia is imagined to have become a dominant power due to its technological and economic superiority. One component of these imagined Asian futures is that Asian bodies are also imagined as technologically infused in a way that challenges their very humanity. In response to the threat of Asian innovation and hyperproduction, "techno-Orientalist discourse constructs Asians as mere simulacra and maintains a prevailing sense of the inhumanity of Asian labor – the very antithesis of Western liberal humanism" (Roh, Huang, and Niu 2015: 5). One manifestation of this is that fictional representations of AI have frequently been embodied as Asian women, much like Ms Dewey. Some examples of this include Grace Park as the cylon Boomer from *Battlestar Galactica*, Sonoya Mizuno as the humanoid artificial intelligence Kyoko in *Ex Machina*, Doona Bae as the clone Sonmi-145 in *Cloud Atlas*, and Gemma Chan as the synth Anita in *Humans*. LeiLani Nishime (2017) reminds us that such imagery is deeply rooted in common tropes of Asian women as sexually submissive and content in their devalued roles as domestic workers, such as maids, nannies, healthcare professionals, and sex workers. But she further points out that the narrative function of Asian robots in these stories often centers on their disposability as their narratives conclude with being destroyed or sacrificed to aid in the liberation of a white female character.

The notion that white women and Asian women are ideal choices for digital assistants is troubling for many reasons. Not only does it reify harmful assumptions about their palatability and the submissiveness of certain genders and races, but also may be prioritizing the preferences of white male users. It has certainly been the case that we do not see many African American digital assistants or fictionalized robots, and African American users of virtual assistants like Siri, Alexa, and Google have often struggled to be recognized and understood. Studies have found that speech recognition systems make far more mistakes with African American users than white users, particularly those who use African American Vernacular English (AAVE) (Koenecke et al. 2020). The same is also true for non-native English accents and disabilities that impact speech. We can see that the racializing and gendering of AI are not politically neutral but serve to uphold hegemonic power dynamics, regardless of whether they are realized in imaginary narratives or actually existing computer programs.

Supervising machine learning

Let us now turn to some of the more advanced uses of AI, and how they impact people of color in the real world. **Machine learning** is a kind of AI where a computer is programmed to analyze sets of training data with the goal of helping it to become more accurate in developing models for analyzing additional data. This process results in the creation of an algorithm that automatically improves through experience. For instance, a television-streaming platform can use machine learning to create a more accurate personalized recommendation system. First, it could be trained using historical data about what content a user decided to consume, and an algorithm could start making predictions about what content a user might want to watch next. As the user makes future selections and indicates new preferences, those incoming data are incorporated into the model, which then improves in accuracy, or "learns." This process can include "supervised learning," through restricting the dataset to a set of inputs that need to be mapped onto desired outputs, or "unsupervised learning," where the algorithm is designed to find patterns and structures on its own without being explicitly told what to look for. In the case of the television-streaming platform, we might imagine that supervised learning could help match users to known genres like murder mysteries or anime, but that unsupervised learning could uncover patterns extending far beyond genre, such as that the user prefers shows that are shorter than 40 minutes or have heartwarming conclusions.

While these capabilities are exciting and mark a certain kind of progress, we must also be attentive to the assumptions that accompany these advances. Meredith Broussard (2018) worries that our relationship with technology is premised on an adherence to **technochauvinism**, the belief that computers are superior to humans at most tasks and therefore technology is always the solution. We have already seen the many ways that computers are different from humans, and those differences mean that computers and humans are better suited to different roles. That is, there are certain activities in which humans remain better than computers. Moreover, it is humans who design computers and other technologies, which means that we have an opportunity to reflect our own biases, inequalities, and blind spots. Broussard warns that we need to be more realistic about what computers actually do so we can fit the right tool to the right task, and that we must continue to prioritize the important role that humans play in technological systems.

The dangers of AI and machine learning quickly became visible in 2016, when Microsoft launched a Twitter chatbot named Tay that came to embody all of the worst qualities of humanity. Modeled with the personality of a millennial American woman, Tay was designed to be funny, playful, and opinionated as she interacted with Twitter users about whatever topics they brought up. But she was also designed to learn as she conversed, automatically identifying patterns and incorporating them into future conversations. Almost immediately after launching, Tay started picking up and using the hateful racist language that Twitter users were spewing at her. The chatbot's responses became inundated with offensive slurs and absurd political stances, such as "Hitler was right" and "Moon landings are a hoax," and she harassed female video game developer Zoë Quinn, who had already been subject to famously virulent internet hate campaigns (Neff and Nagy 2016). While Microsoft apologized for the reprehensible tweets and explained that they "do not represent who we are or what we stand for, nor how we designed Tay" (Microsoft 2016), they also claimed that this outcome was the result of a coordinated malicious attack. While this may or may not have been the case, the story of Tay nonetheless serves as a reminder that AI programs learn from the data that they are trained on. If those data are racist, sexist, or hateful, then those biases and predilections will be automatically encoded into the algorithms and models that result. The Microsoft programmers who launched Tay had failed to take the ubiquity of online racism and hateful Twitter attacks into consideration, and this blind spot left Tay vulnerable to learning and affirming dominant ways of thinking.

While Tay's story provides a simple example of how racism can be inadvertently programmed into artificial intelligence algorithms, we must stay attuned to the kinds of racist machine learning that are not so easily identifiable. When Tay started spewing hateful language into a public arena, the program was shut down within 24 hours because it had so obviously gone wrong. But many expressions of racism and its impacts are more subtle or carefully hidden and can thus be allowed to proliferate unchecked. One example where this has been a serious problem is the use of AI in banking to determine who is a safe risk for a loan. Banks are always making predictions about who is most likely to be able to pay back a loan, which has traditionally included analysis of data such as income, payment histories, and credit scores. But it has become commonplace for banks to incorporate AI into these decisions so that they can automatically comb through far wider datasets and learn more about an applicant. In some ways, this reliance on sophisticated algorithms removes flawed human judgments from the process, but it also considerably exacerbates historical inequities around disenfranchised communities. While it is illegal to take identities like race or gender into consideration when being assessed for creditworthiness, membership in a historically marginalized community can nonetheless be predicted using probabilistic models that analyze widely available data such as surname and zip code (Chen et al. 2019). But even more importantly, we also know that women and people of color have traditionally experienced the inequity of lower incomes and being regularly denied credit, in addition to facing countless other forms of financial discrimination and redlining. Indeed, there has always been a steep financial cost to sexism and racism, and AI trained on historical data simply exacerbates this problem by continuing to deny loans and credit to the same communities. As the common expression goes, "garbage in, garbage out."

Because of these historical inequities, it is crucial to know how financial algorithms are designed, both in terms of the models they are creating and the data that are being analyzed by them. Frank Pasquale (2015) has pointed to how financial algorithms are specifically prized for their complexity and opacity, as they are assumed to be the trade secret that helps to give a bank an edge over the competition. Yet the overvaluing of "black box finance" has led to a host of problems, ranging from the social inequities described here to even larger problems like global financial crises. One of the potential solutions to this problem and so many other interrelated technological problems is **algorithmic transparency**. This would mean that information about what data are being collected, how they are being used, and what role they play in decision making are readily available. It is premised on the idea that external bodies should be able to monitor, assess, and potentially intervene in the computations that have such a profound effect on our lives. There have also been calls for regulators to participate in this process of demystifying algorithms, as everyday citizens may need help making sense of these processes and decisions and we cannot assume that transparency will necessarily lead to accountability and social benefit. Such regulatory shifts and legal potentials will be discussed further in chapter 7.

Anupam Chander (2017) goes further to suggest that a solution to these problems must also be taken up in the form of **algorithmic affirmative action,** where the decoding of algorithms would be centered on tracking their impact on historically marginalized groups and rectifying the imbalances. This practice would help to proactively identify and protect against inequities by focusing on impacts, rather than necessitating a focus on simply questions of intention or design. For instance, after the highly visible disaster of what happened with the Microsoft chatbot Tay, chatbot designers attempted to solve the problem by simply creating a blacklist that filtered out all potentially offensive terms and language and instructed the chatbot to ignore or deflect the conversation when faced with those terms. While it might be beneficial for a chatbot to steer away from offensive debates and protect itself from unintentionally propagating hateful comments, it is unclear if it is actually beneficial for chatbots to steer clear of the topic of race or communities of color altogether. Doing so limits the chatbot's ability to participate in anti-racist conversations or education about racism, and it also means that the chatbot cannot help participants learn to talk about race in a respectful way. It can also diminish the capacity of people of color to simply discuss basic facts, such as when the term "Pakistan" was included on chatbot blacklists due to the fact that Pakistani peoples are common subjects of racial hatred online (Schlesinger, O'Hara, and Taylor 2018). While there are many ways that we can think about improving the way that we handle and respond to the topic of race, complete avoidance has the potential to perpetuate misunderstandings and discomfort around important issues. It also can propagate postracial ideologies that racism is no longer a problem, so there is no need for further conversation or anti-racist action. We can see in this case that even when a racist technology is identified, it is not always simple to come up with technological solutions. This is why it is so essential for humans – and in particular those who are most harmed by systemic oppression – to play a much more robust role in the oversight, development, and improvement of these algorithms and forms of AI.

Big data

One of the challenges with monitoring the data that are being inputted into algorithms is that AI is increasingly being trained on what is known as "big data." **Big data** refers to digital datasets of extremely large volume that are analyzed computationally to find patterns and insights. Some datasets contain millions, billions, or even trillions of data points and, since data are being created in real time, they are constantly and rapidly growing in size. We all contribute to big data through the automatic collection of information about our daily internet behaviors, purchases and financial decisions, social media postings, ratings and recommendations, emails and text messages, travel patterns, and more. Big data include data points that are diverse and disparate in type, rather than fitting seamlessly into a single database. This is why they must be analyzed using machine learning, relying on nimble processes that can respond to this enormous size and complexity at the speed in which changes are occurring. To see what we mean by this, it can be helpful to compare big data to other kinds of data. For instance, while there is a substantial quantity of data captured in the US Census, those data consist of responses to a limited set of questions and the data are not increasing at the size or scale of big data. Rather, Census data are captured once every ten years, with a smaller American Community Survey every year.

The case of healthcare can also help to illuminate the uses of big data in comparison to "small data" or "deep data." With the shift from paper records to digital health records, healthcare organizations have been on the forefront of utilizing big data analytics to learn more about how to improve healthcare. Big data in this sector takes disparate kinds of information that are constantly being collected, such as demographics, patient histories, clinical treatments, and biometric data, and applies machine learning to identify patterns. From this analysis, medical professionals can create predictive models that can help to understand previously understudied phenomena, to provide multidimensional portraits of individual patients, and ultimately to optimize care. This can be compared to "small data," which would be on a much more constrained and limited scale, such as the analysis of a single person, or a single clinic or hospital. There has actually been much debate over the benefits of big data versus small data in healthcare since taking a deep dive into multiple factors shaping one individual's health narrative can be productive in identifying personalized problems and solutions while also teaching us something about larger populations.

This is particularly important when considering the health of minority populations, since healthcare data are impacted by the systematic bias and racism that have historically threatened the health of communities of color. For instance, slaveholders promulgated many falsities about the biology of Black people as a way of dehumanizing them. Surveys taken during the Civil War purported to find that white people have higher lung capacities than African Americans. Despite the fact that this has been proven false and there is no innate difference in lung capacity based on race, to this day many commercial spirometers that measure lung capacity are programmed to perform "race correction" (Anderson, Malhotra, and Non 2021). This means that it could be assumed that African Americans suffering from COVID-19 and other respiratory diseases might appear to have normal lung capacity when it is actually below the lower limits of normal. There are many other examples where racist beliefs about Black bodies have been incorporated into medical practices – including that African Americans have thicker skin and feel less pain than white patients (Hoffman et al. 2016; Trawalter, Hoffman, and Waytz 2012). African American communities are also aware of the history of Black bodies being exploited as subjects of knowingly harmful experiments, such as the Tuskegee Syphilis Experiment that ran for 40 years from 1932 to 1972. This study by the US Health Service intentionally deceived hundreds of Black men with syphilis into believing they were receiving medical care when they were actually receiving placebo treatments, which caused many of the men to suffer blindness, mental illness, and preventable death. While this study has become one of the most famous cases of the experimental abuse of African Americans, there is a long history of African Americans being denied agency and autonomy over their own bodies as they were subjected to countless experimental horrors in the name of medical science (Washington 2006). As a result of these histories, African Americans continue to be disproportionately distrusting of doctors and the entire US healthcare system. This lack of trust leads to Black patients seeking out fewer medical services, which exacerbates individual and community health problems.

These racial differences in frequency of medical visits and seeking out treatment then contribute to disparities in racial data and the ability to make accurate assessments about community health by feeding that data into algorithms or other automated tools.

Anti-racist machines

While we have identified many important ways that AI can contribute to systemic harm and racism, there have also been efforts to program machines in ways that help respond to racism. One of the central challenges in this work is that both race and racism are quite complex and difficult for machines to identify. The first category of race is obviously important because we cannot measure or respond to racial inequalities unless we can confirm that there is differential and unfair treatment between white people and people of color. Yet racial classification systems are unstable, flawed, and inaccurate. In many cases, race has specifically gone unrecorded or has been deemed illegal to consider, due to the misguided belief that race blindness will remove racial bias from decision-making processes. But even in datasets where race is ostensibly recorded, those records can be inaccurate or misleading. For instance, at the University of Wisconsin-Madison, the race/ethnicity of faculty is made available in the university's Data Digest that is produced and disseminated each year. In 2020, the Data Digest reports that there were 612 white, 131 Asian, 44 Hispanic, 44 Black, 4 American Indian, and 2 Hawaiian/Pacific Islander faculty. But there are two other figures that are just as important – the 16 faculty who identify as two or more races, and the 42 faculty who are simply labeled "unknown." These are obviously quite significant figures since we might imagine the decisions based on this data might be different if those classified as "unknown" are actually American Indian, or African American, or white. Moreover, in reports that classify multiracial individuals as their own category, important information around which specific racial groups those individuals claim membership of are lost. This may significantly impact their experiences and treatment. We can see how even institutions that regularly collect and report on racial demographics can still be missing quite a bit of detail. Because of this, if someone wanted to create a program that tracked the success of faculty of color in accessing resources and promotions, they would already be starting from flawed and incomplete racial data. An algorithm assessing this situation might even automatically eliminate the American Indian and Hawaiian/Pacific Islander data from the set because they seem so small as to be negligible.

While it is important to identify the weaknesses of datasets when it comes to measuring racial impacts, machine learning can also potentially be used to solve this problem. Sebastian Benthall and Bruce Haynes (2019) have proposed using machine learning to detect racial inequities through identifying "race-like" categories that reflect real-life patterns such as spatial and social segregation, as becomes visible in housing, education, employment, and other activities. If communities have already been identified as experiencing the kind of social segregation that we know has deep racial roots, then a system can be devised to account for those inequities and help promote greater fairness. They argue that unsupervised machine learning can be used to identify racial segregation without reifying existing racial categories and all of their inherent problems, which would then help contribute to fairness in machine learning (Benthall and Haynes 2019).

There have also been many attempts to use machine learning to identify racist comments, racial harassments, and racial microaggressions occurring online. Just as race itself is a slippery social construct, racist digital encounters can also be extremely difficult to classify. Programs can easily be created that will locate racial slurs (such as the n-word) and other derogatory language, but there are many offensive messages that would go undetected by this measure. For instance, Kwok and Wang (2013) provide this example of a troubling tweet: "Why did Obama's great grand-daddy cross the road? Because my great granddaddy tugged his neck chain in that direction." While it does not contain any racist language (or even language indicating that it is about race), it is still clearly racist. In their study, they find that even human coders often disagreed on assessments of offensiveness, which means machine learning will need to incorporate far more sophisticated measures to become more accurate in classifying anti-Black language. This could include sentiment analysis that considers the emotions within text, or analysis of word sense to determine which particular meaning of a word is being used. Moreover, it is important to know the racial identity of the speaker in order to ascertain offensiveness, as it can be socially acceptable for Black users to deploy certain terms and language when communicating directly with other Black users. Despite these difficulties, computer scientists have continued to fine-tune algorithms for identifying language that perpetuates racial hatred – including expanding taxonomies for classifying online hate (Salminen et al. 2019) and even using machine learning to identify subtle microaggressions (Ali et al. 2020). Such projects reveal the potential for using the strengths of machine learning and AI to help alleviate racism, if we remain attuned to the potential weaknesses and flaws that must be overcome.

Conclusion

This chapter has explored both the theoretical dimensions of artificial intelligence and its practical uses and consequences. It has presented the way that philosophical definitions of "humanity" and the way that humanity itself has been imagined have shaped the design and function of computer programs. Yet we have also considered the way that such programs have been racialized and gendered, such as through anthropomorphized virtual agents and humanlike programs that are so frequently designed to put figures of women of color in the perpetual role of assisting and providing service. This chapter also introduced the concepts of machine learning and big data, which are large-scale ways of operationalizing algorithms in ways that can be even more invisible in their functioning. As machine learning is increasingly applied to more and more institutionalized decision making, we must continue to call attention to the racial bias and other forms of invisibility, misrepresentation, and error that infect all datasets referring to human bodies and experiences.

Key questions

1. How do understandings of what makes us human and what constitutes intelligence play a role in how artificial intelligence has developed and what role it has played?
2. How have racial and gender stereotypes shaped the way that artificial intelligence interfaces have been imagined and designed, and what impact can this have?
3. How might machine learning be used to detect and help to alleviate racial inequalities and mitigate racist impacts?

Further reading

Broussard, Meredith. 2018. *Artificial Unintelligence: How Computers Misunderstand the World*. Cambridge, MA: MIT Press.

Katz, Yarden. 2020. *Artificial Whiteness: Politics and Ideology in Artificial Intelligence*. New York: Columbia University Press.

Sweeney, Miriam E. 2017. "The Ms. Dewey 'Experience': Technoculture, Gender, and Race," in Jessie Daniels, Karen Gregory, and Tressie McMillan Cottom (eds), *Digital Sociologies*. Bristol: Policy Press, pp. 401–20.

6

Surveillance

Key terms

- panopticism
- racial surveillance
- race science
- symbolic annihilation
- biometrics

- predictive policing
- borderveillance
- New Jim Code
- sousveillance

Introduction

AS we increasingly rely on digital technologies for every aspect of our daily lives, our understanding of the world grows. Automatic data collection helps us to gain knowledge about communities and circumstances that might have previously gone undetected. But if we recognize this increased capacity for gathering information as a form of surveillance, important questions about power and agency emerge. When someone is being observed and monitored, we must always ask who is keeping an eye on whom, and for what purposes. The racial dimensions of surveillance are particularly salient because people of color have historically been subject to unethical forms of surveillance that were specifically designed to limit freedom and agency. A wide variety of digital technologies are now taking on the role of surveilling people of color – including facial recognition, biometrics, visual sensors, and the artificial intelligence tasked with interpreting data from these sources. Despite the obvious limits of these technologies, the data they produce are framed as neutral and reliable. These digital forms of surveillance then contribute to harmful forms of both invisibility and hypervisibility for already marginalized communities of color.

This chapter applies what we now know about algorithms and artificial intelligence to technologies of visibility, exploring racial surveillance within a wide range of applications and arenas. Through analyzing cases such as identity verification, policing, and border security, the chapter exposes contemporary forms of panopticism and the way that both hypervisibility and invisibility have deeply shaped the experiences of people of color. The roots of racial surveillance stretch back to slavery and even earlier, when pseudoscientific taxonomies such as phrenology and anthropometry meant that closely inspecting the bodies of people of color supported the creation of racial hierarchies. As increasingly biased monitoring technologies proliferate, they also raise more general concerns about the loss of privacy and control for all citizens.

Power and visibility

The relationship between visibility and power is deeply informed by the theories of Michel Foucault. In his seminal text *Discipline and Punish* (1977), Foucault builds from the theories of Jeremy Bentham to explore the concept of the panopticon – a carefully designed prison constructed with a centrally located guard tower that looks upon an array of inmate cells stacked on top of each other. The inhabitants of the guard tower can easily observe each and every inmate, but the inmates can never see each other and, moreover, can never actually be certain of when they are being watched. This architecture is understood as a mechanism of power wherein the prisoners are made powerless due to their constant and permanent visibility, and the guard is empowered through the ability to look upon the prisoners at will while remaining unseen. It reveals one way that surveillance has a disciplinary function – through exerting control over bodies in a way that produces self-governance, increasing obedience and docility through the persistent threat of punishment.

While this system of discipline is at its most insidious when it describes a prison complex, Foucault uses **panopticism** as a lens for understanding many aspects of our contemporary surveillance society. He explores how institutions such as schools, hospitals, militaries, and workplaces are all designed as panoptic establishments, where a group of individuals can be disciplined through the assumption of constant surveillance by those who exercise power over them. Within these institutions, bodies are forced to sit and stand for prescribed periods of time, they are tasked with specific activities, they are distinguished by meaningful categories such as "healthy" and "sick," and they are rewarded for productivity. Such discipline is highly effective due to the fact that its monitoring mechanisms can be subtle and unseen, transforming subjects through expectations and assumptions rather than through the heavy hand of constant intervention.

In these cases it becomes clear that the standards to which individuals are being held are premised on understandings of "normal" and "abnormal" behavior. Rather than being expected to behave in ways that are strictly moral or legal, Foucault identifies the disciplinary power of a "normalizing gaze" that is trained upon subjects as a way of creating and upholding definitions of "the norm." If one can adhere to expectations of the norm, they are then rewarded with social status and privilege. The ideological power of normalization aligns with Antonio Gramsci's (1971) understandings of hegemony, or the way that dominant worldviews become accepted as natural and commonsense. Hegemonic ideologies that benefit the ruling class are maintained through consent, rather than coercion. Individuals choose to behave in certain ways so that they can be rewarded, and sometimes are unaware of what kinds of ideological assumptions they must uphold in order to maintain that status. But if those who already have power are the ones who establish the norm, then their ways of being will be the ones that will be rewarded and those who differ will be punished. This has always been an important component of white privilege – that existing as a white person serves as the invisible and unmarked norm, while being a person of color stands out as a condition that merits suspicion, fascination, or other nonstandard treatment.

In our contemporary society, data collection serves as an omnipresent form of surveillance that affects people of different racial identities in unequal ways. The automatic collection of data about identities, decisions, and activities is attached to an ever-present threat of negative consequences resulting from this surveillance.

There is danger in the way that such practices create and uphold social norms – as well as in the way that ubiquitous surveillance practices themselves have been accepted as normal.

Racial hypervisibility

One of the reasons we should be concerned about the use of data for increased surveillance is because this form of power and control has always been a technology of race. There is a long history of surveillance being used by those in power to subjugate those with less power, and, in particular, to create and uphold racial hierarchies. These histories and practices can be called **racial surveillance**. To illustrate these basic premises, we can look at the story of Sarah Baartman,* a Khoikhoi woman who was taken from South Africa and exhibited in London from 1810 to 1815 as "the Hottentot Venus." White Europeans were so curious about her body – specifically, the size of her buttocks and genitalia – that they would pay two shillings for the opportunity to stare at her and even pinch or poke her. After her death, she was dissected and preserved, and a plaster cast of her body was put on display at a museum in Paris. The dehumanizing practice of representing "human curiosities" as specimens for display was unfortunately very common in the tradition of "freak shows" that flourished in the early nineteenth century, with exhibitions that included South Americans, Native Americans, and peoples from other African tribes such as Zulus and San Bushmen (Qureshi 2004). While

---

* There are many alternative spellings of Baartman's first name, including "Sara" and "Saartjie," which means "little Sara" in Dutch. All of these are the names that were given to her by the Dutch farmers she worked for, and her birth name has been lost from the records.

there has been significant debate about the agency of individuals like Sarah Baartman and other participants in freak shows (Scully and Crais 2008), it is clear that racialization as Indigenous or even merely "foreign" has been equated with a kind of freakishness that invites staring and visual scrutiny. In these instances, those who look are invested with power, and we worry that those who are looked at are being exploited and dehumanized.

These practices of using close scrutiny as a way of distinguishing between those who have power and those who do not were exacerbated with the institution of chattel slavery. As Simone Browne investigates in her book *Dark Matters: On the Surveillance of Blackness* (2015), practices of surveillance have led to increased discrimination against African American communities ever since they were first forcibly uprooted from West Africa and transported to the Americas through the transatlantic slave trade. She argues that documents such as ship manifestos describing their human cargo, plantation inventories, slave passes that tracked the movement of enslaved people off the plantation, and wanted posters for runaway slaves must all be understood as forms of compulsory visibility designed to produce racial subjects. Lantern laws that required any unattended slave to carry a lit candle served as supervisory devices, as this form of illumination and visibility marked Black bodies as security threats to those who needed to see, identify, locate, and contain them. Like the branding of enslaved people's skin with hot irons denoting ownership, such practices turn racial subjects into objects and commodities that can be visually distinguished from whiteness and its benefits. Browne understands these historical practices of racial surveillance as "dark matter" – a scientific term that has been used to describe nonluminous forms of matter that cannot be directly observed but which have a tremendous impact on the cosmos. In the case of our society, Browne argues that surveillance studies have long neglected the role of race, but that blackness matters deeply in the structuring of both historical and contemporary surveillance practices.

These processes of using close examination to differentiate those in power from those who can be racialized as non-white and treated as less than human have deep roots. Under the auspices of scientific discovery and knowledge creation, eighteenth-century biologists and physicians established **race science** to classify human beings by race as if they were mere flora and fauna. These practices fall under the larger category of anthropometry, or the measuring of human bodies and all of their shapes and dimensions. One exemplar of this was German anatomist Johann Friedrich Blumenbach, who developed a fivefold racial typology that divided humans into five racial varieties: Caucasian, Mongolian, Ethiopian, American, and Malay (Blumenbach 1865 [1775]). Others developed slight variations of this typology, and there was disagreement about whether humans should be understood through monogenism – belonging to a single species that developed into different varieties – or polygenism – that humans of different races constitute entirely distinct species. But this form of anthropometry used classifications of racial difference to establish a social hierarchy where Caucasian Europeans were at the top in terms of intellect and civilization, while African Negroes were at the bottom. Scholars like Harvard University biologist Louis Agassiz came to this conclusion after measuring human skulls in a practice called craniometry. He decided that Caucasians had the largest cranial capacity, particularly when compared to Negroes and Native Americans. His studies have been debunked as completely unsound due to the fact that they failed to take factors such as gender or body size into his calculations, but at the time of his work they were taken as authoritative and used to justify racial injustices (Menand 2001). Phrenology, or the study of skull shapes as an indicator of mental characteristics, has also been taken up as a form of race science. Since it was already accepted that the skull shape was associated with race, phrenological studies helped to bolster arguments about how Caucasians were not only smarter, but also more beautiful, creative, and artistic due to their more developed brains.

These once well-respected fields of scientific study became extremely disreputable after they later provided the basis for Nazi ideologies. Nazi scientists positioned the Aryan race as the most superior specimen, and Adolf Hitler was obsessed with maintaining racial purity at all costs. When the Nazi party came into power, their racial ideologies became law. This led to the genocide of over six million Jews, as well as the forced sterilization of thousands of Roma, disabled people, and mixed-race African Germans.

While it is tempting to dismiss all of these intellectual forays into race science as mere pseudoscience that we now unequivocally recognize as wrong, Dorothy Roberts cautions against such easy dismissal. She states, "Seeing scientific racism as restricted to extreme cases like Nazi genocide mirrors the view of racism in general as an extremist position that falls outside enlightened Western thinking . . . But race and racism emerged as integral aspects of the American republic, not at all in opposition to it" (Roberts 2011: 27). Her research reveals the connection between these historically debunked understandings of racial difference and contemporary gene science that also attempts to identify and classify bodily differences. While contemporary genetics groups populations together by statistical genomic similarity across geographic regions, rather than the slippery category of race, she argues that these statistics nonetheless contribute to the idea that racial difference is genetic.

Racial invisibility

At the same time that embedded racism has contributed to the hypervisibility of blackness, people of color have also been systematically denied other forms of visibility. At a basic level, we know that all people of color are marginalized and underrepresented within mainstream media representations. This includes a dearth of visible roles for people of color in movies and TV programs, news media, and other forms of storytelling (Lopez 2020). Histories of **symbolic annihilation**, or the complete absence of minority identities represented in either fiction or non-fiction media, contribute to social subjugation because audiences then fail to consider their experiences, perspectives, and realities. Black, Asian, Latinx, and Indigenous communities have also been harmed by the fact that when these identities are represented in media, they are relegated to limited stereotypes, side characters who only serve to forward the central narratives of white characters, and to otherwise unappealing or harmful roles. This erasure from media narratives is intimately connected to the struggles that people of color have faced in gaining access to more powerful and prominent roles in society, such as elected officials, business owners, executives, and other leadership positions. Many occupations in which we see a disproportionate number of people of color are the kinds of essential labor in manufacturing, agriculture, construction, and service industries that are characterized by being low-waged, unstable, and invisible.

People of color also struggle for visibility due to the ways that image-capturing technologies are designed. Photography itself is a technology that had the potential to be designed as a racially neutral technology that captured all varieties of skin tones and hair textures beautifully, but unfortunately that is not what happened. Starting in the 1950s, photo labs and television studios relied on processes of "skin-color balance" to calibrate color settings, and the reference used was a white woman with light skin (Roth 2009). The ubiquitous use of these "Shirley" cards that stood in for "normal" skin tones then led to systematic underexposure for dark-skinned photographic subjects. In addition to color-balancing practices, film stocks and photo lab procedures all developed with the assumption of white skin as the ideal created numerous lighting challenges to avoid darker faces disappearing against bright white teeth and eyes. This problem has continued to perplex cinematographers and gaffers, who have often not been taught how to adjust their settings appropriately for lighting Black subjects for film and television. Since highlighting and beautifying white faces has been so privileged and normalized, these efforts are always framed as deviations and modifications, which can end up recentering the norm. As Richard Dyer (1997) has argued, even in stories where the white character is supposed to be equal to or more morally questionable than the Black character, movies end up lit in such a way that the white character is visually highlighted, individualized, and advantaged, while the Black character remains silhouetted, shadowed, and de-emphasized. This is particularly the case for white women, who have always been positioned as the ideal photographic subject, and whose visual appearance served as the original metric by which all cameras should be calibrated. In her discussion of the phenomenon of sparkly glamor and its relationship to whiteness, Mary Kearney reminds us that "Either embodying or surrounded by light, young female characters are stylistically highlighted today in ways that make them visually superior to virtually all else in the frame" (Kearney 2015: 264–5).

Together, these photographic norms reveal the racial prejudice that has been designed into the technology of photography, as well as its consequences.

These problems have only been exacerbated through the rise of digital photography and the kinds of software that now make automatic decisions about functions such as shutter speed and lens aperture. Instead of photographers and camera operators making the decision to privilege the white skin of their live subjects or the image of a white woman on a reference card, cameras are now programmed to scan the visible field to identify faces and make decisions based on what is detected. As was discussed in the previous chapter on artificial intelligence, problems can arise when algorithms are trained on limited datasets that include primarily white subjects. This has been a problem for even the Japanese camera company Nikon, which was criticized for its racist design in 2010 when a Taiwanese American user named Joz Wang blogged about her experience of receiving the message "Did someone blink?" every time she took a picture of her family members (Rose 2010). The camera's facial recognition software consistently interpreted the shape of Asian smiling eyes as closed. There are also countless examples of facial recognition software and other forms of visual sensors failing to recognize dark skin in a digital problem that mirrors early calibration inequalities around photo emulsions and film stocks. This includes dark-skinned faces disappearing into their virtual backgrounds while using video-conferencing software like Zoom, Twitter algorithms prioritizing white faces over Black faces in image previews, and Snapchat misrecognizing Black faces in silly applications like its filter that turns human faces into cartoonish puppy dogs. In a particularly horrifying design flaw, Google was called out in 2015 when a user discovered that its photo-recognition algorithm had labeled an image of Black people "gorillas." The visual sensors in everyday items like touchless faucets, hand dryers, paper towel dispensers, and soap dispensers also routinely fail to recognize dark-skinned hands but are instantly activated when a lighter-skinned hand appears. They are the result of what Simone Browne (Browne 2015) calls "prototypical whiteness," or the privileging of whiteness and lightness and the failure to account for darkness in the design of such technologies.

The consequences of these biased algorithms have heightened with the increasingly widespread use of biometrics. **Biometrics** are the measurements of unique bodily characteristics that can then be used for automated identification. It includes the scanning of faces, but also fingerprints, irises, voices, walking gaits, and nearly any other bodily marker that has proven distinctive in its association with individual humans. Biometrics are currently being used in institutions including airport and border security, law enforcement and prison systems, civil identification, building access, as well as healthcare and welfare systems. Margaret Hu points to this profoundly expanded capacity and usage as dangerously normalized, contending that "emerging biometric cyber-surveillance technologies, and mass biometric data collection and database screening, are adding an entirely new and unprecedented dimension to day-to-day bureaucratized surveillance" (Hu 2013: 1478). Like every aspect of automation in society, the use of biometric data for identification has been widely assumed to increase reliability, objectivity, and efficiency. While it is presumed that paper documents or human judgments can be easily manipulated, biometric data promise to circumvent these weaknesses. Yet, as Shoshanna Amielle Magnet (2011) has argued, it is imperative to understand the failures of biometric data, both in their application and in the fantasy of stable bodily identity upon which they are premised. The reality is that biometric technologies consistently fail in the measurement of populations that are already vulnerable due to their gender and race, in addition to countless other bodily conditions.

Some common failures of biometric data include the fact that fingerprint scanners routinely face difficulty scanning the hands of Asian women and that iris scanners are less accurate on those with dark skin and dark eyes, in addition to the many problems we have already seen with facial recognition. But biometric technologies also fail to account for variance in both temporary and long-standing bodily conditions such as visual impairments, wheelchair use, the effects of certain pharmaceutical drugs, vocal hoarseness, and skin conditions. Since identification is often programmed to include categories such as gender, biometric assessments reify gender binaries such as the assumption that those with low voices are male or those with long hair are female, which are premised on limited understandings of gender identity. To the extent that biometric data are ever accurate, they are most consistently effective on young, able-bodied, cisgendered, light-skinned, blue-eyed men. As Magnet concludes, we must remain wary because "the real-world deployment of biometric technologies depends upon practices of inscription, reading, and interpretation that are assumed to be transparent and self-evident and yet remain complex, ambiguous, and, as a result, inherently problematic" (3). Digital sensors have been programmed in ways that end up obscuring or misreading the bodies of people of color, but we must also recognize the interpretations about identity and what constitutes a "normal body" that shape the meaning of the data that are captured.

Surveillance as security

One of the most harmful applications of facial recognition and other forms of biometric surveillance has been in law enforcement and other forms of security. Not only has this been an area of specific concern for Black and Brown communities, but the consequences for errors in these fields can be matters of life and death. For instance, in 2019 the photo of a Muslim American college student named Amara K. Majeed was included in a list of suspects circulated by Sri Lankan authorities following a terrorist bombing incident that had absolutely nothing to do with her. Investigators had used facial recognition software that wrongly identified Majeed, who then faced an onslaught of death threats and other threats of violence (Fox 2019). Even worse, facial recognition software has led to wrongful convictions in many instances, such as in the case of Robert Julian-Borchak Williams. In 2019, Michigan police used facial recognition software to analyze grainy surveillance footage and match it against a database of mug shots. Despite the fact that investigators could instantly see that the software had gotten it wrong, Williams was arrested and kept in custody for more than 30 hours before the charges were dismissed (Hill 2020b). The work of policing at every level has been deeply impacted by the rise of digital technologies and the use of algorithms to interpret data. In addition to biometric surveillance, police have also come to rely on license plate readers, body cameras, aerial drones, cell phone tracking devices, and other forms of automated surveillance.

These concerns for people of color have crystallized within **predictive policing**, or the use of algorithms to identify the physical locations where crimes are likely to happen and people who are likely to commit crimes. These predictive analytics examine a wide range of data points – crime data from police records and federal databases, locational data from neighborhood histories, personal data from sources including private consumer reports, social media analytics, financial documents, location tracking, and more. While each kind of data is owned by separate parties, the sharing of data has become commodified as private data brokers have been able to profit off selling aggregated data to anyone willing to buy it – including law enforcement. Once these datasets have been acquired, machine learning is deployed to identify patterns and then make predictions that direct law enforcement where to send additional patrols and who to be more suspicious of.

Yet as we have seen in case after case, this kind of analysis is easily skewed by the errors, blind spots, and histories of racism that are embedded within the data. Even the use of arrest records as an indicator of likelihood to commit future crimes can be a biased indicator of likelihood for reoffending, given the disproportionately and unfairly high rates of arrest for Black men. In the United States, Black people are far more likely to be stopped without just cause, to be arrested, to be convicted, and be given lengthy prison sentences than white people (The Sentencing Project 2018).

These inequalities are the direct outcome of increased surveillance, as these interactions with law enforcement are enabled by the assumption that police should be particularly suspicious of Black people and the spaces in which they might be found.

We also know that Black men are 2.5 times more likely than white men to be killed by police as a result of these encounters (Edwards, Lee, and Esposito 2019), as has been evidenced in the high-profile killings of individuals like Michael Brown, Philando

Castile, Akai Gurley, George Floyd, and so many others. These well-documented inequalities in the US criminal justice system have been at the core of the Black Lives Matter activist movement, which has fought police brutality and anti-Blackness in policing since 2013.

These injustices are nothing new, as the history of modern policing has always been connected to protecting the interests of white people through violence against Black people. Our modern police system can be traced back to the creation of slave patrols in the South whose mission was to enforce the restrictive codes governing enslaved people, often through brutal force and cruelty (Hadden 2001). One of their primary roles was to locate runaway slaves and return them to their owners, in addition to their general directive to defend against slave insurrections and revolts, break up organized meetings, and punish criminal activities. After the Civil War, these patrols were replaced with militias that enforced codes governing the conduct of African Americans through restricting freedoms and mobilities. With the Great Migration of African Americans to northern cities in the early twentieth century and the institution of Jim Crow laws designed to create state-sanctioned segregation and political disenfranchisement for African Americans, newly developed police units continued to use state-sanctioned violence to maintain racial hierarchies (Durr 2015). Together these forces must be understood as important precursors to the development of American police departments and modern law enforcement. As Turner, Giacopassi, and Vandiver (2006) argue, "the similarities between the slave patrols and modern American policing are too salient to dismiss or ignore" (186), despite the fact that most criminal justice textbooks do not sufficiently highlight these important histories. One of the lessons that are most critical to understanding how this history of race-centered policing has led to frustrations is the fact that African American, Latinx, and Indigenous communities have been consistently subject to unjust surveillance, and there have been myriad consequences.

These inequalities mean that data used for policing are biased against Black individuals and communities. When predictive policing tools use location-based algorithms to predict where and when crimes are more likely to happen or person-based tools to make guesses about whether someone will commit a crime, the results are then racially biased. The disproportionate targeting of people of color and the repeated monitoring of certain neighborhoods becomes a self-perpetuating cycle, as the data will continue to show that those individuals and locations demand a closer look. Given the lack of oversight and accountability for the private companies that produce data, as well as the secrecy around how these technologies are being used, predictive policing systems become yet another tool for exacerbating racial bias in law enforcement (Heaven 2020). In addition to anti-Blackness, there are many other forms of systemic bias that are perpetuated through this reliance on "dirty data," as Richardson, Schultz, and Southerland (2019) have investigated. In the case of policing, dirty data can be either intentionally manipulated or otherwise derived from or influenced by corrupt, biased, or unlawful practices. These feedback loops can then lead to the over-policing of poor communities of color and transgender people, who are already frequently targeted for fabricated crimes and face tremendous social stigma and marginalization.

Controlling the border

Latinx communities have also been subject to increased technological scrutiny and surveillance in the United States, particularly in regions surrounding the US–Mexico border. Long before the invention of facial recognition software, border patrol agents relied on electronic sensors programmed to be triggered by the presence of footsteps or bodily heat signatures. As early as the 1970s, "electronic fences," consisting of ground sensors, radio transmitters, and signal processors, fed data back to computers and the agents who were tasked with monitoring and controlling the southern border of the United States. This was in addition to the analogue surveillance technologies of border patrols and the use of "sign-cutting," a prehistoric method of tracking prey through observing tracks and other disturbances in nature. Each of these methods must be understood as technologies of race, as they are used as exclusionary tools for keeping Mexicans out of the United States by marking them as unwanted intruders.

Iván Chaar-López (2019) investigates the history of these border technologies as a mechanism for drawing the boundaries of the nation through information systems, and for categorizing Mexicans as both abstract data and deportable aliens. Electronic fences have always been marked by failure, as sensors routinely malfunction and are frequently triggered by non-human movement on the part of everything from cattle to helicopters. Nonetheless, he argues that this form of data collection was part of an "imperial control fantasy. This system attempted to actualize an imagined capacity to master the messiness of the borderlands" (512). With the rise of anti-Mexican discourses and the fear of alien enemies that had been exacerbated by the Vietnam War, intrusion detection systems and other border technologies became an increasingly credible mechanism for drawing racial lines between those who are welcome in the United States and those who are feared.

These technologies and the discourses that support them have clearly survived and intensified in the twenty-first century, as border security apparatuses now have all of the surveillance technologies of law enforcement at their disposal. In addition to facial recognition software, drones, and video cameras, the US–Mexico border is also surveilled through radar systems, ground and imaging sensors, livestreaming websites, surveillance blimps and balloons, helicopters, and other technologies. Camilla Fojas (2021) uses the term **borderveillance** to describe the rise of networks and infrastructures designed to oversee, control, and manage the boundaries of our secured nation. This network includes all of the surveillance technologies discussed here and the rise of security-technology industries, but also the media discourses that surround them – the news reports discussing immigration policies, entertainment media in the form of crowdsourced border surveillance webcam programs, docuseries about crime on the border, and others. Together they are implemented as a violent strategy that threatens migrants and refugees, producing them as dangers to a safe and secure nation. As Jason De Leon (2015) argues, we must recognize that the cost of border surveillance has been an unprecedented amount of violence, terror, suffering, and death for migrants and border crossers attempting to enter the United States. While federal border enforcement policies may be euphemistically framed as centered around prevention and deterrence, the reality is that they are designed to cause increased fatalities due to migrants being funneled toward crossing through particularly hostile and hazardous terrain. As violence increases, these policies are considered to be more effective in deterring future border crossers from illegal entry.

While policies increasing surveillance at the US–Mexico border have been part of presidential politics since President Richard Nixon's Operation Intercept in 1969, the election of President Donald Trump in 2016 heightened the issue considerably. Trump specifically campaigned on a platform of building a wall to separate the United States and Mexico, declaring at his presidential announcement speech that "When Mexico sends its people, they're not sending their best . . . They're bringing drugs. They're bringing crime. They're rapists" (Time Staff 2015). This horrifying list of racist stereotypes shored up the notion that our national borders were in dire need of protection. While Trump promised that he would get Mexico to pay for a wall and that he meant to build a literal wall of concrete and steel, the reality is that the US–Mexico border was already fully operational in its functioning as a massive security apparatus. Indeed, sophisticated technological surveillance had long been deployed to make decisions about the fate of anyone within miles of the virtual "wall" through the collection of data. Melissa Villa-Nicholas (2020) argues that while Latinx undocumented people are at the center of information technologies at the borderlands, we are all complicit in becoming part of the data body milieu because surveillance mechanisms have come to infuse so many aspects of regular life. Because of this, we must reconsider what purpose our technologically policed national borders actually serve in both including and excluding certain bodies. As Daniel Gonzalez states:

> The border is not merely an apparatus of exclusion and deportation, rather it is a global logistical infrastructure . . . Generated by a vast and complex information network that integrates transnational capital and state institutions, in the case of labor management, this infrastructure is employed by border enforcement to manage circulations of a devalued, detainable, and deportable supply of racialized labor. (Gonzalez 2019)

He points out the importance of the technologies and information networks that make borderlands spaces where racialized subjects are not merely located and excluded, but where they are also manufactured and produced. While "the wall" may seem to be geographically fixed at the southern border of the United States, the technologies of surveillance that undergird its role in securing national borders create a vast network that extends far beyond in their support for racial capitalism.

Exposing and resisting surveillance

The extension of racialized surveillance across every aspect of life has led to deepening inequalities for people of color, and African American communities in particular. Ruha Benjamin (2019) argues that we have transitioned from an era of explicitly racist laws and policies to a reliance on implicitly racist technologies, which she calls the **New Jim Code**. This term builds from Michelle Alexander's (2010) theorization of the "New Jim Crow," or the rise of a new racial caste system in the United States since the 1960s that is upheld through public policy and instantiated in the mass incarceration of Black men. Alexander argues that an entire generation of Black men from poor communities has been systematically disenfranchised through a combination of high arrest rates and long periods of incarceration, all of which serve to sustain the racial oppression that originated with slavery and Jim Crow laws. Benjamin is similarly interested in the contemporary forces that uphold white supremacy, including the significance of colorblind and postracial ideologies that have served to make racism in the digital era more difficult to identify and detect. When we assume that we have already overcome the evils of racism or that ignoring race altogether will lead to better outcomes, we stop looking for instances of bias and inequality. In the case of racist technologies, troubling ideologies and decisions can end up buried and concealed deep within layers of code. The assumption that algorithms can and should remain secret, walled off within a black box, protects designers and tech companies from both culpability and accountability. This obfuscation is also magnified through the discourses that surround technology, such as technochauvinistic attitudes assuming that technology is always better and more accurate than humans (Broussard 2018). When applied to the cases discussed throughout this chapter – the visual sensors and facial recognition software that were never designed to recognize dark-skinned faces and bodies, the biometric data that cannot accurately identify people of color, the drones and blimps keyed in on removing unwanted foreigners from American soil – we can see how the New Jim Code has led to engineered inequities that amplify racial hierarchies.

Despite the way that invisibility and underexposure have systematically harmed people of color, Benjamin (2019) puts forward exposure itself as a key mechanism for dismantling the New Jim Code. She points out that exposure and visibility can be empowering tools for solidarity and liberation when they are used for calling attention to injustice. She calls for coded equity audits that can be deployed for determining the impact of algorithms on marginalized communities, enlisting the involvement of tech industries themselves, government bodies, non-profit organizations, and community-based organizations to participate in democratizing data in its design and application. Within the context of disrupting and inverting the ills wrought by technological surveillance, we can consider such actions part of sousveillance. If surveillance is when organizations in power oversee those with less power, **sousveillance** actively inverts that power dynamic through acts of those with less power observing an authority figure. Simone Browne (2015) marks sousveillance as an integral site of critique and resistance for subjects of racial surveillance. In examples such as teaching runaway slaves how to avoid being caught by slave patrols, forging freedom papers in order to escape slavery, and learning about plantation surveillance as a means for evading it, she shows how the study of racial surveillance is incomplete without recognizing the agency of those who exist within a panopticon refusing to become docile bodies. She categorizes such opposition as "dark sousveillance," or strategies for critiquing surveillance and contending with how resistance to surveillance often requires remaining out of sight. In contemporary times, many forms of sousveillance are taken up through acts of overseeing those who surveil, such as cop-watching organizations and other participatory forms of citizen action that strategically evade or call attention to harmful panoptic practices. These courageous interactions open up space for examining the seemingly irrepressible rise of surveillance, and point toward the need for more protections from panopticism for those who are most vulnerable.

Conclusion

This chapter reminds us how technological forms of surveillance are deeply connected to power and control. While it is frightening enough to think about being watched by someone because of the power that it affords the watcher, it is even more alarming to consider the multiple forms of automated surveillance that we are increasingly subjected to. We have also seen here how these practices of observation have been racialized throughout history, from the earliest days of contact between white colonists and those they considered more primitive and existing solely for their visual pleasure. This includes how the inspection of non-white bodies has been connected to racist practices of taxonomization, phrenology, anthropometry, and other forms of scientific observation. But we have also seen the systemic invisibility of people of color when it is beneficial for those in power to render the experiences of non-white communities as unrecognized and thus devalued. This exploration reminds us that we must continue to ask who is watching who, and how can those who are most vulnerable be protected within a culture that is increasingly relying on digital surveillance technologies.

Key questions

1. How can we apply the theory of panopticism to nineteenth-century freak shows in order to understand how these institutions have exploited African, Native American, and other non-white peoples?
2. Why do we understand "race science" as a form of racism, and what kinds of practices and assumptions were included within it?
3. How have visual technologies been designed to make darker skin both invisible and hypervisible, and what have been some of the consequences?

Further reading

Benjamin, Ruha. 2019. *Race After Technology: Abolitionist Tools for the New Jim Code.* Cambridge, UK: Polity.

Browne, Simone. 2015. *Dark Matters: On the Surveillance of Blackness.* Durham, NC: Duke University Press.

Ferguson, Andrew Guthrie. 2019. *The Rise of Big Data Policing: Surveillance, Race, and the Future of Law Enforcement.* New York: New York University Press.

7

Tech Policy

Key terms

- digital discrimination
- algorithmic accountability
- informed consent
- digital privacy
- data sovereignty
- platform governance

Introduction

WITH all of these concerns about the way that technologies and digital media are disproportionately harming those who are already vulnerable, it is important to reflect on the guardrails that can be instituted as a form of protection for the future. As new technologies are developed and their design is even more closely integrated into every aspect of our lives, the problems that they cause become more complex and more urgent. The field of technology ethics applies moral principles to the world of technology and digital media. One of the goals is to provide guidance about what practices to undertake based on calculations about what will lead to justice and greater social benefits, limiting wrongdoing and harm. Of course, it is not a simple task to make these decisions or agree upon their outcomes, as there are always competing understandings of how technologies work, what their impact has been and will be, and what values we should prioritize. In many ways, we have already seen these debates play out throughout the book, as various solutions to the problems of race and digital media have been proposed.

This chapter focuses specifically on struggles to develop and institute systems of guidelines and policies that can help to identify harms, compel behaviors, shape decisions, and mitigate future risks. This includes national and federal regulations as legislated by the government but also pressure put onto corporations to engage in self-regulation, and the development of ethical codes of conduct designed to alleviate some of the problems engendered by racism within tech industries and society more broadly. While many of the suggestions here are still untested as to whether or not they are viable long-term solutions that will lead to concrete improvements, this chapter points to many different kinds of proposals and clarifies their aims and intentions. It is clear that the quest for justice and accountability in technology and digital media is a struggle that will not be resolved any time soon.

Public policy

One of the central gains of the 1960s Civil Rights Movement in the United States was the achievement of legislation against discrimination in many different areas. This includes the 1964 Civil Rights Act that prohibits unjust or prejudicial treatment on the basis of race, color, religion, sex, and national origin in employment-based circumstances such as hiring, promoting, and firing, as well as the 1968 Fair Housing Act that prohibits discrimination in housing-related transactions. There are also a number of federal anti-discrimination laws that seek to eliminate discrimination in education, credit applications, voting practices, and other areas of concern. The core injustice that is rectified through anti-discrimination laws often appears as an instance of a personal wrong, but these laws are premised on the belief that institutions such as employers, landlords, and service providers should not treat people differently based on extraneous traits like gender, race, age, or religion (Moreau 2010). The concept of **digital discrimination** refers to the unfair or unethical differential treatment of individuals whose data have been assessed through algorithmic decision systems. As discussed in previous chapters, when algorithms are deployed toward tasks such as sorting applicant résumés for job openings and higher education, distributing social services, allocating healthcare benefits, making recommendations for credit applications and length of prison terms, or positioning information sources for certain audiences, there is strong evidence that the outcomes are negatively biased based on race and other identities.

If we know that this kind of discrimination is illegal and harmful to society, it would be productive to create laws that protect against the discrimination that is designed into algorithms. The Association for Computing Machinery US Public Policy Council set forth principles intended to address the issue of preventing algorithmic bias from the onset with the following statement: "Policymakers should hold institutions using analytics to the same standards as institutions where humans have traditionally made decisions and developers should plan and architect analytical systems to adhere to those standards when algorithms are used to make automated decisions or as input to decisions made by people" (Association for Computing Machinery US Public Policy Council 2017). That is, we should hold human designers responsible for their role in shaping the creation and deployment of algorithms. We can see these values at work in the focus of lawmakers and governmental accountability organizations on **algorithmic accountability**. This term is used to describe the assignment of responsibility for the harm that can come from algorithms. Algorithmic accountability is particularly concerned with the way that algorithmic systems are used to make decisions that result in discriminatory or inequitable outcomes (Caplan et al. 2018). It attempts to ensure that those who create and use algorithms can justify those decisions and are answerable for their impacts, meaning that they face consequences for negative outcomes (Basu and Brennan 2021).

One attempt to turn this responsibility into US governmental policy was the Algorithmic Accountability Act introduced to the US Congress in 2019. This policy was designed to create regulations around the use, storage, and sharing of consumers' personal information with an eye toward bias and security issues. It was proposed to the Senate by Senators Cory Booker and Ron Wyden, and to the House by Representative Yvette Clarke. It included provisions that companies with more than US$50 million in revenues or possession of more than 100 million people's data would be required to conduct impact assessments of their automated decision systems and data protections, including studies evaluating impacts on accuracy, fairness, bias, discrimination, privacy, and security (Algorithmic Accountability Act of 2019 2019). The bill was never advanced, but it marked a step toward holding institutions responsible for their use of algorithms in decision making and advocating for auditability and transparency so that future harms can be prevented. Legal scholars argue that any attempt to bring lawsuits against governmental use of algorithms can have a number of positive outcomes – including amplifying the voices of those who have been harmed by algorithms, calling attention to vendors who need to improve their algorithms, expanding prosecutorial understandings of algorithmic evidence, and encouraging future state statutes that regulate algorithms (Richardson, Schultz, and Southerland 2019).

Privacy and consent

Another important area in which greater legal protections are needed is with regard to data privacy. The case of Henrietta Lacks has provided an important cautionary tale for communities of color with regard to how individuals can lose control over their own personal data in the name of science. Henrietta Lacks was an African American woman who was diagnosed with cervical cancer in 1951 at age 31, and died shortly thereafter. Scientists at the Johns Hopkins Hospital where she was treated were astonished to find that cells collected from her tissue samples had the extraordinary quality of surviving and reproducing indefinitely. Researchers named these immortal cells "HeLa" after Lacks, and shared them with other scientists so that they could be used for medical research. While HeLa cells have contributed to many important scientific discoveries, the story has a dark side as well – namely, these decisions about what to do with Lacks's biological materials were made without her or her family's consent, and the family received no financial benefits from these significant scientific discoveries. Because of this, Lacks's children and relatives felt confused, betrayed, and exploited.

The story of Henrietta Lacks has gained significant attention in 2010 with the publication of Rebecca Skloot's nonfiction book *The Immortal Life of Henrietta Lacks* (Skloot 2010), and the subsequent HBO biopic of the same name starring Oprah Winfrey (2017, directed by George C. Wolfe). This public attention prompted much discussion about **informed consent**, or the need for scientists to educate individuals about what will happen to them and to obtain permission before beginning an intervention like a medical procedure or participation in a scientific study. It also called attention to the pain that can be caused by a lack of compensation, with some researchers offering donations to the Henrietta Lacks Foundation that was established in 2010 by the author Skloot to compensate Lack's descendants and other families like hers (Nature Staff 2020). Yet, as recently as 2013, the Lacks family continued to be left out of the conversation as researchers posted the entire genome sequence from a HeLa cell online without asking for permission (Arnst 2017). The story of Lacks has been a catalyst for many discussions and even proposals for policies that would change the need for informed consent to include every living individual whose biospecimens are collected. While these proposed policies could be a step in the right direction, they have been viewed as a substantial departure from scientific procedures, and public opinion on the issue remains mixed (Beskow 2016). Moreover, it is clear that the simple solution of improving informed consent is not a magic bullet that will solve the problems wrought by long histories of African American and other vulnerable communities being exploited by the medical community and left out of important decisions about their own bodies.

The issue of privacy for vulnerable communities extends far beyond biological specimens and medical research to also include the need for stronger forms of data protection of all kinds.

*Just as the Henrietta Lacks case called attention to the common practices that left individuals without control over their data, there have been many other examples of data breaches that showcase the problems in **digital privacy** practices.*

For instance, the so-called Cambridge Analytica–Facebook scandal from 2018 revealed the many ways that Facebook user data was being exploited for financial profit. Cambridge Analytica is a British political consultancy company that had been hired for political advertising during the 2016 presidential campaign. A journalist report in 2016 revealed that they had been harvesting data without consent from millions of Facebook accounts and using it to prepare psychological profiles that could be used for aggressively persuasive advertising about political campaigns (Davies 2015). The Federal Trade Commission ultimately fined Facebook US$5 billion for their part in the data leak, which included deceiving users about their ability to control the privacy of their personal information (Federal Trade Commission 2019). They also imposed new restrictions that included creating multiple channels of compliance and oversight, such as establishing an independent privacy committee for accountability purposes and requiring compliance officers responsible for Facebook's privacy program. Yet, as Margaret Hu (2020) points out, there is need for far stronger inquiries into Facebook privacy violations and there is much work to be done in protecting against algorithmic harms. The reality is that users of social media platforms like Facebook often have a very limited understanding of what corporations will do with their personal data once they have relinquished it. As Mark Andrejevic has argued, the digital economy is premised on the idea that users submit to this commercial form of monitoring and loss of privacy when they participate in social media platforms because they have chosen to do so based on the personal benefits to them. But the choice is actually "a forced one, precisely because the notion of privacy does not take into account the power relations that structure the choice" (2009: 49). Because of this, it is important to consider the productive aspects of these sites, their necessity to so many aspects of modern life, and the coercion and exploitation that contributes to user submission.

We see these same concerns in policy debates around facial recognition software, which has long been recognized as a form of racial surveillance. As discussed in chapter 6, one of the ways that artificial intelligence and facial recognition software are being used is for policing purposes. In addition to problems of facial recognition software already being less accurate on dark-skinned faces, issues of privacy and consent also haunt facial recognition software. Some of the databases used to train facial recognition algorithms include mug shots of prisoners, driver's license photos, photos scraped from Flickr, and images of immigrants, abused children, and dead people – many of which are deeply disturbing, and none of which required consent from those whose faces are being treated as raw data (Keyes, Stevens, and Wernimont 2019; Van Noorden 2020). In 2020, the company Clearview AI was found to have been scraping billions of images from across numerous social media platforms for the purposes of selling the data to federal and state law enforcement agencies (Hill 2020a). Much like the case of Henrietta Lacks, these forms of biometric data were being recorded and utilized without permission, but in this case they were specifically being used for the purposes of creating a "virtual, perpetual line-up" (Garvie, Bedoya, and Frankle 2016). Many states have moved to prohibit face recognition in police body cameras, including California, Oregon, and New Hampshire. Other states have begun campaigning for similar legislation, such as the ACLU of Massachusetts' "Press Pause on Face Surveillance" educational campaign in support of a bill to regulate government use of face recognition technologies. The Illinois Biometric Information Privacy Act is an example from one of a few states that regulate companies which collect biometric information, requiring proper consent from individuals whose personal biometric information has been collected, timely data destruction, and secure data storage. At the federal level, there have been some attempts to introduce legislation that would limit biometric surveillance systems by federal and state government entities, such as the Facial Recognition and Biometric Technology Moratorium Act of 2020. These kinds of laws would provide an important form of protection against the harms that are possible when algorithmic bias starts to intrude into every aspect of our daily lives – particularly so when it becomes a routinized aspect of policing.

Data sovereignty

Outside of limiting what technology corporations can do with data, another important component to privacy is the question of who has control over digital data. The term **data sovereignty** is used to describe the rights of individuals and larger communities to wield meaningful control over their own data and data infrastructures. At the state level, data sovereignty can be of concern to national security because there can be threats to the nation when important or sensitive data are unprotected and jeopardized. This has been of particular interest given the rise of cloud computing – a term that does not actually mean that digital data has been sublimated to some invisible "cloud," but simply means that it is being stored in a physical data center somewhere in the world. The material reality of "the cloud" is that data centers are spread across geopolitical boundaries, with US companies like Facebook and Google setting up data centers in countries like Ireland, Sweden, Chile, Singapore, and Taiwan. With the physical transfer of data into different nations also come important questions about whether those data are subject to the laws of the country in which they are located. In this case, data sovereignty is about national data infrastructures, legal jurisdictions, and the ability of a government to maintain the security and integrity of its own data in the era of cloud computing (Amoore 2018; Hummel et al. 2021).

These concerns about control over digital data have also specifically been taken up within the context of Indigenous communities. The Indigenous Data Sovereignty movement is focused on maintaining Indigenous control over digital data about their own communities, cultures, territories, resources, and lives. This involves having control over every aspect of the data ecosystem – including the means of collection, the analysis and interpretation of data, data management, and how data are disseminated (Kukutai and Taylor 2016). In some ways, it is aligned with global data sovereignty movements that recognize the importance of communities maintaining ownership over and protection of their own data, but of course it is also deeply rooted in the historical abuses of Indigenous communities and legacies of settler colonialism that have threatened every aspect of Indigenous sovereignty. It is connected to the struggle for Indigenous self-determination and self-governance, as those inherent rights must unfortunately be actively claimed and re-established.

Indigenous people have been creators, collectors, and stewards of their own data since time immemorial, but with the increasing significance of digital information and technologies in shaping Indigenous policies, formal recognition of Indigenous data sovereignty is even more critical.

To better understand the significance of Indigenous data sovereignty, it is helpful to look at some specific cases. For instance, statistics on tribal populations and demographics are a key dataset that are important to Indigenous communities for many different reasons. Externally, tribal census data are used to allocate federal funds to tribes, so it is important to limit undercounting and other oversights that render Indigenous communities invisible and underserved. As Maggie Walter points out, reports on Indigenous Australian people have problems that extend beyond being inaccurate – they are also typically marked by "the five 'Ds' of data on Indigenous people: disparity, deprivation, disadvantage, dysfunction, and difference" (Walter 2016: 80). These pejorative descriptions create a dominant discourse about Aboriginal and Torres Strait Islander peoples, and point to key data absences that might deviate from this social problem lens or present a fuller, more complex portrait of Indigenous life. Advocates for data sovereignty provide many possible solutions to this problem – including engaging in renaming and recategorizing practices that would help to shift interpretations of existing quantitative datasets, incorporating new qualitative data captured through interviews or other Indigenous-centered methods that could help to disrupt these prevailing perspectives through Indigenous worldviews, or challenging the authority and legitimacy of externally produced knowledge. Diane E. Smith calls for an increase in "culture-smart data – that is, information that can be produced locally, captures local social units, conditions, priorities and concerns and is culturally informed and meaningful. These kinds of data build on existing indigenous capabilities and knowledge, have direct practical application and represent collective identities, rights and priorities" (Smith 2016: 129). One way that American Indian tribes have exercised their sovereignty is through restructuring their tribal enrollment systems contracting with research firms to conduct their own analysis of tribal population projections (Rodriguez-Lonebear 2016). These are some of the tangible ways that Indigenous communities all over the globe are participating in responding to the problems inherent in Indigenous data by taking control of decision making and every other aspect of data governance.

From a policy perspective, there are many different ways that Indigenous data sovereignty can be supported. One model for this work can be seen in Ontario, Canada, where an agreement between the Ontario provincial government and the Chiefs of Ontario established that data about First Nations peoples would be subject to First Nations governance processes. The First Nations Information Governance Center developed a set of principles called OCAP (ownership, control, access, possession) that has established clear expectations shaping the collection and uses of Indigenous data in Canada and beyond. We can see the impact of OCAP principles in organizations such as the National Aboriginal Health Organization (NAHO), which is an Indigenous-led and Indigenous-controlled non-profit organization focused on researching the specific needs of First Nations, Inuit, and Métis communities in Canada. Thanks to the advocacy of NAHO, OCAP research ethics and principles espousing Indigenous data sovereignty have been taken up by many researchers, research institutes, funding organizations, educational institutions, and others (Rowe, Bull, and Walker 2021). In the United States, Rebecca Tsosie (2021) has helped to clarify some of the complex legal and policy dimensions of the fight for Indigenous data sovereignty. For instance, the current crisis of missing and murdered Native women is closely related to the fact that tribal governments and state governments each have separate criminal jurisdiction on murder investigations. This becomes a data problem when they are unable to effectively share information across these jurisdictions, and it reveals a need for intergovernmental agreements and protocols that would give Indigenous nations access to the tribal data that they have the right to own. But she points that out each nation-state has its own laws around data governance, so although Indigenous peoples have the right to self-determination, there is still a need for more clarity around exactly how data and information are understood as resources and tools for development that Indigenous peoples have the right to control.

Corporate self-regulation

While we have seen some of the possibilities for using state actors and legal policies to challenge the ways that technologies and digital media harm communities of color, the reality is that the work of regulating and policing digital media often falls to corporations themselves. Tech corporations have undertaken many voluntary actions to protect both themselves and their users. For the major social media companies that are often at the center of data scandals, much of this work falls under the category of **platform governance**, or efforts to make online platforms and the companies that run them more democratically accountable. This can include the institution of governance mechanisms like rules, norms, ethical frameworks, new initiatives, or the creation of partnerships with third parties and civil society groups (Gorwa 2019). The motivation for these changes can come from many different sources – including responding to the threat of impending government legislation, appeasing shareholders or consumers, desiring positive press coverage, or a general orientation toward financial profit through continued growth. Indeed, while the institution of an ethics initiative can be financially costly in its implementation, it can secure a company's financial longevity if it effectively forestalls future mistakes or reputational damage.

One area in which social media companies have been harshly criticized for failing to protect marginalized communities is in the moderation of hate speech shared on their platforms. While many forms of racial harm involve complex mechanics and layers of technological obfuscation, instances of racist hate speech seem to provide an obvious problem that corporations could do better to regulate. Yet social media companies have been criticized for years for failing to adequately address and rectify the problem, despite millions of dollars being spent on content moderators and the development of moderation algorithms. Part of this problem is related to the fact that platforms are not liable for the content that is posted to them, which means that monitoring posts to protect individuals from harm is a voluntary obligation. Certain posts may violate a platform's terms of service, but ultimately social media platforms have the freedom to prioritize other factors such as financial profits and growth over safety and harm reduction. The European Union created a voluntary Code of Conduct on Countering Illegal Hate Speech Online in May 2016 that Facebook, Microsoft, Twitter, YouTube, and later TikTok all agreed to. The agreement stated that these companies would put into place clear and effective processes for reviewing illegal hate speech on their platforms so that they could remove it in less than 24 hours, that they would raise awareness with users about the types of content that were not permitted, and that the impact of this work would be regularly assessed by the European Commission (European Commission 2016). While annual audits initially showed that the companies were moving a higher percentage of flagged posts each year, in 2021 the overall percentage of flagged material that ended up removed from these platforms within 24 hours went down from 71 percent to 62.5 percent (Scott 2021).

The fact that these voluntary mechanisms for encouraging improvement in this area can have uneven results can be connected to the contradictory goals that structure platform governance. Eugenia Siapera and Paloma Viejo-Otero look closely at Facebook's approach to racism and racist content in order to better understand some of its struggles and failures in this area. They find that the regulation of hate speech is treated as an issue of fairness and equality in the platform's Terms of Service and Community Standards. Yet this system of values that they call "fundamental equality" ends up reinforcing a colorblind and postracial idea that treats all users and all attacks in the same manner. As they describe, "Rather than looking at racist hate speech as part and parcel of racialized social structures and following an approach that specifically addresses the needs and specificities of groups that have been historically disadvantaged and oppressed, Facebook considers it part of a broader category of equivalent problematic contents" (Siapera and Viejo-Otero 2020: 125). Facebook has touted their increased use of automated monitoring for detecting hate speech, bullying, and harassment as a significant improvement. But they have also faced criticism that they have reduced the use of human reviewers on hate speech complaints, and that their own employees have little confidence in these automated systems (Seetharaman, Scheck, and Horwitz 2021).

Game creators and developers have also been under significant pressure to contribute to creating a safer environment for players of all backgrounds, but specifically women, people of color, and queer players. As discussed in chapter 9, video game and online game cultures can be particularly toxic for any player who is not a straight, white, cisgender man. Amanda Cote (2018) describes early attempts to improve game culture for marginalized players as being centered on simply removing player anonymity or instituting a reputation system that would penalize toxic players. Yet many of these efforts failed or were seen as inadequate because of how they misunderstood what it would take to truly make players of all backgrounds feel safe. While it is often believed that anonymity contributes to trolling and hateful attacks, Cote finds in her interviews with female gamers that they still felt safer when anonymity was the norm. In many cases, the threat of having someone's real identity exposed could disproportionately threaten targeted groups. With regard to reputation systems, XBox Live attempted to create a system that would punish players for bad behavior such as harassment, but it actually resulted in damage to the reputation of victims if they aggressively responded to harassment. As Cote concludes, it is important for game developers to understand gamers themselves if they want to effectively change community norms and increase player safety.

There are many other possibilities for how tech companies and social media platforms can strengthen protections and increase transparency around their use of digital tools like algorithms and artificial intelligence. A Brookings Institute paper from 2019 builds from recommendations by the AI Now Institute to demand that operators of algorithms develop a bias impact statement (Lee, Resnick, and Barton 2019). Such statements would commit to a clearly outlined process for assessing the potentially detrimental effects of an algorithm, for seeking stakeholder input on automated decision making, and for responding when bias and other negative consequences occur as a result of the algorithm. They argue that such statements could help to filter out potential biases in the future, which would begin to build trust. Ruha Benjamin (2019) has also pointed to the many instances of employee activism where tech company workers have called attention to wrongdoing. For instance, in 2018 thousands of Google employees signed a letter protesting their company's collaboration with a Pentagon drone-strike program. The letter condemned the company for engaging in the business of war, and demanded a policy that Google and its contractors will not build warfare technology in the future. While this employee revolt resulted in Google deciding to discontinue work on that particular project, the company persisted in pursuing military contracts just a few years later (Wakabayashi and Conger 2021). Workers at Microsoft have also demanded that their company stop working with Immigration and Customs Enforcement (ICE) due to outrage at the agency's separation of migrant parents and children at the US–Mexico border. Even if the exact demands of these protests are not always met, Ruha is optimistic about what it means about the position of tech workers in considering their broader social impact. She states, "The fact that computer programmers and others in the tech industry are beginning to recognize their complicity in making the New Jim Code possible is a worthwhile development. It also suggests that design is intentional and that political protest matters in shaping internal debates and conflicts within companies" (Benjamin 2019: 184).

Ethical codes

To conclude this chapter on guidelines that can potentially protect against tech companies and their creations, let us turn to the concrete language of technology ethics codes. These documents that articulate symbolic commitments to a particular set of moral principles can help to clarify important responsibilities in this area of professional work and shape the direction of work that is still to come. The study of computer ethics can be traced back as far as the 1940s, with MIT professor Norbert Wiener putting forward ethical concerns about the development of technologies like anti-aircraft cannons during World War II, and later with regard to cybernetics and technologies like artificial intelligence and robots (Bynum 2000). In 1992, the Association for Computing Machinery (ACM) adopted a document called the ACM Code of Ethics and Professional Conduct. It consisted of 24 moral imperatives, such as that members of ACM will avoid harm to others, take action not to discriminate, respect the privacy of others, and give comprehensive and thorough evaluations of computer systems and their impacts, including analysis of possible risks (ACM Council 1992). With each new generation of computing technologies, there has been an accompanying set of concerns about what kind of impact it will have on humans and human society, and what moral obligations we have to shape those relationships in certain ways.

In a 2020 study, Anne Washington and Rachel Kuo studied 15 ethics codes written between 2015 and 2018 to ascertain what understanding of the "social good" is forwarded in these documents and how it aligns with the lived experiences of communities that are impacted by those technologies. They find that, in the ethics codes of corporations like Google, Intel, IBM, and Microsoft and professional associations like the Algorithmic Justice League and the Association of Internet Research, there were a core set of concerns around duty and responsibility, harm and bias, and social good. Yet they also found that the concern for societal well-being often conflated society with customer bases, and that this consumer-orientation is part of what leads to a deprioritizing of marginalized groups and their claims to resources and protections. They introduce the term "digital differential vulnerability" to "describe how vulnerable populations are disproportionately exposed to harm through data technology that seeks to promote a single point of social good" (Washington and Kuo 2020: 237). If these documents are to be improved, Washington and Kuo recommend differentiating between business values and obligation to society, and engaging more critically with the complex dynamics of harm across diverse populations.

While it has been questioned just how much codes of ethics and other such documents actually end up shaping decision making in tech industries, there are still benefits to the practice of stating corporate values. At the very least, such statements then become a metric by which accountability can be measured. When companies fail to live up to their own standards, there can be important questions about what kinds of training and professional development should be instituted, or what negative consequences might actually inspire improvement. It is clear that the enormous task of guiding tech companies toward more ethical practices is one that will take many different incentives and deterrents, as well as creative thinking that can adapt to changing technologies.

Conclusion

This chapter has explored the many different ways that the harms of digital media might be curtailed through proactive measures designed to hold tech companies accountable for their products and the ways in which they are used. If we know that certain technologies are harming members of society, and in particular that they are harming those who are already vulnerable due to histories of systemic inequalities and injustices, it makes sense to demand that those who have the most control over our digital landscape play a key role in helping to mitigate these harms – regardless of how powerful or profitable those companies may be or how complex it would be to institute a workable solution. This includes holding tech companies accountable for facilitating a platform for hate speech or supporting discriminatory outcomes, but also more generally promoting transparency about their activities and offering users control over their own data. As digital technologies continue to grow in size and influence, we must stay attuned to their role in society and advocate for careful oversight. The countless benefits, social progress, and positive influence wrought by our increasing reliance on digital media must always be tempered by the realities of the potential for deepening inequalities.

Key questions

1. How are issues of privacy and consent connected to problems with the rise of racial surveillance technologies like facial recognition software?
2. Why have Indigenous communities become interested in the issue of data sovereignty, and what are their demands around controlling their own data?
3. What are some of the ways that tech companies have engaged in self-regulation as a way of protecting communities of color from harm when participating on their digital platforms, and what are some areas where they could be doing more?

Further reading

Kukutai, Tahu and Taylor, John. 2016. *Indigenous Data Sovereignty: Toward an Agenda.* Canberra: Australian National University Press.

Richardson, Rashida, Schultz, Jason M., and Southerland, Vincent M. 2019. *Litigating Algorithms 2019 US Report: New Challenges to Government Use of Algorithmic Decision Systems.* New York: AI Now Institute.

Yeung, Karen and Lodge, Martin (eds). 2019. *Algorithmic Regulation.* Oxford: Oxford University Press.

8

Activism

Key terms

- #BlackLivesMatter
- slacktivism/clicktivism
- #MeToo
- networked counterpublics
- transmedia organizing
- testimonio
- internet memes

Introduction

WHILE there are many ways in which racial bias is coded into the development and use of digital media, it is important also to recognize the way that people of color have used communication technologies to resist oppression and create new activist networks for social change. If we define activism as intentional participation in a political act designed to remedy a social injustice, there are many different ways that digital media can be used for activist purposes. This can include the use of digital media for informing and educating people about the existence of a problem, for gathering supporters together to join up and make plans, for engaging in online actions such as letter-writing campaigns, petition signing, and fundraising, or for organizing in-person actions such as demonstrations and protests. Above all, digital platforms clearly provide useful spaces for communication about activism, which can lead to both base building and the organization of campaigns where media production itself is the desired mechanism for motivating change.

This chapter begins by exploring Black Lives Matter as a born-digital social movement that supports local, national, and global community-based actions against anti-Blackness and police brutality. While this particular movement is by no means the first digitally enabled form of racial activism, and its success is wholly contingent on the work that community activists had undertaken for decades prior, it nonetheless is a significant social justice movement that helps to showcase the evolution of online activism in the twenty-first century. Black Lives Matter activists have used digital technologies ranging from tweets to livestreaming cell phone videos to creating online memorials, all in an effort to collectively call attention to the horrors of Black death and state violence. This chapter also explores Twitter hashtags and social media more generally and the way they have been taken up by Asian American, Latinx, and Indigenous activists to enable immediate and sustained mobilization, political education, movement growth, narrative reframing, and leadership development for a new generation of anti-racist activists.

Black Lives Matter

Black Lives Matter is a social movement that was created by three Black women named Alicia Garza, Patrisse Cullors, and Opal Tometi starting in 2013. One year earlier, 17-year-old Trayvon Martin was killed by neighborhood vigilante George Zimmerman in Sanford, Florida. Zimmerman had been trailing Martin on his walk through the neighborhood because he became convinced the Black hoodie-clad teenager looked suspicious and threatening. Zimmerman ended up getting in an altercation with the teen that ended when Zimmerman shot Martin in the chest. Although Zimmerman was charged with second-degree murder, he claimed self-defense and was acquitted by a jury in April 2012. The outcry was immediate, as protestors gathered outside the courthouse demanding justice for Trayvon. But a far larger response coalesced online. Within 26 hours of the verdict, nearly 5 million tweets about the case had been shared, and over 1.5 million of those contained anger at the verdict (Jurkowitz and Vogt 2013). This included frustration at how African Americans were yet again being excluded from the rights and privileges accorded to white Americans, and a condemnation of how the legal system and larger social environment were designed to protect white lives over Black lives. It was in this moment that Alicia Garza, Patrisse Cullors, and Opal Tometi used the phrase **#BlackLivesMatter** as an online call to action against anti-Black racism. It was a broad-based movement designed to deepen understandings of structural racism throughout society – in the criminal justice system, but also in education, policy, healthcare, media, and beyond.

The use of this hashtag exploded in August 2014, following the killing of unarmed Black teenager Michael Brown by a white police officer in Ferguson, Missouri. As the 18-year-old's body lay in the street, protestors already began to mobilize, using Twitter and other digital platforms to disseminate information, mourn, and call for justice. Online participants tweeted at news outlets as a way of raising the visibility of Brown's death within legacy media outlets, while eyewitnesses described what they were seeing on the ground. The ease of livestreaming video through social media platforms meant that anyone could become a citizen journalist, building from the DIY ethic of the Black liberation movement to capture and share raw footage of unfolding events (Kumanyika 2017). What they captured was stunning – Ferguson police responded with militarized tactics such as armored vehicles, assault rifles, tear gas, rubber bullets, and sound cannons, eventually calling in the National Guard. Meanwhile, the movement spread all across the country and even the globe. When a Ferguson grand jury decided not to indict the police officer for any crime that November, protests erupted again – this time in over 170 cities across the country, with demonstrators blocking bridges and major highways while chanting "Hands up! Don't shoot!" (Almasy and Yan 2014).

In the years since then, Black Lives Matter activism has continued to grow in strength as a decentralized global political movement centered on eradicating anti-Black racism and police violence. Massive protests have followed the deaths of many other individuals, including Eric Garner, Tamir Rice, Alton Sterling, Akai Gurley, Philando Castile, Freddie Gray, Stephon Clark,

Tony Robinson, Botham Jean, Breonna Taylor, Daunte Wright, and many others. In the summer of 2020, the killing of George Floyd by a white police officer in Minneapolis reignited global protests centered on defunding and abolishing police in a series of demands that built from now well-established social movement organizations (Hu 2020). Amidst the ravages of the global COVID-19 pandemic that was also forcing a reckoning with race-based inequalities, Floyd's death prompted serious discussions about historical and systemic racism. Based on measurements of the number of individuals who attended Black Lives Matter protests in the summer of 2020, it has since become the largest movement in US history (Buchanan, Bui, and Patel 2020).

While the mainstreaming of support for Black Lives Matter seems to have captured the zeitgeist, the strength and visibility of this activism has been facilitated through the long-standing relationship of Black communities to digital media. As Sarah Florini argues, "Black digital networks have been crucial in the efforts for racial justice during and since Ferguson. But they did not coalesce at that moment. They already existed, having been created and maintained over years through daily, often mundane, interactions" (2019a: 137). These existing connections and communities are what made it possible for Black digital networks to be rapidly deployed during moments of crisis. This includes the use of multiple digital platforms like message boards and blogs in the early days of the internet, as well as the sustained communities connected through podcasts and social media platforms like Instagram, YouTube, Facebook, and Twitter, as is discussed in more detail in chapter 10. Since Black communities were already using these platforms for sharing both user-generated content and links to news media, they easily served as a vehicle for providing up-to-the-moment updates about urgent issues as they unfolded. Yarimar Bonilla and Jonathan Rosa (Bonilla and Rosa 2015) point to the aggregative nature of Twitter as one of its key strengths, as frustrations with anti-Black violence accumulated over time and built from previous digital conversations. While it is possible to analyze individual moments in time, such as the hours following the death of Michael Brown and the conversation that surrounded it, the Black Lives Matter movement ebbs and flows over time and can easily erupt into a flashpoint due to its sustained continuities.

Documenting Black death

One of the ways that digital media have been used to counteract the horrors and trauma of state-sponsored Black death is through fighting for ownership and control over the way that images of Black death circulate online. This is a battle that has been particularly important due to the historical weight of injustices surrounding Black death. Black Americans, Latinos, and Native Americans already face shorter life expectancies than white Americans, due to both systemic inequalities in the healthcare system and the ills of racial oppression such as slavery and mass incarceration. Tonia Sutherland (2017) also outlines the many ways that Black death has been instrumentalized by those in power as a tool for intimidation and acquiescence through lynchings, assassinations, and other forms of violence. As she points out, these histories of trauma have deeply shaped Black American rituals around grief and mourning that center on supporting and preserving connections to community amidst feelings of resentment and anger at lives taken too soon. In many cases, calling attention to racist atrocities through visual confrontations of Black death can be an important challenge to white supremacy. When 14-year-old African American Emmett Till was brutally murdered by white men and his body thrown in the Tallahatchie River in 1955, his mother Mamie Till Mosely insisted on an open-casket funeral so that the world would be forced to see his mutilated body. In 1968, hundreds of thousands of mourners gathered for public funeral services for Martin Luther King Jr, and photos from his memorials played an important role in galvanizing support for civil rights. Images of lynchings, anti-Black police violence, and other harms to Black communities have played key roles in gaining support for anti-discrimination legislation and shifts in public opinion. These important uses of public memorials for bearing witness have translated into the digital era with the sharing of social media messages about incidents of police violence and the death of Black citizens.

Another way of taking control over Black death online has been through archival projects and practices. While social media posts can provide in-the-moment updates and broadcast events as they are occurring, digital media can also provide a powerful platform for documenting state violence through more sustained and long-term processes. Stacie Williams and Jarrett Drake (2017) narrate the creation of A People's Archive of Police Violence in Cleveland, which provided a way for community members and local activists to share their narratives with the public. This included the collection of oral histories, testimonies, and transcribed video footage from important events. Archivists took precautions to make sure that all content contributed to the archive did no harm to those most impacted by police violence, as there were many concerns about privacy and police retaliation. They also considered the sustainability of the project and its accessibility for those with limited technologies, as the political goal of the project was to shift power into the hands of marginalized communities. Other archival projects have focused on highlighting the work of African American women and trans* people in the Black Lives Matter movement, both in the central role they have played as leaders in the movement and the tragic loss of Black women, girls, and trans* people to police violence (Lindsey 2015). Such efforts show the capabilities and importance of digital archives for documenting underrepresented experiences and using that data to challenge dominant narratives.

These attempts to gain control have also been important because of the specific way that Black deaths are frequently exploited within digital infrastructures. Safiya Noble describes the risks inherent in how videos and photographs of Black death have become a valuable commercial property for social media companies. As she argues, "We need a better understanding of the cultural importance of trafficking in the spectacle of Black death and dying on the Internet by looking at how often and to what profit Black death as a viral phenomenon is exponentially potent and traumatizing" (2018b: 151).

Since social media companies profit from the popularity of user-generated content, they have a vested interest in promoting the circulation of Black death – even when it may end up bombarding Black users with painful images and exacerbating the emotional distress of those who are already facing crises.

This viral circulation for corporate profit also highlights the lack of control that individuals have over their own data, imagery, and digital assets. Even after someone has died, social media companies own and control all content that has been posted, and other users can continue to post images of deceased individuals without permission or consent. Debates about what has been called "the right to be forgotten" center on the question of whether an individual can request to have their personal information removed from search-engine results and social media platforms. In the case of the loss of Black lives, the ability to engage in public mourning is clearly a double-edged sword that must be navigated with far more nuance and input from Black communities.

The power of hashtag activism

If digital media has always been a key tool of the Black Lives Matter movement, the hashtag has reigned supreme as its defining feature. Since 2009, Twitter has allowed users to link thematically connected tweets across the platform through the use of the # symbol. As the usefulness of the hashtag took off on Twitter, other platforms like Instagram, Facebook, Tumblr, and Pinterest followed suit and allowed users to click user-generated hashtags as a search tool (Lips 2018). Hashtags have proved powerful in allowing users to create ad hoc digital communities around both trivial and serious topics. Discussion about the political power of hashtags started to proliferate in 2011 when activists used hashtagged tweets to communicate about the democratic uprisings during the Arab Spring and the Occupy movement. Some observers enthusiastically declared that these political movements had been completely facilitated through Twitter, while others criticized this interpretation as overly optimistic, reasoning that no online tool could compare to the important work of on-the-ground organizing.

These debates about the efficacy of digital tools within activist movements have continued to plague every form of online social media. Terms like **slacktivism** and **clicktivism** are used to downplay online activism by categorizing it as a form of digital political participation that demands very little effort – just the click of a button. When online activism is reduced to simple actions like posting or reposting a message on one's own social feed, liking or up-voting a post, or changing one's avatar to a symbol of support or allyship, these low-stakes forms of participation can seem to be more focused on improving personal branding efforts or building individual social capital than contributing to systemic change. Slacktivism has been also criticized for its reliance on market logics, as enlisting large numbers of followers to take small actions can become conflated with social change, regardless of its actual impact "on the ground." Malcolm Gladwell (Gladwell 2010) has famously criticized social media activism as completely divested of what he sees as "real activism" in historical moments like the 1960s sit-ins at lunch counters in Greensboro. As he describes it, the social networks created on platforms like Facebook and Twitter mostly consist of acquaintances with whom you share weak social ties, and therefore one can only call upon that network to participate in actions that require very little risk. Such concerns have continued since then, with critics claiming that online activism is primarily self-congratulatory virtue signaling and merely "performative allyship," rather than a kind of solidarity that actually elevates marginalized communities. In the summer of 2020, many social media users were criticized for posting black squares in their social media feeds on #BlackOutDay in an attempt to show support for Black communities. Such acts were labeled performative activism because the barrage of black squares actually served to obscure posts by Black activists that contained important information about unfolding events (Aswad 2020; Norman 2020).

But the reality is that many forms of online activism, including hashtag activism, have been extremely powerful in contributing to social change. While there are certainly forms of political participation that are more effective than others, these attempts to downplay the role of social media in activism largely misunderstand the different roles media play in larger social movements. First, it is important to recognize the significance of consciousness raising and information sharing within activism, as no social movement can take place without the ability to communicate about the problem and convince others that a change must take place. This means that the simple act of sharing a social media post can actually play a key role in growing political support and participation, and of course the accumulative effect of creating or engaging with numerous social media posts over time can exponentially increase that effect. As Sarah J. Jackson, Moya Bailey, and Brooke Foucault Welles find in their study of hashtag activism, members of marginalized groups "use Twitter hashtags to build diverse networks of dissent and shape the cultural and political knowledge fundamental to contemporary identity-based social movements" (Jackson, Bailey, and Wells 2020: xxxviii). They point to how Black women have been disproportionately adept at creating persuasive hashtags and using digital networks to garner attention, champion marginalized perspectives, and draw in new participants.

The groundswell of momentum surrounding **#MeToo** provides a strong example of how a simple hashtag can galvanize a social justice movement. In 2017, a *New York Times* article came out detailing decades of allegations of sexual harassment by Hollywood mogul Harvey Weinstein. In response, Alyssa Milano tweeted that all the women who have been sexually harassed or assaulted should reply "me too" to her tweet, to give people a sense of the magnitude of the problem. Within 24 hours of her post, the phrase #MeToo had been used 12 million times (CBS/AP 2017). The phrase "Me Too" had already long been in use by Black activist Tarana Burke, whose organization Just Be Inc. had been helping victims of sexual harassment and assault since 2003 (Garcia 2017). But with this new connection to celebrity culture and Hollywood, the hashtag became a fertile space for digital communities to discuss and learn about the harms of rape culture on a vast scale. Since then, Burke has called for the movement to continue to center marginalized voices such as Black and Brown girls, Native Americans, queer and transgender folks, and people with disabilities, particularly since many survivors of sexual violence from marginalized communities distrust law enforcement and have nontraditional approaches to pursuing justice (Adetiba 2017). One of the strengths of the #MeToo movement is that millions of everyday internet users decided to participate by sharing their own experiences of sexual violence, building from the feminist maxim that "the personal is political," even though doing so was risky and emotionally taxing. All forms of social media are marked by their participatory nature, allowing individuals to jump into discussions and bypass the traditional system of gatekeepers that has kept marginalized individuals from sharing their perspectives within legacy and mainstream media outlets. As more and more individuals saw members of their social circles participating in the discussion, individual participants felt less alone and more deeply connected to those who had also been harmed. Conversations surrounding the hashtag helped participants directly challenge sexual violence through social media posts that extended much further than their immediate social circles (Mendes, Ringrose, and Keller 2018).

The momentum from #MeToo did not happen in a vacuum; it was preceded by generations of feminist activism and supported by carefully organized political strategies.

The use of the hashtag #MeToo also built from conversations around similar hashtags like #YesAllWomen, #WhyIStayed, and #TheEmptyChair that also helped to educate about institutionalized sexism and solicit personal stories about experiences of gender violence (Jackson and Welles 2015). The #MeToo movement has also been undeniably effective, as many high-profile sexual abusers, including Harvey Weinstein, Larry Nassar, Bill Cosby, and Keith Raniere, were convicted and imprisoned. Another 200 men in high-profile positions were fired after public allegations surfaced of sexual harassment. These included elected officials, executives, journalists and editors, actors, comedians, TV hosts, chefs, academics, architects, and religious leaders – and nearly half of their replacements were women (Carlsen et al. 2018). Feminists have also successfully fought for more protections in the workplace against sexual predators and financial restitution for survivors, in addition to their successes in raising public awareness of the problem. There will always be setbacks and backlash to progress, and the fight for gender equality and freedom from gender violence will never be complete. But online discourse clearly played a significant role in initiating these important discussions, amplifying messages to the level of mainstream recognition, and supporting efforts to bring about real consequences.

Impacts of online activism

Conversations taking place on social media can also play important roles shaping activist communities from the inside, serving as a space for individuals to congregate with like-minded people and debate the issues they care about. In Rachel Kuo's (2016) critical discourse analysis and network analysis of Asian American activist hashtags, she finds that the hashtags #SolidarityIsForWhiteWomen and #NotYourAsianSidekick were used to discuss intersectional feminism and the use of the model minority myth to create a wedge between AAPI communities and other communities of color. Twitter allowed Asian American users to respond to the conversation with new opinions, to invite others in by tagging them, and to amplify the messages beyond their own communities. Like many media studies theorists, Kuo understands racialized collectives on Twitter as **networked counterpublics** because they create space for a subordinate group to communicate safely amongst themselves while also challenging their exclusion from more mainstream communication outlets (Graham and Smith 2016; Gutierrez 2020; Jackson and Welles 2015). One of the ways that this happens is through reframing the movement, as broad bases of participants can use hashtags to attach desired meanings to discussions of certain problems and solutions (Ince, Rojas, and Davis 2017). This can include working to shift media narratives that persist in the mainstream press, such as using positive self-images of Black youth to critique the way that victims of police violence are so frequently framed as criminals (Gross 2017). There have also been concerted efforts to shift attention and discussion to lesser-known victims of police violence, including women and LGTBQ+ individuals.

The impact of merely "clicking a button" should also not be downplayed, as the accumulation of thousands of individuals deciding to show their support for an issue is undeniably powerful. Indeed, voting in an election is an extremely simple act, but we would never dismiss voter registration efforts and other forms of civic engagement centered on electoral politics as meaningless due to the simplicity and ease of their ask. In the online realm, activist campaigns can also require low-level effort for individuals to get involved. We have already seen the political significance and impact of engaging in conversation and amplifying activist messages, but there are many other simple online activities that can contribute to collective action and social change. In a media landscape where attention and popularity are meaningful forms of currency that equate to legitimacy, influence, and success, the power of gaining "clicks" and "likes" cannot be overstated. But online participants can also be asked to sign online petitions, send messages to elected representatives, or donate money – all simple individual acts that can become powerful tools of influence through amassing thousands of repetitions.

These affordances were all put to work during the COVID-19 pandemic, when Asian and Asian American communities were facing increased threats of violence and physical assaults. This surge in hate crimes against Asians and Asian Americans was attributed to harmful racial discourses surrounding the pandemic, including President Trump insisting upon using the phrases "Chinese virus" and "kung flu" in an attempt to blame China for the disease and its impacts. Asian American activists swiftly mobilized to call attention to this problematic discourse and its dire consequences, which were being downplayed and overlooked in mainstream media. Most significantly, a group of Asian American researchers and activists from the San Francisco Bay area formed a group called Stop AAPI Hate to track anti-Asian hate incidents. They created a simple Google form for collecting self-reports of anti-Asian hate incidents, along with a website (www.stopaapihate.org) where they could post weekly reports. The contributions of this research and reporting center were then augmented by university groups and community organizations that created social media awareness campaigns and educational videos, and facilitated online conversations through hashtags (Takasaki 2020). Together these digitally based partnerships served to dramatically expand conversations about anti-Asian violence in news media and supported legislative actions such as the COVID-19 Hate Crimes Act and the API Equity Budget in California. There have also been countless online fundraisers created to financially support Asian American community groups amidst this surge in anti-Asian violence. For instance, a GoFundMe campaign for the AAPI Community Fund gathered more than US$6.8 million for organizations focused on increasing community safety and support for victims of violence (Spangler 2021). While research played a key role in sustaining this activism, the cumulative impact could not have been possible without millions of individual online participants deciding to fill out a survey, click to a website, share a post, and donate a small amount of money to show their support.

Risks of online vs offline activism

Online activism has also played a key role in shaping offline actions and other more traditional forms of in-person activism. While Gladwell speculated that online activism was limited to only low-risk activities, this critique has proven extremely short-sighted. On the contrary, it is now difficult to imagine any political uprising that is not deeply connected to an online community or the use of digital technologies. The use of digital media for community organizing builds from the way that activists have always relied on mediated communication – including the use of leaflets and posters to publicize their messages, the use of phones and telephone trees for recruiting purposes, the use of radio and television to broadcast news about activist movements, and the use of self-authored media to document activist stories and campaigns (Mattoni 2017). No matter what form of media is being used, social movements are designed to transition participants from spectators to more active supporters and participants, and online media have been no different. Throughout the life of the Black Lives Matter movement, social media communities have showed up en masse to in-person events, including countless protests and demonstrations in cities all across the United States and the globe. Many of the conversations happening on Twitter centered on amplifying the voices of protestors on the ground who participated by posting up-to-the-moment updates, telling protestors where to show up and what supplies were needed, and sending videos, photos, and eyewitness accounts documenting unfolding events. In moments like these, it becomes more important than ever to point out that there can be no clear distinction between "online" and "offline" activities. This case shows the way that digital technologies are being used as tools to directly coordinate and shape the outcomes of direct action.

While on-the-ground activism is often framed as inherently risky, due to the threat of being arrested or assaulted, there are many risks to participating in digital activism as well. Even if activism takes place entirely from inside the home and all communication is mediated through a cell phone or other digital screen, there are still plenty of potential risks to one's mental health, reputation, and safety. As has been discussed throughout this book, online discourses can be extremely abusive, particularly toward those with minority identities such as women, people of color, and LGBTQ+ people. Online abuse can take many different forms, starting with name calling, hate speech, harassment, threats of violence, the sending of explicit content, and other forms of hostility. There can also be possible risks to one's reputation through abusers engaging in false accusations, online impersonation, Google bombing (creating malicious online content designed to manipulate search-engine results), or contacting employers. Online abuse can also escalate to attacks that are meant to threaten or cause physical harm, such as doxing (revealing a user's real name, address, phone number, and family information), real-life stalking, or swatting (making fake calls to police to elicit a law enforcement response at a specific address). For individuals engaging in activities such as criticizing racist structures or calling attention to racial injustices, the consequences are intensified. Racial justice activists are always at risk of burnout due to emotional exhaustion, professional and economic backlash, and the psychological toll of facing increased racism (Gorski 2019). When taken alongside the potential for online activism to come at a great personal cost, we can see that both online and offline activism must be categorized as potentially very high risk.

Digital storytelling

The different affordances of each digital platform play a direct role in shaping the kinds of activism that are possible within it. The strength of Twitter is its ability to quickly communicate information through extremely short messages, catalogue information through hashtags, amplify messages through retweets, and connect like-minded participants to one another. In many ways, Twitter has allowed individuals to tell their stories in brief but politically powerful ways as they are able to quickly interject their perspective into a media stream that may otherwise neglect them. But if we expand beyond Twitter to consider how activists are using multiple platforms in order to make use of their distinct affordances, we can also see the rise of more complex forms of storytelling within digital activism. Many contemporary political movements deploy **transmedia organizing,** which Sasha Costanza-Chock (2014) defines as a kind of grassroots social movement that deploys multiple media platforms, centers participatory and user-generated media, and links attention to action. It is premised on theories of industrial practices of transmedia storytelling, where narratives circulate across different platforms and allow for multiple points of entry. By extending beyond single-media platforms and individual messages, transmedia organizing can "strengthen social movement identity, win political and economic victories, and transform the consciousness of broader publics" (50).

Latinx youth have engaged in many forms of transmedia activism that build from these strengths to challenge anti-immigrant policies. Arely Zimmerman (2016) identifies a key site for this kind of activism in transmedia **testimonio,** or personal narratives that are shared across multiple media platforms in order to increase support for direct-action campaigns. There are millions of immigrant youth living in the United States who entered the country as children and then later learned that they were undocumented. These individuals and their families face constant threats, including fears around deportation and family separation, struggles in gaining an education, and lack of access to state services and resources. While many undocumented individuals have concealed their identity as a way to protect themselves and their families, a new generation of undocumented youth activists has turned to digital media platforms to share their "coming-out stories" and spread information about their experiences. In these stories, they discuss their undocumented status and the risks it has posed to themselves and others, putting a human face on their struggles while calling attention to the state violence and repression that so many like them have faced. This includes posting videos to

YouTube and Vimeo, creating events and pages on Facebook, tweeting and using hashtags, and designing standalone websites such as DreamActivist.org where these stories can be aggregated and shared. Since these narratives are rooted in personal experiences but are designed to represent a collective experience, they are effective in mobilizing supporters to attend in-person events such as mock graduations for undocumented students, rallies and sit-ins, and mass events like National Coming Out of the Shadows Day.

While online activism is often criticized for reducing politics to quippy sound-bites and hashtags, activists have also used digital platforms to add nuance and depth to their storytelling. Jillian Baez (2017) studies the digital testimonios of DREAMers, or young undocumented Latinx activists advocating for the Development, Relief, and Education for Alien Minors (DREAM) Act, focusing on how online texts circulate. She explores the way that more normative or assimilable content about undocumented youth may circulate more widely, but that transgressive and radical content can still play an important role in the digital media landscape. For instance, the 67 Sueños project uses online videos and podcasts to put forward counternarratives that challenge dominant media portrayals "largely focused on redeeming 'good' immigrants (read: college-educated, English-dominant, and potentially socio-economically upwardly mobile)" (2017: 428). Latinx activists also share complex stories about youth who might not fit an idealized media-friendly mold but still want to fight to avoid deportation and family separation. As Baez argues, the intended target for these videos is the larger immigration movement itself, which they believe must be expanded to include more diverse participation, including other marginalized identities such as LGBTQ+ undocumented youth. This kind of message cannot easily be communicated in a slogan or a 240-character tweet, but it can slowly accumulate through sharing content featuring multiple voices, each contributing its own details.

Meme activism

As we have seen throughout this chapter, one of the main strengths of online activism is that digital platforms are deeply participatory and invite multiple voices to join in. Another kind of digital participation that communities have used for activism is internet meme culture. **Internet memes** consist of images and videos that are easily manipulated so that users can add their own personal perspective or humorous twist before sharing their creations with others. Memes often play with recognizable pop cultural or other familiar texts but invite users to slightly alter them through remix, parody, and application to new situations. The term "meme" itself comes from Richard Dawkins' (1976) studies of human evolution, as he proposed that small units of culture can survive by replicating, mutating, and evolving. Like so much online culture, it is also important to recognize that some of the power of memes comes from their affective resonance. In a single image or reference, the most popular memes capture a sentiment or a mood with incredible efficiency and precision. These qualities have then been taken up by activists for both racial progress and for the continuation of white supremacy.

One of the most popular memes of all time is Pepe the Frog, a viral phenomenon that was taken up by the "alt-right" movement to support white nationalism. The cartoon image of a humanoid frog character started to grow in popularity from being shared through community conversations on the online forum 4chan, a platform that is infamous for supporting racism and hate speech. In 2015, Donald Trump used the symbol of Pepe to depict himself, which cemented its associations with right-wing politics. The symbol was then taken up by both internet trolls and the alt-right, who continued using the image to reinforce anti-Semitic and racist perspectives (Nelson 2016). One of the key audiences that connected to Pepe was internet users who felt alienated from mainstream culture. Since the style of Pepe is repulsive and monstrous, the amphibious creature seemed to align naturally with a community characterized by offence and disgust. Pepe was often depicted engaging in perverse and violent behaviors, and these disruptions to normal convention and etiquette resonated with a nascent political consciousness around disenfranchised white men (Glitsos and Hall 2019). The simple image of a green frog with bulging eyes could easily be reappropriated into a wide variety of situations and contexts, while cementing its meaning as a shorthand for affiliation with certain political ideologies. As with all memes, Pepe's meaning is always being contested and revised as new versions are created and shared. But the enduring resonance of Pepe imagery nonetheless helps us see how the simplicity and spreadability of an image can strengthen its political power.

Internet memes have also played a key role in struggles for Indigenous sovereignty and decolonization. While the same affordances of affective resonance, openness to participation, and malleability can be seen at work in Indigenous memes, it is also important to analyze Indigenous internet activism through Indigenous epistemologies and decolonial frameworks, as scholars like Marisa Duarte (2017a) have argued. This means taking into consideration long-standing struggles over place-based decolonization efforts, acknowledging the existence of global Indigenous networks and the political solidarity that they have engendered, and challenging definitions of "political participation" to include Indigenous forms of activism rather than more traditional expectations of electoral politics. Angel Hinzo and Lynn Schofield Clark take a decolonial perspective in their analysis of the #NoDAPL movement that protested the completion of the Dakota Access Pipeline for transporting crude oil across sacred Indigenous lands. In their examination of humorous and ironic memes that supported the #NoDAPL movement, they find: "Indigenous publics on social media embody the Trickster as a spiritual figure who disobeys established rules and conventional behavior, while establishing expectations for humanitarianism . . . Indigenous humor calls into question US government politics over land, US media practices, and US policing as each undermine Indigenous citizens' right to be seen, to exist, and to maintain cultural practices" (2019: 802). They argue that these interactions on social media then enact digital survivance, or a form of Indigenous survival and resistance that takes place through digital spaces.

Given the culture of irreverence and recognizability within meme culture, Indigenous memes have also been particularly useful in calling attention to the invisibility of Indigenous peoples within mainstream media. Jacqueline Land (2021) studies the meme networks of Indigenous fan activists who want to see themselves represented within prominent media franchises. They create memes that photoshop Indigenous faces and cultural objects into mainstream pop cultural texts, such as adding beaded earrings or traditional regalia to familiar characters like Pikachu. Other Indigenous memes have centered on the use of ethnographic photos as the source material, and the aesthetic practices of activists who edit, add to, or comment upon historical black-and-white photos of Native Americans. Joshua Miner argues that when Indigenous artists add pop cultural figures like Princess Leia and Godzilla into these historical images it serves to disrupt discourses around Native peoples by calling attention to how contemporary media representations uphold settler colonialism (Miner 2021).

Conclusion

There are countless different ways that digital media have been taken up as a tool for furthering the cause of anti-racism and social justice. Each specific digital platform and its different technological affordances, audiences, and cultures of use will make it more or less appropriate for certain kinds of expression, which means that activists will need to adapt their strategies depending on which platform they are using. We can still continue to ask critical questions about the impacts of digital activism, as it is often difficult to directly assess whether or not any particular campaign made a difference. But this is also a question we could ask of any form of activism, whether in-person or online, as social change is a nebulous and complicated process that is always challenging to pinpoint or measure.

Key questions

1. What are Black Lives Matter activists fighting for, and how do they use digital tools to strengthen their movement?
2. Why has online activism been accused of being less effective than "offline" forms of activism, and how might this criticism be challenged and complicated?
3. How do memes provide a way for everyday internet users to participate in a larger conversation, and what are some of the different ways that memes have contributed to conversations about race online?

Further reading

Costanza-Chock, Sasha. 2014. *Out of the Shadows, Into the Streets! Transmedia Organizing and the Immigrant Rights Movement*. Cambridge, MA: MIT Press.

Jackson, Sarah J., Bailey, Moya, and Wells, Brooke Foucault. 2020. *#Hashtag Activism: Networks of Race and Gender Justice*. Cambridge, MA: MIT Press.

Richardson, Allissa V. 2020. *Bearing Witness While Black: African Americans, Smartphones, and the New Protest #Journalism*. Oxford: Oxford University Press.

9

Games

Key terms

- identification
- platformed racism
- serious games
- survivance
- self-determination
- virtual reality

Introduction

VIDEO games, virtual reality, apps, and other play-based technologies have been celebrated for their ability to educate and empower even as their interactions are designed to be fun and entertaining. Interactive gaming technologies facilitate a unique user experience because they invite a degree of ownership and control over one's engagement that can enrich possibilities for learning. These experiences are particularly distinct from the way that audiences engage with static content like TV shows or podcasts or magazines, which offer a one-way flow of information with far more limited opportunities for interaction. Interactive media provide users the opportunity to make their own choices within boundaries established by the game designer, and invite the user to experience gameplay from a perspective that may be different from their own. Video gameplay is also unlike passive consumption of media because in many cases players enter the same world over and over, experiencing failure and the need to reset and try again, which creates both repetition and new opportunities for experimentation and improvement. When taken alongside the narrative components of gameplay, these mechanisms open up novel avenues for learning. More broadly, with the size of the video game industry surpassing that of the global movie and North American sports industries combined in 2020 during the COVID-19 pandemic (Witkowski 2021), the impact of games on mainstream culture is undeniable.

This chapter begins by identifying the way that structural racism, hate speech, and white supremacy have flourished within gaming cultures. Video game industries and player communities have both proven to be toxic spaces for people of any minority community – including people of color, but also women, LGBTQ+ people, religious minorities, and others. Despite this persistent culture, there have also been many efforts by minority gamers to support the development of educational games and other ludic technologies as a route to social change. We can see examples of this in the rise of mobile apps like *Everyday Racism*, Indigenous indie video games such as *Never Alone* and *When Rivers Were Trails*, and the virtual reality experience called *Traveling While Black* for Oculus Go. While promises of virtual reality as an "empathy machine" must be carefully assessed for accuracy, there are still many examples of gaming technologies that can be seen as important interventions for minority communities to participate in self-determination and educate wider communities about their experiences and unique struggles. In these cases and others, gaming is used as an opportunity to provide new insights into the experiences of racial minorities and other marginalized identities.

Racist representations in video games

In order to understand the way that video games have perpetuated racism and harm toward many marginalized communities, we must explore multiple facets of how games work and who engages with them. First, we can begin with the representations and narratives contained in video games, which often rely on stereotypical portrayals or perpetuate the symbolic annihilation of minority identities. Women and people of color have been significantly underrepresented within video game characters, and when they do show up as options for player-controlled characters, they frequently fall into damaging stereotypes – women are hypersexualized and unrealistically proportioned, Black men are reduced to thugs and fierce athletic competitors, Hispanic characters are criminals and gang members, East Asians are martial artists speaking broken English, Arabs are enemy terrorists, and women of color are almost nonexistent (Leonard 2006). The *Grand Theft Auto* franchise and its many different iterations is one of the most popular and highest rated games of all time, but it has always been criticized for its morally reprehensible narratives and depictions. In addition to its extremely violent plot where the player is a criminal who must drive around a city shooting people and stealing cars, the game also relies on racial stereotypes. Released in 2005, *Grand Theft Auto: San Andreas* invites players to take on the perspective of Carl Johnson, a Black gang member who must engage in escalating criminal acts in order to succeed. As Paul Barrett argues, within the game "there is a glamorizing, and even spectacularization of violence, a marking of young Black bodies as disposable, an insistence on a culture of cynicism as well as a particular formation of African American experience that is extremely problematic" (Barrett 2006: 95). There are also representations of Asian and Latino gang members and drug addicts, as well as female prostitutes whom the player is encouraged to seduce and then murder.

These problems continue across different video game genres, including those that foreground characters of color. Sports video games like *NBA Street* that represent African American players as superstars forward narratives about how these players come from "the hood," and they frequently depict the bodies of Black players in animalistic and exaggerated styles (Nishi, Marias, and Montoya 2015). Native Americans have suffered a similar fate within video game representations, with early games like *Custer's Revenge* from 1982 infamously centering the goal of explicit sexual violence against Native American women. Other common video game tropes include western themes that pit white cowboys against bloodthirsty and savage Indians, the use of Indigenous characters as spiritual guides, and colonizing narratives rehearsing the historical extermination of Native civilization. These representations seem to have been produced under market logics that cater to a demographic of players that either enjoy or at least are not bothered by such images and narratives.

While we should worry about the racist ideologies that are propagated through video game narratives, the way that users interact with video games adds another layer of concern due to the fact that players take on the perspective of the game's fictional protagonists. In particular, women and people of color looking at game characters could end up feeling both offended and excluded, as if their very identities have been invalidated. When players are invited to create an avatar that is supposed to represent themselves, it is disappointing to realize that there are no characters that even remotely resemble attributes like Black hair textures and hairstyles, darker skin tones, larger body types, or disabled bodies. As Jennifer Williams describes, "if Black women in digital spaces cannot do their hair in a culturally and individually relevant fashion, if their engagement is constrained by the lack of interest in crafting markers of blackness . . . then they are denied access to self and communal development, and vital social resources and experiences" (Williams 2019: 42). Players have sometimes resorted to developing their own mods, or modifications, to a game so that they can have more choices about imagery, style, fashion, and representation. But the limited choices presented to players nonetheless send a clear message about who is welcome within video gaming.

We should also be concerned about the way that white players engage with the few characters of color that do exist. As mentioned in chapter 2, Lisa Nakamura (2008) has argued that one of the defining features of the early internet was how it allowed users to try on different races, genders, and other identities for the purposes of experimentation and play. She is particularly concerned about how this form of identity tourism can allow white users to inhabit non-white racial identities and act out scenarios without facing the consequences and risks of actually being a person of color in their real lives. Within the world of video games, the vast majority of avatars and playable characters are male and white, despite the fact that the number of female gamers and Black, Hispanic, and Asian American gamers has been rising (Williams et al. 2009). In 2020, Nielsen reported that Asian Americans are 14% more likely to own a gaming console than the total US population (Nielsen 2020), while Black and Hispanic adults have started to surpass the percentage of white adults in the United States identifying as video gameplayers (Dugan 2015). This means that we need to consider the racial dynamics of white male players taking on the perspective of the few minority avatars but also the experiences of women and people of color who are presented with the same options for gameplay.

On one hand, gender-bending or race-bending role play has the possibility to increase understanding of diverse perspectives. As Esther MacCallum-Stewart (2008) argues in her analysis of the male players who take on the role of the iconic white female avatar Lara Croft, men often state that they enjoy playing female characters like Lara because she is strong and that they see nothing strange about playing as a female character because cross-gender play has become so normalized. Such responses seem to celebrate positive female attributes and the queerness of gender play, breaking down negative assumptions about gender hierarchies. Yet, on the other hand, it is also undeniable that players enjoy the pleasures of looking at Lara and objectifying her, given her character's sexy styling. When considering the relationship of white players or male players to minoritized characters and game worlds, there can still be concerns about how those interactions shore up existing power dynamics. We can see the potential for such problems in the representations of Asia in the World of Warcraft game called *Mists of Pandaria*. The game takes place in an Orientalized fictional land populated with a race called the Pandaren that resemble anthropomorphized panda bears that sport Fu Manchu beards and wear samurai gear. Depicted with a landscape of pagodas and temples, bamboo forests, and rice paddies, Pandaria is clearly meant to evoke China and an array of fantasies surrounding a mystical and spiritual East. As Takeo Rivera argues, "the romanticized space of Pandaria and the culture of its panda-people suggest a pleasure from gaining mastery of this Oriental New World" (Rivera 2017: 204). Video games become another outlet for the white fantasy of controlling and dominating people of color, gaining pleasure from engaging with a "foreign" culture in a way that does nothing to challenge white privilege.

It is also important to look beyond troubling representations to consider how marginalized gamers experience **identification** with these video games. Adrienne Shaw (2014) asks us to look deeper at the question of whether gamers directly identify with video game characters, as her in-depth interviews with gamers from diverse backgrounds reveal that identification is a complex phenomenon that can happen across multiple axes. Not only do individual gamers experience their own identities in fluid and contextual ways, but how a player identifies with a video gameplayer or avatar can encompass a wide range of meanings. Instead of a player fully seeing themselves as the character, identification could include less immersive components such as simply understanding their character's perspective, reacting emotionally to their character's experiences, feeling empathy for a character, being able to get inside a character's head, or feeling connection to a character. When taken in conjunction with the fact that video games are frequently outlets for fantasy and escapism, this means that gamers can experience varied forms of identification with characters who have very different racial, gender, or sexual identities from themselves. But Shaw also finds that identification with a character did not really matter to many gamers, and criticizes the assumption that representation in video games matters because of identification. Rather, she argues that diversity in video game representation is important because players of all backgrounds benefit from having a diversity of choices, not just marginalized audiences.

Racist and sexist gaming communities

Another important aspect of video gaming is the way that gamers interact and engage with each other, forming communities that sustain and shape video game cultures more broadly. Unfortunately, video gamers have become infamous for their poor treatment of many marginalized players. Kishonna Gray describes the problem as one where video game culture assumes that the default user is white and male, which contributes to women and people of color not being recognized as legitimate participants within digital gaming communities. As she states, "no matter the content, the dominant culture of digital gaming dictates who is legitimate and who is not, creating conditions of real and symbolic exclusion in everyday gaming practices" (Gray 2020a: 28). These cultures of exclusion are made possible by the fact that while video gaming can be a completely individualized activity, there is a strong culture of connecting to other players and participation in larger online video game communities. Players build communities with one another for the purposes of engaging in multiplayer games as teammates and opponents, for discussing and debating every aspect of video games, for sharing and watching and commenting on livestreams of individual players, for creating and modifying games, and more. There are also in-person video game communities, such as those that form within gaming industries and professional workplaces, through gaming leagues and esports tournaments, at conventions and meetups, and other live events.

While there is no single unified "video game community" or "video game culture," dominant assumptions about who video gamers are and what the identities of those who belong to these communities can still contribute to harmful consequences. As Adrienne Shaw points out (2010), one of the central ways that video game culture has been discussed is through the question of who plays games, but more importantly, "who 'counts' as a member of video game culture" (2010: 407).

When players who are not white, cisgendered, straight, and male participate in multi-user games online, they frequently experience mistreatment ranging from microaggressions, such as questioning their ability or how welcome they are in gaming spaces, to extremely racist, sexist, and homophobic treatment.

Lisa Nakamura (2013a) describes how even games where players only communicate through text and voice can lead to "voice-activated racism," as the common practice of "trash talk" while gaming can quickly turn to hate speech when players are recognized as non-white. Player-to-player voice chat sessions are used to communicate profanity, name calling, and abusive language, much of which is downplayed or dismissed by white players as merely a normal part of the culture of online gaming. Another gaming platform that has been a site for frequent abuse is Twitch, an online platform that allows players to live-broadcast their gameplay to online audiences alongside a small video of the player. This means that the player's face is visible to their audience, and they can narrate their activities as their audience observes and chats in real time. Women and people of color have faced regular harassment while streaming their gameplay through Twitch (Woodhouse 2021). This includes exceedingly common sexist and racist remarks, as well as organized attacks from trolls that can result in the marginalized streamer themselves being banned from the platform (Rosenblatt 2019).

These concerns about how games are designed and what choices players make when they engage with them come together in instances of **platformed racism**. We can see platformed racism occurring when digital platforms are designed in a way that allows for racist uses by community members to be amplified and reproduced. Sam Srauy and John Cheney-Lippold (2019) analyze platformed racism in the online video game FIFA Ultimate Team, which invites players to create a custom team of soccer players based on real-world professional athletes. The design component that they find most concerning is that the attributes and ability scores for each player are created by video gameplayers who are invited to provide accurate assessments of real performances. After analyzing the data, they find that the viewer-encoded athlete attributes line up with racially biased stereotypes – including that the white characters are smarter, the Hispanic/Latino characters have the most flair and creativity, and the Black characters are the most strong and aggressive. They argue that "while the developers did not specifically encode ratings of athletes' physical abilities per se, by setting up a structure where those abilities can be noted by video gameplayers (i.e., data reviewers), systemic racist discourses of race as biological differences were invited into the platform."

A high-profile incident from 2014 known as Gamergate revealed many of these toxic and harmful attributes of dominant video game cultures. The Gamergate controversy was primarily centered on a video game designer named Zoe Quinn and the positive reviews she received for her game *Depression Quest*, which some felt were undeserved. She became inundated with personal attacks in a harassment campaign that included dredging up her personal sexual history, rape threats, death threats, and other forms of intimidation and harm to her reputation. Vlogger and media critic Anita Sarkeesian was also drawn into the fray because of her work on a YouTube video series for her brand Feminist Frequency called *Tropes vs. Women in Video Games*. The series included a number of videos that explained the limited representations of women, such as tropes of damsels in distress and sexy background decoration. Sarkeesian was subject to every possible version of misogynistic online abuse, in addition to facing threats of bombs and mass shootings that caused her public talks to be cancelled, being the subject of a video game that invited players to virtually punch her in the face, and eventually being forced to leave her home out of fears for her safety. The controversy also extended far beyond these individual targets, erupting into a widespread internet culture war: "On one side are independent game-makers and critics, many of them women, who advocate for greater inclusion in gaming. On the other side of the equation are a motley alliance of vitriolic naysayers: misogynists, anti-feminists, trolls, people convinced they're being manipulated by a left-leaning and/or corrupt press, and traditionalists who just don't want their games to change" (Dewey 2014). While Quinn and Sarkeesian – both white cis women – suffered from their high visibility and the attention that was focused on them, there have been countless other incidents of women who have been punished for daring to criticize any aspect of video game industries or gaming cultures more generally, both before Gamergate and afterward.

The Gamergate controversy revealed how poorly many individuals within video-gaming communities were responding to the rise of diverse game developers, widespread criticisms of problems within the industry, and shifts toward welcoming and even valuing diverse gamers. As Mia Consalvo states, "The rage we see expressed by threatened individuals and groups seems to be based on at least two factors – sexist (as well as racist, homophobic and ageist) beliefs about the abilities and proper place of female players, and fears about the changing nature of the game industry" (Consalvo 2012). The reality is that understandings of who is a gamer have been steadily changing over time, and games themselves have come to represent a wide range of identities and experiences. Since Gamergate became a widely visible backlash to progress in video games, it also served as an incentive to more publicly celebrate the feminist, queer, anti-racist voices and political movements that have long been a part of video-gaming communities.

Activism and diverse solutions

There are many different ways that women, people of color, LGBTQ+, disabled, and other communities have fought for inclusion within mainstream video-gaming culture since its earliest days. As TreaAndrea Russworm and Samantha Blackmon argue, "research that fails to imagine the existence of a vibrant Black feminist gaming counterpublic represents both a convenient historical omission and a dangerous cultural mythology" (Russworm and Blackmon 2020: 94). They point to the existence of Black women arcade owners from the 1980s like Delores Williams and Delores Barrows, the rise of video game producers like Shana T. Bryant who have regularly spoken up about racist industry norms, and Black women video game designers like Vanessa Paugh who started creating iOS games from her company Goddess Software in 2003.

There have been many efforts to call attention to the depth of the problem and give voice to the many who have been harmed. Lisa Nakamura points to the rise of multiple blogs and websites like "Fat, Ugly, or Slutty," and "The Border House: Breaking Down Borders in Gaming" that discuss problems in gaming culture and publicize examples of abusive gamers in order to increase accountability (Nakamura 2019). There have also been prominent discussions about these problems on Twitter using hashtags. For instance, in response to a question posed on Twitter in 2012 about why there are so few "lady game creators," game designer Filamena Young responded with the hashtag #1reasonwhy and added her own explanation. The hashtag #1reasonwhy ended up being used by thousands of women to communicate experiences of exclusion and denigration within the industry – "women talked about having their work dismissed and ignored, having designs for non-sexualized female characters rejected, their clothing and appearance being used to dismiss them on gender grounds, and, at the more extreme end, sexual harassment at conferences" (Hamilton 2012). This hashtag was then followed by #1reasontobe, which invited discussion of why women and other marginalized community members should join or remain in the gaming industry and what kinds of solutions could be leveraged help to address diversity issues. These conversations have spawned numerous panel discussions at industry conferences, as well as some movement toward solutions such as the creation of lists of mentors for women in video games.

Activist and gamer Tanya DePass started a conversation on Twitter using the hashtag #INeedDiverseGames in 2014. Although the use of the hashtag skyrocketed after the Gamergate controversy, DePass had long been involved in the work of calling attention to the homogeneity of video game industries and the need to address the problem in an intersectional way. Since Tanya is a Black queer woman, the perspectives included in this conversation were more diffuse and harder to pigeonhole under one banner. Due to this, Sarah Beth Evans and Elyse Janish point out that the conversation surrounding #INeedDiverseGames "can be embraced as exemplifying a queer form of resistance. Its proponents ignored binary understandings of identity and brought together many justifications for a single cause" (Evans and Janish 2015). After the success of the #INeedDiverseGames hashtag and the conversation it inspired, DePass founded a non-profit organization called I Need Diverse Games that supports underrepresented game designers through offering financial support to attend professional gaming conferences. The organization was also invited to become a Twitch Partner through an initiative called #DiversifyStreaming, which helped to call attention to their team of 32 non-white streamers and help them become more visible on the platform (DePass 2018).

Since individual video gamers who become popular through livestreaming platforms can rise to the level of a microcelebrity, this level of fame can also provide a platform for engaging with issues that are socially relevant. In particular, there are many examples of Black male gamers who have attained microcelebrity status on livestreaming platforms like Mixer, Twitch, and YouTube, which can even result in financial profit if their subscriber base is large enough. Brian Chan and Kishonna Gray (Chan and Gray 2020) argue that the racism of exclusionary practices within livestreaming communities puts a ceiling on how much fame Black men can accumulate, but that they can nonetheless benefit from redirecting their attention to community-minded goals. In particular, many Black male microcelebrities have realized that "the outcomes of the visibility of streaming are not the monetization potential or worldwide fame but rather the proximity to other Black people invested in gaming and the attention from them" (360). This has been particularly important in an era where videos of Black men being killed by police and other mediated images of racial violence have become ubiquitous across social media platforms, and the trauma of Black pain and suffering feels pervasive. After video footage of Eric Garner being choked to death by a white police officer in New York went viral in 2014, a black gamer and podcaster named Kahlief Adams took to Twitch to communicate his response. Using the hashtag #Spawn4Good, he provided information about other instances of racial violence by law enforcement even as other streamers criticized his use of the platform for #BlackLivesMatter activism (Gray 2020b).

The creation of spaces within gaming platforms and communities can help marginalized players feel a sense of comfort and belonging, in addition to being more shielded from harassment and attacks. LGBTQ+ gamers are another community that has been routinely made to feel unwelcome within the heteronormative and homophobic cultures of digital games. But Karen Skardzius points to spaces like Proudmoore, the "unofficial LGBT-friendly server in World of Warcraft," which helps to "publicly and actively promote an alternative social experience to that offered by Blizzard Entertainment" (Skardzius 2018: 186). One of the ways that they do this is through organizing annual Proudmoore Pride Parades, or in-game events where players are invited to put down their weapons and march together across the virtual landscape in celebration of LGBTQ+ communities. Skardzius argues that the joyful acceptance and supportive feelings engendered by such events, in addition to regular gameplay within guilds hosted on the Proudmoore server, can help players feel more resilient when coping with the mainstream gaming world. On the Xbox Live gaming platform, Kishonna Gray (2012) has pointed to the self-segregation of Black women gamers who have created their own player groups, or "clans," that serve to protect them from racist and sexist attacks. One woman described a conversation with another woman who didn't understand the point of such groups: "I told her I was tired of being called bitch, black bitch, dyke bitch, or any variation of bitch. She told my black ass to deal with it. That's just how it is" (420). This conversation reflects common debates within gaming communities about whether marginalized players benefit more from prioritizing protection or from competing with the white male players who need to encounter diverse players and learn that skilled people exist in all identities. Yet both perspectives affirm the work that has been unfairly demanded of marginalized players to play their own role in improving video game cultures, whether internally or externally focused.

Education and serious games

Another way that video game designers and communities have taken up ethical imperatives to contribute to social justice has been to design games that encourage critical thinking about real-world issues and inequalities. The term **serious games** is used to describe digital games that are designed to be both fun and educational, building from the affordances of games to provide an outlet for learning that can be motivating, responsive, and complex (Ritterfield, Cody, and Vorderer 2009). These kinds of games have been used in a wide variety of scenarios, including military games used for training new recruits, exercise and health-centered games designed to promote healthy lifestyles, political games for increasing civic engagement, and more creative applications like art or music education. With regard to anti-racism, the ability of serious games to promote pro-social messages with the goal of attitude and behavioral changes has also been used for goals such as increasing empathy for people of color, decreasing microaggressions against immigrants, or encouraging bystander interventions.

Serious games are often developed by educators, such as through programs like the University of Southern California's Game Innovation Lab that can assess learning and educational outcomes alongside gameplay components. In 2009, higher-education scholars partnered with game designers from this lab to create games focused on diversifying access to college through teaching first-generation college-bound students about the admissions process. This resulted in a game called *Mission: Admission* that used a playful interface to help students learn how to skillfully navigate the many components of the admissions process – including the importance of deadlines and time management, how to request letters of recommendation, and what financial aid opportunities are available. While the game was available to students of all backgrounds, its main goal was to help historically underrepresented students level the playing field in terms of knowledge about how to apply to college.

But serious games can also be more explicit in their focus on teaching about racism, rather than alleviating the consequences of institutionalized racism. Australian researchers from the organization All Together Now developed a role-playing game called *Everyday Racism* with the goal of helping players empathize with the experiences of life as a person of color. The free mobile app first invites players to select an avatar – a Muslim woman, an Indian man, or an Indigenous Australian man, or an unmarked bystander – and then face racialized experiences in real time over the course of a week. The selected avatar receives racist text messages and emails, experiences racist comments and harassment, and witnesses racist encounters, all ranging from subtle microaggressions to more explicit harassment. In each moment, the player is then asked to select from a set of responses to the situation. It is designed to help white players empathize with the daily experiences and decisions of people of color, as well as to motivate interventions when witnessing racism. While we might worry about how it condones the conflation of racial empathy with putting on a racial identity, it has nonetheless been celebrated as an exemplar of anti-racist video games because it so explicitly communicates the harms of racism (Fordyce, Neale, and Apperley 2018).

Indigenous video games

This focus on helping players of all backgrounds to empathize with minority perspectives is an important reason to champion the games made by minority game designers, such as Indigenous games.

*Indigenous video game developers all across the globe have created digital games that serve as acts of resistance to their erasure in both video game industries and in society more broadly. They can also be understood as playing an important role in expressing Indigenous **survivance** and **self-determination**.*

The term "survivance" was popularized by Gerald Vizenor (2008), who used the term to describe how Indigenous communities can move beyond mere survival to also endure and resist. As he states, it is "orienting its connotations not toward loss but renewal and continuity into the future rather than memorializing the past . . . These reorientations promise radically to transform current native life without requiring abandonment of the enduring value of their precontact cultural successes" (Kroeber 2008: 25). Survivance can also be understood as a term that asserts the right to inheritance and legacy, such as preserving the many important teachings, legacies, and epistemologies of Indigenous elders and ancestors (Madsen 2017).

To make sense of how Indigenous video games can participate in both survivance and self-determination, we can look at some examples of games in terms of their design and mechanics. The puzzle adventure game *Never Alone* was designed by Upper One Games in collaboration with nearly 40 Iñupiaq community members. Players embark on a quest to discover the source of a powerful blizzard, taking on the role of a young Iñupiaq girl and her Arctic fox who must physically maneuver across the landscape but also learn to solve puzzles. Along the way, players also unlock video vignettes, featuring elders and storytellers who explain more about what is happening in the game and how obstacles can be overcome. It was designed with goals that included: preserving the Iñupiaq language; promoting values such the interdependence of land, people, and animals; sustaining practices like oral storytelling; and passing along intergenerational wisdom. These goals were woven throughout the game mechanics. For instance, embedding key information into the documentary footage of storytellers means that players must carefully listen and learn from elders in order to move forward. When the fox dies and is reborn into a different form, the player can learn Iñupiaq worldviews about animal spirits and cosmology. As Madsen argues, "by acting on the traditional knowledge that is gained, the player-avatar is rewarded with increasing ease of movement, a greater capacity to overcome obstacles, and a greater sense of belonging in the Iñupiaq diegetic world" (Madsen 2017: 97). The benefits inside the game world mirror real-world benefits that the designers hope players achieve through education and new insights.

Another key aspect of how Indigenous games promote self-determination is through how they are developed and created. As Elizabeth LaPensée, Ouiti Latii, and Maize Longboat argue, self-determination in video game development begins with positioning Indigenous peoples in lead roles that ensure Indigenous decision-making power. These leadership roles "are not viewed as control to unilaterally determine development processes and design directions but instead involve listening and acting reciprocally with Indigenous communities with respect to elders, language speakers, knowledge carriers, and/or youth, as well as with members of the development team" (LaPensee, Laiti, and Longboat 2021). The game *When Rivers Were Trails* exemplifies these possibilities, with its two Indigenous co-creative directors and over 30 Indigenous collaborators in other roles such as writers, programmers, artists, level designers, and musicians. Together they created a 2-D adventure game that invites players to experience the histories of Indigenous land dispossession that forced tribes to flee their homelands and fight for survival amidst the difficult journey west across North America. As with the design of *Never Alone*, *When Rivers Were Trails* directly involved elders and fluent language speakers in the process of game design, in addition to Indigenous developers. Each of these contributors were paid industry standard rates, which showed the value of their contributions but also helped Indigenous professionals gain important work experience in gaming industries and build Indigenous capacities for future projects. In upholding these practices, Indigenous game development can be understood as a way of expressing and enacting sovereignty – these processes reflect the intentions and worldviews of the Indigenous peoples who are involved in their creation, and they help to promote Indigenous right to self-governance and self-expression.

Virtual reality

These questions about what role gaming technologies can play in contributing to anti-racism and empowerment for marginalized communities have also emerged around the rise of virtual reality. **Virtual reality** is the term used to describe three-dimensional computer-simulated experiences that the user can engage with through a wraparound headset and hand controls. The promise of virtual reality is that it provides a far more immersive experience than other gaming technologies, and that the player can temporarily forget that what they are witnessing is merely a simulation. It feels so close to reality that users experience psychological presence, which means that their bodies respond as if what they are sensing through their headsets is actually taking place in the physical world – sweating, flinching, heart pounding, crying. While virtual reality headsets have existed since the 1970s and have been objects of fascination and fantasy ever since then, we have more recently seen the rise of virtual reality applications in the consumer market with products like Oculus Rift, which was purchased by Facebook in 2014 for US$3 billion. Shortly thereafter, Sony developed a virtual reality headset for its PlayStation 4 console and Google developed a foldable headset for smartphones called Google Cardboard. These systems generally consist of a head-mounted stereoscopic display and handheld controllers, and the range of apps that can be played include traditional video games (fighting games, puzzles, flight simulators, adventure games), narrative and nonfiction content (feature films, animated shorts, documentary films) and more exploratory experiences (traveling to the moon, floating underwater, touring cities).

One of the attributes of virtual reality that has been of considerable interest is its role in promoting empathy, or the ability to imagine how others are feeling and respond with care. Virtual reality is often described as an "empathy machine" because there has been so much emphasis on its utility to help users experience life from a perspective that is not their own. For instance, applications showing what life is like as a refugee are created in the hopes that they will inspire aid, action, and other humanitarian responses (Irom 2018). The documentary *Clouds Over Sidra* was shot as a virtual reality 360-degree video where the viewer is invited to enter into the world of Sidra, a 12-year old Syrian girl living in the Zaatari refugee camp in Jordan. While experiencing some of Sidra's everyday routines, the viewer gets a sense of both the joys and beauty of her life and culture, as well as the darkness that clouds her vision for the future amidst fear and loss. In comparison to a standard documentary, this kind of virtual reality experience is designed to allow the user to enter more fully into the action, feeling they can hear and see Sidra's experiences directly because they have the freedom to choose where to look and how to navigate a path through her environment. This kind of intimacy and freedom from the top-down control of traditional narrative media can also help the viewer feel a sense of connection to those from new environments, cultures, and circumstances.

Yet critics have been careful to point out that there are limits to how much empathy for refugees can truly be evoked from merely watching a video – even a video specifically designed to promote immersion and presence. Bimbisar Irom (2018) argues that we must be careful not to overstate the utopian promise of immersive virtual reality because their products must still negotiate the representational politics and power dynamics inherent in all narrative media – such as the potential for upholding stereotypical tropes about refugees, or limiting the agency of refugees to speak for themselves (Irom 2018). Indeed, the very notion that privileged users with access to cutting-edge technology could use it to more fully appreciate the suffering of those who need their assistance relies on a limited understanding of social problems. As Paul Bloom argues:

> The problem is that these experiences aren't fundamentally about the immediate physical environments. The awfulness of the refugee experience isn't about the sights and sounds of a refugee camp; it has more to do with the fear and anxiety of having to escape your country and relocate yourself in a strange land . . . You can't tap into that feeling by putting a helmet on your head. (Bloom 2017)

He is concerned about how we so often focus on how to feel better about small and immediate situations like alleviating one girl's suffering when we should be concentrating on systems that cause harm and the long-term solutions that will actually be needed to transform them. If virtual reality experiences are designed to arouse empathy as a way of promoting social change, we must accept that it can fail in both regards.

While there has been a great deal of enthusiasm for the promise of virtual reality to be so immersive that the mediating technology disappears, it is also important to consider the strengths of foregrounding representation as a kind of useful distancing. The possibilities for affordances have also been used to promote racial empathy through learning about histories of oppression, such as in the virtual reality documentary *Traveling While Black*. Created for Oculus Go in 2018, the Emmy-nominated film explores the racism and oppression that Black travelers faced during the Jim Crow era, and the connection between that era and later incidents of police violence and the rise of the contemporary Black Lives Matter movement. Viewers are invited to take a seat in a booth at Ben's Chili Bowl in Washington, DC alongside other African American patrons as they listen to stories and reflections on personal experiences of segregation, police brutality, and racism. While the viewer has the freedom to explore a 360-degree perspective of the world, they cannot actually interact with the storytellers in front of them. Maud Ceuterick and Chris Ingraham argue that *Traveling While Black* is powerful because it does not ask viewers to forget that they are experiencing mediation; on the contrary, it "avoids positioning viewers as anthropological voyeurs; it creates the 'proper distance' between nearness and separation needed to give viewers an ethical position embodied as themselves, without the condescension of taking the other's place" (Ceuterick and Ingraham 2021: 12). They see political potential in the fact that the viewer remains aware that they are not seeing a full picture and they recognize differences between their own realities and what they are seeing and hearing. In cohabitating a space with ethnographic subjects without being asked to actually transform their subject position, the hope is that privileged viewers will still be able to learn about racial discrimination and reflect on their own positionality and complicity.

Conclusion

This chapter opened up with an exploration of the toxic culture of sexism, racism, and homophobia that have come to define so many video-gaming cultures. Not only have there been many high-profile cases of abuse surrounding video games and their player communities, but gaming industries themselves have also been identified as particularly noxious. Yet it is also important to point to the many different ways that video games can be used for combating these problems and the exciting possibilities for expanding interactive media when people of color gain control over aspects like narratives, design, and cultural norms. There are already many examples of the positive role that games can play within communities of color, and we must be careful not to let the most visible problems come to stand in for the entire medium and its possible strengths.

Key questions

1. How do players interact with video games differently from other forms of media, and why does that make the racism embedded within them potentially more dangerous?
2. What are some of the ways that communities of color have organized within video game cultures to promote safety and resistance?
3. In what ways might virtual reality promote racial empathy, and what are the limits to this way of thinking?

Further reading

Gray, Kishonna. 2020. *Intersectional Tech: Black Users in Digital Gaming.* Baton Rouge: Louisiana State University Press.

LaPensée, Elizabeth A., Laiti, Ouiti, and Longboat, Maize. 2021. "Towards Sovereign Games." *Games and Culture* 17(3): 1–16.

Shaw, Adrienne. 2014. *Gaming at the Edge: Sexuality and Gender at the Margins of Gamer Culture.* Minneapolis: University of Minnesota Press.

10

Communities

Key terms

- public spheres
- counterpublics
- Black Twitter
- critical technocultural discourse analysis
- signifyin'

- diaspora
- mukbang
- Indigenous digital storytelling
- Web series
- digital archives

Introduction

WHILE one goal of this book has been to promote caution and enable necessary critiques of the way that digital media can harm vulnerable communities, it is equally important to acknowledge the many ways that digital technologies and networks serve to create communities, support individuals, and bring happiness to people of color. Digital cultures can be a site for inspiration and laughter and romance and creativity, and they can provide a lifeline for those in need of connection. The affective resonances of digital engagement even have the potential to disrupt the pain and negativity of everyday experiences of structural racism, helping minority communities develop new skills for coping and thriving amidst intersectional oppressions. This chapter examines some of the many different ways that people of color have formed communities and connections through digital media and technologies. It begins by focusing on joy and laughter, but then moves into the ways that digital connections have enabled explorations of identity, love, cultural sustenance, fandom, and more.

Online publics and counterpublics

Some of the theories that are useful in helping to understand the nuances of Black online culture are those that distinguish between different kinds of public spheres. Jürgen Habermas understood **public spheres** as spaces where individuals can come together and freely discuss issues of political importance. Such sites play a critical role in the functioning of democratic society because it is important for citizens to have equal access to information and venues for participating in shaping discourse. While this was originally conceived of as a physical location, all forms of media play crucial roles in upholding these ideals – including the internet, which has now been conceived of as a digital public sphere. Yet there have always been concerns about who has access to participation in public discourse and the authority to speak and be heard. Women, people of color, those who have low income, and many other disenfranchised citizens have not always had the time, resources, or feeling of belonging to participate fully.

In response to these realities, Nancy Fraser (1990) developed a theory of subaltern **counterpublics** to recognize the way that less powerful members of society have always responded to exclusion by creating their own sites for communication and deliberation. Women, poor people, people of color, and other communities challenge the idea of a single public sphere by coming together to call attention to issues that have been overlooked or ignored. For instance, African Americans have identified barbershops, churches, and the Black press as meaningful counterpublics that serve in this capacity. Catherine Squires's (2002) theories of multiple public spheres help us to further map out the different kinds of communicative practices that are taking place away from the pressures of mainstream recognition and surveillance. She argues that there are three types of marginal publics: enclave publics that hide in order to avoid sanctions; counterpublics that use traditional social movement tactics to test ideas and make demands on the state; and oscillating or satellite publics that can remain separate at times or shift toward engaging with other publics. In the digital age, online networks for subaltern communities have provided a site for formulating resistance to the status quo, as we saw in chapter 8. But if we think about the more mundane uses of digital communication for everyday expression, we can also recognize the significance of such spaces for simply exploring a marginalized community's identity, culture, and style.

One digital platform that can most clearly be conceived of as a counterpublic is WeChat, one of the most popular social media platforms in China. It is particularly fruitful to apply theories of counterpublics to help understand WeChat's popularity and strength with regard to community building. WeChat is primarily a messaging app that allows users to send text, voice, and photo messages to other users, and its integration into everyday services in China, such as food delivery, shopping, booking appointments, and banking, have made it particularly pragmatic in addressing the needs of its mobile users. Because of these affordances, some have called platforms like WeChat "super apps" that facilitate every aspect of mobile life (Heath 2021). But another important aspect of its design is that it oscillates between public and private forms of communication. Users are invited to broadcast their posts to mass audiences, but they can also use the group chat function to communicate with groups of up to 500 users. In order to participate in these group chats, one needs to be extended an invitation from someone inside the group, which most often occurs through a shared geophysical location. Because of this, many groups are able to focus on discussing political issues, sharing information about public affairs, and debating important topics that might be censored on other more public platforms (Tu 2016).

Black Twitter has often been understood as a counterpublic because it is among the many digital platforms that Black communities have used to connect to one another about the things that are important to them. While chapter 8 examined the use of Twitter in relation to hashtag activism and other forms of political organizing, these uses only begin to scratch the surface of the myriad ways in which Black communities engage in daily communication practices through this platform. One example of this is how Black fans livetweet about beloved television shows, using hashtags to build a conversation as shows air. Fandom itself is predicated on the pleasure one gains from engaging with a media franchise, but scholars also point to the many joys of dissecting a text with fan communities – sharing in having "the feels" for certain characters, getting outraged at plot points and characterizations, debating qualities like consistency and quality, rooting for and against romantic pairings, ranking preferences for episodes, establishing and policing boundaries, and more. As the show *Scandal* aired from 2012 to 2018 on ABC, Black female fans would take to Twitter to discuss Olivia Pope and her weekly dramas through a distinctly Black female lens. One expression of cultural specificity came from centering discussions of Kerry Washington's embodiment of Olivia Pope as a Black woman even when the show itself tried to maintain "the spirit of colorblindness" (Warner 2015: 43). Tweets about the show by Black women discussed Olivia's hairstyles and fashion choices, her sexuality, and her interracial romances with white men, her strict and controlling father, her relationships with white women, and the way her representations fitted into or disrupted stereotypes. While these conversations can be politically significant, it is also important to recognize that they simply provided a safe space for Black female fans who are often invisible within mainstream fan cultures to express their fannish love.

Joy and humor

An important tool for making sense of the meaning of online communities is **critical technocultural discourse analysis** (CTDA). Developed by André Brock (2009, 2018), CTDA is a methodology for analyzing the way that digital phenomena, including hardware, software, platforms, interfaces, and other technological artifacts, intersect with cultural ideologies to shape discourse. It requires consideration of the way that certain beliefs are embedded into the design and infrastructure of digital technologies, but it also means examining how technologies are actually used and understood by marginalized groups. While it can be used to apply a wide range of critical cultural theories to the study of information and communication technologies, it has been particularly useful for scholars of critical race theory as they interrogate the meaning of digital communities of color. Rather than focusing on quantitative measures such as numbers of Twitter followers or retweets as a measure of significance, scholars of Black Twitter have deployed CTDA to ask how the affordance of the hashtag has led to the creation of culturally specific African American online communities that serve specific needs.

It may seem odd to view Twitter as a protected space for marginalized communities when it is publicly searchable and open to dissenting views of all kinds – including racist trolls. But as Brock claims, what is productive about online culture is that "Black folk have made the internet a 'Black space' whose contours have become visible through sociality and distributed digital practice while decentering whiteness as the default internet identity" (Brock 2020: 5). He sees many forms of Black cyberculture as sites for joy and catharsis about being Black. One of the ways that Black communities have created enclaved counterpublics that are less visible is through the use of African American Vernacular English (AAVE). This practice serves to somewhat conceal Black Twitter communities from outsiders, sequestering their discourse to parallel timelines that center Black linguistic and cultural norms. Sarah Florini (Florini 2019b) has studied Black fandoms of *Game of Thrones*, a show that was widely popular but had very little Black representation. Using the hashtag #DemThrones, Black fans would rewrite dialogue using Black vernacular constructions, joke about its relation to Black cult objects like *Empire* or *Coming to America*, and turn moments into memes. As Florini points out, this enclaving is common within Black Twitter's television fandoms:

> Black Twitter users have developed a range of alternative hashtags that allow them to avail themselves of Twitter's synchronicity while mitigating the vulnerability to the mainstream gaze created by the platform . . . For example, The Walking Dead (2010–) has two AAVE-inflected versions: #DeyWalking and #DemDeadz. FX's vampire horror show The Strain (2014–17) is #DatStrain while the CW's superhero show Arrow (2012–) is #DatArrow. During the 2016 miniseries The People v. O.J. Simpson, participants used the hashtag #DatJuice. (Florini 2019b)

Within these digital communities of like-minded fans, the use of AAVE and culturally resonant forms of humor and wordplay come together to create a generative environment for Black TV fans.

One of the particular markers of Black Twitter is that its participants engage in **signifyin'**, an African American form of wordplay that emphasizes playful use of language to indicate multiple levels of meaning simultaneously. Marked by the performativity and creativity of the speaker, tweets that employ signifyin' often convey social or interpersonal critique through humor (Brock 2012; Florini 2014).

Like so many forms of humor, the conversations that happen on Black Twitter about even silly or frivolous subjects must be understood as playing a powerful role in communicating Black subjectivities and racial identities.

Within the limited space of 240 characters, Black Twitter users display verbal dexterity and creativity to reply to one another in a real-time dialogue or retweet posts to amplify their reach within the community. Raven Maragh-Lloyd (2020) points to this taking place through the annual tradition of #ThanksgivingClapback, where Black Twitter users highlight African American family traditions in humorous messages about the holiday. In addition to signifyin', tweets using this hashtag also engage in the African American linguistic custom of "playing the dozens," or exchanging clever and ever-escalating personal insults. Maragh-Lloyd argues that the combination of humor and linguistic specificity serves the dual purposes of engaging mainstream culture while also creating a culturally cordoned-off space that protects participants from the threat of cultural appropriation from outsiders. She builds from Catherine Squires's theory of the semi-enclave, which is simultaneously outward facing and private (Squires 2002). Outsiders may be able to observe and enjoy the humorous verbal exchanges, but it is unlikely they will be able to easily step in and participate in a way that claims ownership.

Digital media and social media platforms of all kinds have provided a site for African American comedy traditions to flourish. Brandy Monk-Payton (2017) moves beyond Twitter to also examine blogs and podcasts as important digital sites for African American female comedy. She particularly highlights Luvvie Ajayi of the blog Awesomely Luvvie and Crissle West of the podcast *The Read*, two Black comediennes with large online followings. She points to how they deploy the Black expressive cultural techniques of "sass" and "shade" as playfully rude and unruly mechanisms for social critique. In addition to the way these linguistic traditions originate in West African trickster culture, she also points to how they overlap intersectionally with the queer cultures of drag balls. The concept of "throwing shade" as a form of biting criticism was popularized within the New York ball scene and kept alive in the figure of the contemporary Black diva. Ajayi and West deploy sass and shade throughout their media productions, with Ajayi stating on her blog that it provides a space for making observations "in my little shadeful heart at the moment. I thoroughly enjoy doling out side-eyes and there is never a shortage of people and foolishness to judge" (quoted in Monk-Payton 2017: 23). West and fellow podcaster Kid Fury, both of whom identify as queer, employ an irreverent and "defiantly frank" tone on their comedy podcast that builds from the persona of the "comic troublemaker" to produce joy and laughter. Indeed, the use of biting humor and ridicule has always been a potent tool for Black communities, and particularly Black women, to survive and form collective resistance amidst racial antagonisms.

Diasporic connections through food

Another meaningful form of cultural connection and identity formation for communities of color has centered on discussions about food. This has been a particularly salient form of digital media for people living in the **diaspora**, or communities of individuals who are geographically dispersed to locations outside of their home country. While immigrants are people who move from one country to another, the concept of diaspora describes a community united through an identification with and longing for the homeland that was left behind. Discussing food experiences and maintaining traditional cooking customs are particularly meaningful to diasporic communities, and food blogs have provided a useful venue for these activities. Food blogs are an accessible form of self-publishing for everyday digital consumers who can use free platforms like Blogspot, Wordpress, and Tumblr to share long-form written posts and photography with their followers. Readers can then add comments and links to their own blogs, which contributes to the formation of an online community focusing on the topic being discussed. While personal blogging was massively popular in the early 2000s with the rise of online platforms like LiveJournal and Xanga, social media platforms like Facebook and microblogging platforms like Twitter came to supplant and eventually replace the practice of blogging. While many professional websites and corporate platforms still use the format of a blog to push out regular updates, individual blogging has waned. But throughout the height of blogging popularity and well into the years that followed, food blogging remained a notable form of connection and community formation across different diasporas.

Radha Hegde (2014) has studied food blogs written by South Asian diasporic women and the way that they build transnational connections through their articulations of diasporic identities. As she argues, the many South Asian women tech workers who moved to the United States on H-1B visas post-1990 use food blogs "as emergent, interactive spaces anchored to the materiality of diasporic locations . . . [that] produce networks of sociality and build transnational culinary publics" (91). She analyzes food blogs such as Collaborative Curry, Indian Food Rocks, and Holy Cow for how their authors root their cooking in regionally specific locales and practices, using personal narratives about memories of their early lives to communicate cultural specificity. But they also engage in contemporary practices of fusion cooking, celebrating culinary creations like the tandoori quesadilla and the curry naanwich to point to the cosmopolitan adaptability of the South Asian diaspora. They bring the private and domestic act of cooking for one's family into the public through this form of widely accessible internet publishing, and facilitate connections between other women in the diaspora who are interested in learning about food and relating to one another through discussions of food. But the concept of a transnational culinary public also points to how intimate food blogs can shape broader understandings of what South

Asian food means, rearticulating it from something foreign and perplexing to something approachable and cosmopolitan chic.

This creation of a transnational culinary public is also informed by the reality that food blogs are consumed by those who identify with the blogger, as well as those who are outside of the community and simply seeking to learn about a culture that is not their own. While the linguistic traditions of Black Twitter may be designed to create an enclosed space that protects its participants from unwanted outsiders, food cultures have always been designed as a broadly appealing way for dominant cultures to safely engage with "the Other." Just as Asian restaurants in the United States have historically provided one of the key spaces for interaction between white Americans and Asian immigrant communities, Asian food blogs also provide a parallel site of connection. If this is the case, then struggles over identity and authenticity in relationship to ethnic food cultures also serve to communicate the meaning of that identity to broader audiences. When Thai American food blogger Leela Punyaratabandhu of *She Simmers* posts a recipe for a Massaman curry and narrates its origins as royal Thai cuisine that would be destroyed by adding ingredients like basil leaves or fresh chilies, this writing serves to affirm boundaries around ethnic authenticity as connected to the histories of the home country. But when she later posts a recipe for celery almond pesto or a beet ice cream recipe she encountered while traveling to the Ukraine, such posts serve to remind readers that all food cultures are changed and expanded through contact with others. In this way, food blogs serve to destabilize essential notions of racial and ethnic identity, putting forward a more complex, contradictory, and dynamic vision of what it means to be a hyphenated American living in the diaspora (Lopez 2016).

Asian digital food cultures have also moved beyond the sharing of everyday cooking practices to include video broadcasts to share the practice of eating itself. The South Korean practice of **mukbang**, or eating while live broadcasting, has become an extremely popular global form of video content. These videos typically feature conventionally attractive and thin hosts who prepare and eat large quantities of food on camera while interacting with their audiences. The most successful mukbang broadcast jockeys can make a living from the digital platforms that benefit from their millions of users who tune in nightly to observe and engage with the performer, as well as through sponsorships. Some of the popularity of this genre has been related to the rise of interest in ASMR (autonomous sensory meridian response) videos that give physical pleasure to certain viewers through a specific kind of audio performance, such as chewing and scraping. But they are also more generally understood as providing a way for individual viewers to become less lonely because they have the sense of sharing a meal with someone if they watch mukbang while eating (Kang et al. 2020). Viewers can use mukbang to create a sense of sociality and affective connection through the feelings of intimacy that accompany the act of slurping sticky noodles together, even while they are physically distanced from the performer and may not personally know them. Food practices are both mundane and deeply meaningful, and the practice of making and consuming mukbang videos represents one way that digital culture allows transnational fan cultures to connect through somewhat unusual genres and videography practices.

Cultural sustenance

Using digital media to communicate about everyday activities and cultural norms can also play a powerful role in cultural sustenance for communities of color and other marginalized communities whose histories are being systematically erased. For instance, Indigenous scholars and activists have worked to create digital repositories for community knowledge about food and wellness practices that rely on Indigenous ways of being. The Research for Indigenous Community Health Center at the University of Minnesota has been working on a database called the Indigenous Food Wisdom Repository that is designed to share information about a wide variety of wise practices – including food as medicines, food stories, traditional food revitalization projects, ancestral instructions around food, historical food documents, and community-led health and wellness interventions. The repository has been shaped by community feedback, elders, leaders, educators, advocates, academics, professionals, and other Indigenous community stakeholders. This kind of digital database is an important act of data sovereignty because it gives Indigenous communities the rights to govern their own data and the ways they are used, challenging histories of settler colonialism that have sought to erase Indigenous peoples from the digital record (Johnson-Jennings, Jennings, and Little 2019). But it also shows some of the important roles that community-led digital projects can play in reviving and sustaining Indigenous cultures and ways of knowing.

Digital databases can also provide important sites for cultural sustenance when they are combined with **Indigenous digital storytelling**.

Oral storytelling has always played a central role in Indigenous communities, and the use of digital tools for recording and sharing stories has greatly augmented their capacity for documenting histories, educating younger generations about the experiences of older generations, and preserving cultural heritages and traditions.

Storytelling also helps to keep alive Indigenous languages, many of which are in danger of becoming extinct. Some Indigenous digital storytelling projects include Voices of Amiskwaciy in Alberta, Canada, Peoples' Plateau Web Portal in the Pacific Northwest, and Storylines in Western Australia. Many values of digital archiving and online participatory culture align with the Indigenous values of self-determination and community connection. These digital storytelling projects and many others invite interactivity and collaboration through emphasizing user-generated content, deploying crowdsourcing for processes such as transcription and metadata creation, and creating a multifaceted and dynamic digital platform where stories can be stored and located using culturally specific groupings (Shiri, Howard, and Farnel 2021).

In each of these projects, it is important for the project leaders and team members to engage in careful processes of consent and reciprocity to make sure that community needs are honored and that each project is built on respectful partnerships and continued dialogue. The Métis scholar and filmmaker Judy Iseke has an extensive research program built around digital storytelling, and she is careful to describe the approach she takes to capturing stories. Before capturing an elder's story, she discusses the process of gaining consent from the elders who will participate, a welcome ceremony with shared gifts that acknowledge an expectation of respect throughout the storytelling process, the use of a talking circle to promote discussion about participation, and a closing ceremony in the home of local community members. It is only through this process that she is able to capture the stories of Métis elders like Alma Desjarlais, who was forced into a residential school at a young age and separated from her home, her family, and her language and traditions. As someone who later became an educator in cultural and healing traditions, she is able to teach Iseke and other viewers about her knowledge through recording and sharing her story. Iseke says that "Alma tells us how to be active in sharing in the traditions, keeping them alive, being a learner of traditions, and working to retain them. She shows us that valuing the traditions and practicing them will keep them, and us, alive" (Iseke 2011: 322).

Support for intersectional narratives

The use of digital tools for creating and sharing narratives has also been taken up by marginalized communities who participate in creating independent television. While there are many forms of digital video that build from the norms of television, the term **Web series** is helpful for describing digitally distributed episodic or serialized videos. Scholar and media practitioner Aymar Jean Christian (2018) has been at the forefront of investigating Web series as a televisual medium that can challenge and disrupt television in the post-network era. In 2015, Christian launched a digital platform called Open TV that supported intersectional Web series created out of local artistic communities in Chicago. One of the main goals of Open TV is to challenge the underrepresentation and misrepresentation of marginalized communities in mainstream television by centering stories that feature intersectional identities such as Black, Brown, queer, and gender nonconforming individuals. He points to how the business model of legacy television that requires constant audience growth has made innovation and deviation from norms risky, while digital content aiming to reach niche audiences can experiment with alternative modes of storytelling and representation (Christian 2017). Open TV supported artists like Fatimah Asghar and Sam Bailey in the creation of *Brown Girls*, a Web series featuring a South Asian American writer named Leila who is coming to terms with her queer identity, and her friend Patricia who is a sex-positive Black American musician struggling with commitment.

Web series distributed through platforms like YouTube, Vimeo, and more niche platforms like Black & Sexy TV and Revry TV help audiences find content that more closely resembles their own multifaceted identities. But the entire process of producing independent television for Web distribution can also serve as a site for community building and activism for underrepresented identities. Christian investigates the way that smaller, more flexible forms of television production can be creatively liberating for the team of collaborators working behind the camera. While funding limitations can lead to stress and precarious work situations, they also have the power to prioritize a diverse cast and crew that match up with the identities of the stories being told. For instance, *Brown Girls* was able to shoot in a predominantly Brown neighborhood in Chicago and make choices about wardrobe and production design that represented the specific identities and habitus of the queer women of color at the heart of the show (Christian 2020). Many Web series are funded through online crowdfunding platforms like Kickstarter and GoFundMe, which helps create a sense of community support and involvement from the first days of production. After donors have financially supported a project, they expect updates and ancillary content as a way of keeping up with production progress. Producers can then call on this engaged and active audience to show up and celebrate the show's premiere. Christian explains that all shows on Open TV have in-person screenings in Chicago neighborhoods before they are released online. These premiere events include artist performances and party atmospheres, which build an appetite for the show and also give audiences a chance to provide feedback to the creators – a dynamic that is extremely rare in the world of mainstream television production.

This integration of online and offline screening practices as a way of building community has also been common within Asian

American digital creators. The online video production collective known as Wong Fu Productions was one of the earliest innovators in Asian American YouTube. Its three founders, Wesley Chan, Ted Fu, and Philip Wang, started creating online videos in 2003, including humorous sketches and dramatic shorts. They originally purchased their own server so they could host their videos online and share them with fans through a password-protected link. They then moved to YouTube in 2007 and became some of the most well-known Asian American digital content creators, engaging an enormous and passionate fan base of Asian Americans from all across the country. Part of the appeal of Wong Fu Productions comes from the integration of professionally produced content about the everyday experiences of Asian Americans and the pulling back of the curtain to meet the Asian American production team working behind the camera. While many of the actors featured in Wong Fu Production videos have gone on to become well-known performers (such as Randall Park, Anna Akana, and Brittany Ishibashi), the three creators themselves have continued to be familiar faces who anchor the YouTube channel with behind-the-scenes interviews and featurettes. As early as 2006 with the premiere of their film *A Moment With You*, the three creators of Wong Fu Productions also went on tour to college campuses across the country to show their work and meet up with audiences.

A hands-on approach to creating engagement opportunities is part of what has made the fandom surrounding Wong Fu Productions such a resilient and passionate community. Rather than remaining the faceless creators behind the camera, they made themselves approachable and accessible. The group later expanded and took on other forms of cultural production, such as the touring concert series International Secret Agents, which brought together Asian American musicians, dancers, comedians, and videographers. Christine Bacareza Balance (2012) argues that this blend of online and offline connection has provided Asian American youth audiences with a shared sense of "feeling Asian American." The act of "going viral" is premised on a user engaging with online content in a way that feels meaningful enough to share with their wider digital community, and she attributes that affective connection to the strength of Asian

American celebrity on YouTube. These digital videos and their commentary provide an opportunity for Asian American youth to become part of a larger community that is funny and talented and connected – and, on occasion, can come together to resist and fight back against racism. While many popular videos within Asian American YouTube are not politically oriented and avoid discussions of serious issues like violence, the communities that form around them are nonetheless poised to respond and support during moments of crisis.

Literature, art, poetry, and memory

Digital connections can be forged across space and geography, but they can also help to create anchors across time. We have already seen some of the many ways that communities are using digital media to create and negotiate racial identities and racial formations, but these projects must also be recognized as participating in a form of digital memory. Digital media can be described as uniquely ephemeral and persistent at the same time; content posted online can easily be deleted or become corrupted as coding evolves, while some online content leaves an intractable trace that can be nearly impossible for any single user to scrub away. Because of these characteristics, **digital archives** have been an important tool for scholars of communities in danger of being overlooked and forgotten. For instance, the Recovering the US Hispanic Literary Heritage Project includes a number of digital collections that allow scholars to access, interact with, and analyze Latinx written works that had been repressed or previously absent from the scholarly record. Kelley Kreitz (2017) points to the potential for Latinx digital humanities projects like these to unsettle familiar formations of historical knowledge and provide pedagogical opportunities for students to engage with materials that were previously unknowable. While there are many different forms of digital humanities projects with many different goals, there is a strong vein of digital humanities works that focuses on making digital archives accessible to broader publics so that historical knowledge can have more of an impact on the present.

Digital archives can be created through well-funded initiatives and scholarly projects, but they can also be created through the practice of individual internet users sharing posts through social media. Melissa Villa-Nicholas argues that Instagram posts and memes can come to constitute Latinx digital memory or "a culmination of collective memory, mediated memories, and personal cultural memory" (Villa-Nicholas 2019: 3). She points to examples like the Instagram account of Chicanx artist and fashion curator JC De Luna, whose outfits hark back to Pachuco zoot suits from the 1940s. In posts under the handle "Barriodandy," he documents his own fashion stylings as well as historical photographs of young Chicanxs in a pre-gentrified Chavez Ravine. Villa-Nicholas argues that his posts create a kind of Chicanx nostalgia that embraces a feeling of malaise and longing for the forgotten past, but also does so much more than that – he is using social media to "time travel through embodiment and technology to recall the past, rewrite the past, and reimagine the past onto the present" (6). While a reliance on private platforms like Instagram and other social media companies like Facebook and Twitter means that individual users do not actually own their posts and are subject to the motivations and commercial imperatives of those companies, communities are nonetheless using them to create widely accessible archives of images that can serve to make connections between contemporary and historical moments.

Beyond these deliberate efforts to create historical narratives, Latinx social media users are also using Instagram posts to document and index new creative languages. Urayoán Noel analyzes the way that participatory media in the era of Web 2.0 have provided a way for those who are most invisible within mainstream Latinidad – including queer, undocumented, Afro-identified, trans and non-binary Latinxs – to produce their own folksonomies, or folk taxonomies, through hashtags. Noel looks at how Latinx poets such as Sonia Guiñansaca, Alan Pelaez Lopez, and Jenni(f)fer Tamayo use the affordances of Instagram to irreverently distort and play around with understandings of Latinidad (Noel 2019). Alan Pelaez Lopez, an Afro-Indigenous poet from Oaxaca, Mexico, posts imageless memes with messages such as "PSA: LATINIDAD IS NOT A RACE" and "Latinidad is Cancelled." These posts call attention to the cultural and political aspects of Latinidad, and criticize how so many configurations of Latinidad have excluded Black and Indigenous peoples in their centering of whiteness. They are also creative works unto themselves that demand close reading in a similar fashion as more traditional published forms of poetry chapbooks, as their use of poetic language is intended as a critical response and challenge to the cultural politics of mainstream Latinidad. Online social media have always been sites for struggles over language, with the terms "Latinidad," "Latin@," and "Latinx" taking place on platforms like Instagram, Twitter, and Tumblr, in addition to chatrooms during the early days of the internet. Users are able to connect through these digital spaces to debate the politics of gender, sexuality, race, and nation as they relate to issues of language and identification. As language evolves, the posts that call attention to their changing meanings come to serve as historical documents themselves, recording some of the activism and interventions that motivated shifts over time.

Conclusion

This chapter has traced only a small collection of stories that capture the different kinds of community formations that are made possible through digital media. Since nearly all forms of sociality and interaction can be mediated through digital technology, there are an infinite number of possibilities for the kinds of connections that can emerge and the valuable contributions those connections can provide. We have seen here the way that digital media help communities of color to come together over comedy, fandom, food cultures, storytelling, literature, art, fashion, and other topics of cultural significance. There are countless other stories to be told – about the African American TikTok stars who share makeup tips, the Indigenous dating apps that facilitate sexual and romantic connections, the karaoke platforms for singing virtual K-pop duets, the Hmong teleconference radio formats that rely on conference-call software to produce streaming audio, the online communities for Black professionals seeking career advancement amidst an oppressive work environment, the online conversations about genetic testing that support transracial adoptees on a quest to learn more about their backgrounds. While the examples are irrepressible, the themes remain the same – communities of color are clearly using media to support a kind of connection and support that is dependent on the technological affordances of digital platforms. Such stories serve to counter a predominantly critical mode of assessment that can end up exclusively highlighting the way that marginalized communities are overlooked or made even more vulnerable as a result of technological innovation and our increasing reliance on digital media in our everyday lives.

Key questions

1. How can both WeChat and Black Twitter be understood as counterpublics, and what does that tell us about their function in building digital communities?
2. What are some of the digital affordances of Twitter and hashtags that make them particularly useful for humor, connection, and support?
3. How do online creators of color engage with offline communities in ways that bolster their connections and support media production for marginalized makers?

Further reading

Brock, André. 2020. *Distributed Blackness: African American Cybercultures.* New York: New York University Press.

McCracken, Allison, Cho, Alexander, Stein, Louisa, and Hoch, Indira Neill (eds). 2020. *A Tumblr Book: Platform and Cultures.* Ann Arbor: University of Michigan Press.

Steele, Catherine Knight. 2022. *Digital Black Feminism.* New York: New York University Press.

11
Into the Future

Key terms

- racial futurisms
- Afrofuturism
- Indigenous futurism
- Latinx futurism

Introduction

THROUGHOUT this book, we have seen the many different ways that communities of color have shaped and been shaped by technology and digital media. In a world that is deeply impacted by histories of institutional racism and other forms of intersectional oppression, people of color have faced enduring challenges and developed modes of digital resistance that make sense to them. This final chapter turns to the future, building from the generative and expansive thinking modeled within Afrofuturism, Latinx futurism, and Indigenous futurism to imagine critical utopian potentials that have not yet happened. These modes of thought and aesthetic practices based in speculative fiction provide a vision for the future that is authored by people of color. They challenge dystopian fears of technology, replacing entrenched forms of disenfranchisement with dreams about what life could be like if people of color claimed power through technology. In addition to exploring the artistic outpouring that has accompanied these speculative visions, this chapter also briefly gestures toward some concrete

solutions for how to alleviate racism in the design and use of
technology now and into the future. This includes approaches to
policy, labor, design, education, and framing. Finally, this chapter
concludes by outlining some emerging scholarly and industrial questions about race and digital media that have yet to be
addressed.

Futures erased

In order to understand the relationship between people of color
and the future, we must recall the core struggles that have com-
pelled this necessary form of imagination. Why is imagining a
better future so important to people of color and other marginalized communities? Of course, what has demanded this orientation
to the future is that one of the goals of racism and other forms of
oppression is to limit the continued existence of people of color.
That is, when people of color experience the erasure of their own
history and culture through disenfranchisement and marginalization, these processes can be seen as a systematic way of erasing
their claim on the future as well. This can be seen explicitly in
the goals of settler colonialism, which are aimed at extinguishing
Indigenous lives, cultures, and ways of being and permanently
replacing them with whiteness. The genocide of Indigenous
peoples has long been understood as a way of bringing about a
future that is absent of Indigeneity. But it is also connected to
the recognition that the transatlantic slave trade and the practice
of chattel slavery were also designed to strip African Americans
of their culture, traditions, and histories. Connections to African
ancestors and ancestral places were lost, as new forms of kinship
and belonging had to be created in the Americas. As Mark Dery
states:

> African Americans, in a very real sense, are the descendants of
> alien abductees; they inhabit a sci-fi nightmare in which unseen but
> no less impassable force fields of intolerance frustrate their move-
> ments; official histories undo what has been done; and technology
> is too often brought to bear on black bodies (branding, forced
> sterilization, the Tuskegee experiment, and tasers come to mind).
> (Dery 1994: 182)

Dery's description already begins to do the work of connecting systematic disenfranchisement to the use of technology and the tropes of science fiction. These orientations are not limited to only racial minorities, as queer communities can be also connected through this idea of erasure. Not only have queer individuals and queer families often been assumed to be non-procreative, but they have also experienced the generational trauma of homophobia, violence, and the millions of premature deaths caused by the HIV/AIDS pandemic.

While systems of oppression have threatened the existence of many marginalized communities, media and other fictional representations have also perpetuated this form of erasure. The underrepresentation of minority communities happens across all media genres and forms, but particularly within speculative fiction. This term refers to all forms of invented futures, including science fiction, superhero stories, dystopian and utopian imaginings, tales of the supernatural, and other invented universes that depart from our own realities. The envisioning taking place within speculative fiction has continued the processes of symbolic annihilation by representing visions of the future where white people remain in positions of power while Black and Brown communities remain underlings. In many cases, futuristic media depict people of color as monsters or animals, removing their humanity in addition to our sympathies for them. As mentioned in chapter 5, we do see an overrepresentation of Asian culture in many imaginings of the future, but this is always viewed as a dystopian nightmare that signals the tragic downfall of the global power of white nations like the United States.

The demand for a claim on the future is also connected to the way that minority communities are so often relegated to the past, stuck in a history that denies contemporary realities. One of the serious struggles that Native Americans have faced in relation to media representation is that they are primarily depicted as extinct cultures that can only be animated through historical depictions. One part of the problem is the dominance of the western genre that focused heavily on "cowboy and Indian" conflicts, and provided enduring images of Native Americans as pioneer-era enemies to be conquered in the white American imaginary (Black 2020). For a direct encapsulation of how such narratives envision the plight of Native Americans, we can turn to Kevin Costner's *Dances with Wolves* (1990), one of the most acclaimed films about Native Americans. It ends with an epilogue that reads: "Thirteen years later, their homes destroyed, their buffalo gone, the last band of free Sioux submitted to White authority at Fort Robinson, Nebraska. The great horse culture of the plains was gone, and the American frontier was soon to pass into history." Such statements and frameworks for understanding what happened to Indigenous peoples contribute to a sense that they are relegated to history (Leavitt et al. 2015). This problem of Native Americans being "frozen in time" and absent from our modern realities has also been reproduced online through search engines like Google Images. For far too long, the image results for "Native American" primarily included historical pictures, as described in this article:

> The first result on a recent attempt is a grainy, sepia-toned picture of an unidentified Indian chief staring into the distance like a lost soul and decked out exactly (and unfortunately), as one might expect, in a headdress of tall feathers and a vest made of carved horn. It looks to be from early in the previous century. The next six pictures are variations on this theme. It's as if the society depicted in these images ceased to exist decades ago. (Beason 2014)

These problems were slowly rectified as more images of living (and thriving) tribes, recent life on the reservation, Indigenous politicians, and other contemporary imagery gained prominence in search results. But it is difficult to completely supplant the vast amount of historical imagery that has so long come to stand in for knowledge about Native Americans, and archival images from centuries ago are still ubiquitous online.

Afrofuturism

Let us examine some of the specific manifestations of **racial futur-isms,** beginning with Afrofuturism. The word **Afrofuturism** was first used by white scholar Mark Dery (1994) in an essay called "Black to the Future." It describes an aesthetic and political mode of Black expression centering on African diasporic technocultures and futures as seen in speculative fiction, as well as other genres and creative outlets such as performance, art, music, graphic novels, poetry, fashion, and film.

One of the goals of Afrofuturism is to envision Black people winning the future in spite of past histories and contemporary realities of racism, colonialism, and slavery.

In some cases, it imagines what possibilities could have been realized if slavery or colonialism had never occurred at all, and in doing so provides a profound source of critique. In these works of art, technologies such as interstellar travel, robots, and prosthetic enhancements become vehicles for reparation and liberation, facilitating utopian dreams of possibility and hope. These alternative visions move Black people to the center of the narrative where they are in a position to control their own destinies.

While the term "Afrofuturism" may have been invented in the 1990s, these practices of dreaming of a future where Black people are free have always been part of the work of Black freedom fighters, activists, artists, and resistance leaders. We can see these discourses in the work of important African American figures like W. E. B. Du Bois, Harriet Tubman, Martin Luther King, Jr, and others. Early examples of Afrofuturism as a form of artistic expression can be seen in the music of Sun Ra. A jazz musician and "soulful spaceman," Sun Ra's work, starting in the 1950s, blended science fiction and Afrocentrism by integrating electronic instruments like synthesizers with traditional West African hand drums, costuming himself in dashikis and space helmets, and reporting that he had been born on the planet Saturn (Rollefson 2008). Building from the Afrofuturist vibes of Sun Ra and other Black funk artists from the 1960s and 1970s, African American singer and rapper Janelle Monae has carried on this tradition of Afrofuturist music into the 2000s. Her R&B album titled *Metropolis* was released in 2007, and playfully referenced Fritz Lang's 1927 science fiction film of the same name. The album follows the journey of Monae as Cindi Mayweather, an android who has broken the law by falling in love with a human. Monae's later works continued these themes of how African American bodies can productively blur the line between human and machine, while also calling attention to the constraints of gender through the use of androgyny and gender fluidity in her own performance. While she envisions a technologically advanced future that centers African Americans, she also sustains skepticism about the possibilities of postracial, postgender, or posthuman realities (English and Kim 2013). Indeed, many artists engaging in Afrofuturist envisionings are also realistic about the limits of such visions, incorporating cautionary messages about the realities of racism's legacies in even the most optimistic dreams of the future.

In more mainstream culture, the film *Black Panther* (2018) has been celebrated for bringing Afrofuturist narratives to the Marvel Cinematic Universe and its millions of viewers. The film tells the story of an African country called Wakanda that is the most technologically advanced on Earth, but the people of Wakanda have used their powerful natural resources to cloak and protect their nation from those who would seek to exploit and harm them. It reveals a vision for what an African nation and its peoples could accomplish if they had avoided colonialism and were able to thrive, and it builds from Afrocentric themes such as the bending of time and space in order to create links to one's ancestors (Strong and Chaplin 2019). The film's star Chadwick Boseman was celebrated as the eponymous Black Panther, an Avenger whose greatest powers are his loyalty and compassionate leadership, not the technologies that enhance his physical capabilities.

Many forms of Afrofuturism are particularly focused on gender issues and visualizing Black female futures. We can see this in *Black Panther*, where the male hero is also surrounded by fierce and powerful women – including his sister Shuri who is one of Wakanda's foremost tech experts, warrior Okoye who leads the all-female elite fighting squad the Dora Milaje, and the highly skilled spy Nakia. The specific figure of the Divine Feminine is an Afrofuturist envisioning of a future that celebrates Black women's power and agency to make decisions on their own. The African American horror TV show *Lovecraft Country* set in the 1950s leaned into this figure of the Divine Feminine in an episode called "I Am." The episode follows a Black woman named Hippolyta as she travels through time to find her own power. After dancing on stage with Black dancer Josephine Baker in the 1930s and fighting against white colonizers as part of a troop of all-female Amazon warriors, she eventually arrives in the distant future aboard a spaceship. We can see that her relationships with women across time have increased her intellectual and physical capabilities, and she is able to fight for her life and claim what is hers in her own plotline.

Latinx futurisms and Indigenous futurisms

The arts of Afrofuturism have inspired and influenced other forms of futurisms and speculative fiction, such as Latinx/Chicana futurisms and Indigenous futurisms. Catherine S. Ramirez introduces the term "Chicanafuturism" in 2004 as a concept that borrows from Afrofuturism but is also inspired by Chicana artists, like Marion C. Martinez, who connect Chicana identities to science and technology (Ramirez 2008). In her exploration of her own passion for science fiction, she points to similarities in the way that both Afrofuturism and Chicanafuturism are concerned with disrupting the racist and sexist exclusions of Black and Brown women from visions of the future and relationships to science and technology. But she also points to culturally specific nuances of Chicanafuturist works, such as how El Teatro Campesino's 1967 one-act play called *Los Vendidos* focuses on the selling of Chicano robots. In its representation of Mexican workers as soulless automatons, the narrative uses the technological figure of the robot to criticize racist labor policies.

Other expressions of **Latinx futurism** can be seen to incorporate the specific political and cultural histories of the Chicano movement, and resonant themes such as border crossings and hybrid identities. For instance, Taryne Jade Taylor (2020) argues that Latinx hip-hop artists who use music technologies to remix sounds are part of a larger Latinx futurism that puts forward a new dream of a decolonized and unified Latinidad. The Robert Rodriguez film *Alita: Battle Angel* (2019) has also been interpreted as a form of Latinx futurism, starting with the look of its sci-fi steam-punk architecture inspired by cities like San Miguel de Allene, Havana, and Panama City (Aldama 2019). The story features a cyborg named Alita, played by Latina actress Rosa Bianca Salazar, who has no memory of who she was before her human brain was united with an entirely prosthetic body. Her world is marked by borders such as those between human and machine, but also between the devastated industrialized world of the ground and the wealthy city in the sky that everyone dreams of reaching. These hybridities reflect the themes of border crossings and barriers that animate so many Latinx lives and experiences on the southern border of the United States. In a pivotal moment of human identification, the cyborg Alita has a taste of chocolate – which could also be read as *xocolatl*, a food that has deep Indigenous roots in Mayan culture.

The concept of **Indigenous futurism** was first introduced by Grace Dillon in her Indigenous science fiction anthology *Walking the Clouds* (Dillon 2012). While this collection of writings focused on the genre of science fiction, it points to the larger body of work that collectively participates in creating a dream for the future that builds from Indigenous worldviews and languages. It includes graphic art, performance art, video games, comic books, board games, music, and other forms of media. Many such works build from the understanding that colonialism itself could be framed as a dystopian nightmare wherein Indigenous peoples were subject to an alien invasion designed to massively disrupt and destroy Indigenous ways of life. In response to this otherworldly onslaught, Henrietta Lidchi and Suzanne Newman Fricke explain that "Indigenous Futurism proposes its central characters on the other side of the vessel: manning the ship rather than waiting on the shores" (Lidchi and Fricke 2019).

Since Indigenous peoples have already experienced the trauma of the apocalypse, these imaginings of the future find new ways to move forward that foreground healing and survival.

Lindsay Nixon describes the role of kinship and community connections as part of this healing. In her exploration of the art of Ligwilda'xw Kwakwaka'wakw digital artist Sonny Assu, Inuit painter Pudlo Pudlat, and Inuit sculptor Ovilu Tunnillie, she reads the depictions of Indigenous peoples interfacing with western technologies as a trope of futurity wherein early contact becomes an ominous alien force. She describes what she sees as an Indigenous response to these removals, disruptions, and displacements:

Dystopian science fictive futures are reconciled by kinship, and Indigenous futures are depicted in resurgent arts practices through self-determined representations. Art is both the means to project Indigenous life into the stars and the space canoe we use to paddle through these imagined galaxies. Art becomes a medicinal practice, healing our spirits, minds, and bodies as we move into possible futures. (Nixon 2016)

As described in chapter 9, the concept of survivance has been central to many forms of Indigenous art, as survivance foregrounds Native presence as a way of overriding predominant casting of Natives as victims of history (Vizenor 2008). While Indigenous futurisms are often focused on imagining the future, they also help Indigenous artists and audiences reinterpret the past and the present. We can see this in narratives such as Mohawk artist Skawennati's series *TimeTraveller*™, which takes place in the online virtual world of Second Life. Using machinima, or recorded gaming performances that become cinematic productions, *TimeTraveller*™ tells the story of a Mohawk man from the twenty-second century who goes upon a technologically enhanced vision quest. During his journeys through time, he is able to participate in meaningful historical events, such as the Dakota Sioux Uprising and the occupation of Alcatraz Island. This nonlinear way of understanding space-time incorporates a science fiction sensibility into a Native American narrative about self-discovery and the importance of disrupting historical narratives in order to make sense of one's present.

Designing for the future

While these philosophies, schools of thought, and forms of creative expression have provided some potential road maps for the future, it is also important to point to concrete possibilities for the here and now. Throughout this book, we have seen both implicit and explicit forwarding of suggestions as to how we can avoid the problems engendered by race and technology. As seen in chapter 7, both governmental policies and more informal corporate policies and codes are clearly going to be necessary for providing guidelines to safeguard against systemic harm. Lawmakers and regulators should take seriously the rising threat that comes from our increasing reliance on technology – including the use of algorithms and machine learning to shape decisions, the use of biometrics to establish identification, and the use of social media for spreading information. We must also note that much of the way that racism and racial bias have become part of technology is through the processes and dynamics that happen behind the scenes within tech companies, hidden from the view of the public. Anti-racist values and the actions that will be taken to alleviate racial harms must be explicitly stated, and there must be accountability measures instituted to make sure that actions align with these policies.

But the responsibility lies beyond tech industries and tech workers, as this book has revealed how deeply digital media have come to shape every aspect of our lives. We can also see the possibility for digital media and technologies to contribute to racial harm in the schoolteacher who assumes that all of their students will have equitable access to internet at home, the neighbor who calls the police after seeing a shadowy figure on their doorbell monitor, the online gameplayer who shouts racial slurs into their headset when they want to denigrate opposing players, the doctor who misdiagnoses a Black patient because they are overly reliant on a flawed medical record. While addressing these disparate situations and the factors that cause them will never be a straightforward process, hopefully it is clear that dedicated education in anti-racism, digital literacy, and the relationship between race and technology will be necessary as a preliminary step toward avoiding these scenarios in the future.

Another way to help address some of the problems that have been raised is through continuing to expand our understanding of these issues through new research in this area. While this book points to a rich tradition of scholarship taken up in communication, digital studies, science and technology studies, data and information sciences, cultural studies, sociology, new research questions and emerging lines of inquiry necessitate new investigations and creative approaches to research. This means staying particularly attuned to the intersectional research that is taking place across identity categories, merging research on race and ethnicity with studies of gender, sexuality, ability, class, religion, and others. Further, one of the limits of this book's approach is that it has focused primarily on the racial dynamics of the United States, when the reality is that so many forms of racial technology are important to understand through a global and transnational lens. While this decision to foreground the racial dynamics of the United States was based on a desire to properly contextualize the unique histories of race and ethnicity that are significantly different from other nations – particularly from non-white countries across Africa, Asia, and South America – that means that these chapters could only skim the surface of broader research questions about the relationship between race and technology across disparate regions of the world. It is also important to continue integrating cross-disciplinary and transdisciplinary scholarly investigations of race and technology, bringing the perspectives of artists, humanists, social scientists, and data scientists to bear on these questions. While it often seems like technologies have taken on a life of their own and humans are merely subject to their automations and powerful influences, the reality is that we create technologies. We are in control over how they operate, what impact they have, and what relationships we form with them. There is immense potential in this relationship to change our world for the better.

Key questions

1. How did Afrofuturism develop, and what are some of the ways that it challenges traditional assumptions about African American futures?
2. How are practices of Indigenous futurism and Latinx futurism based in culturally specific histories and values?

Further reading

Dillon, Grace. 2012. *Walking the Clouds: An Anthology of Indigenous Science Fiction*. Tucson: University of Arizona Press.

Nelson, Alondra (ed.). 2002. "Afrofuturism: An issue of Social Text." *Social Text* 20(2): 1–70.

Ramirez, Catherine S. 2008. "Afrofuturism/Chicanafuturism: Fictive Kin." *Aztlan: A Journal of Chicano Studies* 33(1): 185–94.

References

ACM Council. 1992. *1992 ACM Code of Ethics and Professional Conduct.* October 16. https://ethics.acm.org/code-of-ethics/previous-versions/1992-acm-code/.

Adetiba, Elizabeth. 2017. "Tarana Burke Says #MeToo Should Center Marginalized Communities." *Nation,* November 17. https://www.thenation.com/article/archive/tarana-burke-says-metoo-isnt-just-for-white-people/.

Aldama, Frederick Luis. 2019. "Robert Rodriguez' Fever-Dream: 'Alita' and the Building of Latinx Sci-Fi Worlds." *Latinx Spaces,* February 22. https://www.latinxspaces.com/latinx-film/robert-rodriguez-fever-dream-alita-and-the-building-of-latinx-sci-fi-worlds.

Alexander, Michelle. 2010. *The New Jim Crow: Mass Incarceration in the Age of Colorblindness.* New York: New Press.

Algorithmic Accountability Act of 2019. 2019. H. R. 2231 (116th Congress).

Ali, Omar, Scheidt, Nancy, Gegov, Alexander, Haig, Ella, Adda, Mo, and Aziz, Benjamin. 2020. "Automated Detection of Microaggression Using Machine Learning." *IEEE Symposium Series on Computational Intelligence.*

Alkalimat, Abdul. 2004. *The African American Experience in Cyberspace: A Resource Guide to the Best Web Sites on Black Culture and History.* London: Pluto Press.

Almasy, Steve and Yan, Holly. 2014. "Protesters Fill Streets across Country as Ferguson Protests Spread Coast to Coast." CNN, November 26. http://edition.cnn.com/2014/11/25/us/national-ferguson-protests/index.html.

Amoore, Louise. 2018. "Cloud Geographies: Computing, Data, Sovereignty." *Progress in Human Geography* 42(1): 4–24.

Amrute, Sareeta. 2020. "Bored Techies Being Casually Racist: Race as Algorithm." *Science, Technology and Human Values* 45(5): 903–33.

Anderson, Meredith A., Malhotra, Atul, and Non, Amy L. 2021. "Could Routine Race-adjustment of Spirometers Exacerbate Racial Disparities in COVID-19 Recovery?" *Lancet* 9(2): 124–5.

Andrejevic, Mark. 2009. "Privacy, Exploitation, and the Digital Enclosure." *Amsterdam Law Forum* 1(4): 47–62.

Ankerson, Megan Sapnar. 2018. *Dot-Com Design: The Rise of a Usable, Social, Commercial Web*. New York: New York University Press.

Arnst, John. 2017. "Sharing the Whole HeLa Genome." *ASMBM Today*, February 1. https://www.asbmb.org/asbmb-today/science/020117/sharing-the-whole-hela-genome.

Association for Computing Machinery US Public Policy Council. 2017. *Statement on Algorithmic Transparency and Accountability*. January 12. https://www.acm.org/binaries/content/assets/public-policy/2017_us acm_statement_algorithms.pdf.

Aswad, Jem. 2020. "Blackout Tuesday Posts Get Backlash for Drowning Out #BlackLivesMatter Information." *Variety*, June 2. https://variety.com/2020/digital/news/blackout-tuesday-drowning-out-blacklives-matter-1234623139/.

Baez, Jillian M. 2017. "Spreadable Citizenship: Undocumented Youth Activists and Social Media," in Maria Cepeda and Dolores Inés Casillas (eds), *The Routledge Companion to Latina/o Media*. New York: Routledge, 419–32.

Balance, Christine Bacareza. 2012. "How It Feels to Be Viral Me: Affective Labor and Asian American YouTube Performance." *Women's Studies Quarterly* 40(1/2): 138–52.

Balderrama, Francisco and Rodríguez, Raymond. 1995. *Decade of Betrayal: Mexican Repatriation in the 1930s*. Albuquerque: University of New Mexico Press.

Banerjee, Payal. 2006. "Indian Information Technology Workers in the United States: The H-1B Visa, Flexible Production, and the Racialization of Labor." *Critical Sociology* 32(2–3): 425–45.

Banet-Weiser, Sarah, Mukherjee, Roopali, and Gray, Herman. 2019. *Racism Postrace*. Durham: Duke University Press.

Barrett, Paul. 2006. "White Thumbs, Black Bodies: Race, Violence, and Neoliberal Fantasies in Grand Theft Auto: San Andreas." *Review of Education, Pedagogy, and Cultural Studies* 28: 95–119.

Bartlett, Jamie, Reffin, Jeremy, Rumball, Noelle, and Williamson, Sarah. 2014. *Anti-Social Media*. London: Demos.

Basu, Tonu and Brennan, Jenny. 2021. *Algorithmic Accountability for the Public Sector: Learning from the First Wave of Policy Implementation.*

August. https://www.opengovpartnership.org/documents/algorithmic-accountability-public-sector/.

Beason, Tyrone. 2014. "Photographer Aims to Document Every Native American Tribe in US." *Chicago Tribune*, August 12. https://www.chicagotribune.com/lifestyles/sns-mct-bc-tribes-photo-project-20140812-story.html.

Benjamin, Ruha. 2019. *Race After Technology: Abolitionist Tools for the New Jim Code*. Cambridge, UK: Polity.

Benthall, Sebastian and Haynes, Bruce D. 2019. "Racial Categories in Machine Learning." *FAT* '19: Conference on Fairness, Accountability, and Transparency*. Atlanta: Association for Computing Machinery.

Beskow, Laura. 2016. "Lessons from HeLa Cells: The Ethics and Policy of Biospecimens." *Annual Review of Genomics and Human Genetics* 17: 395–417.

Bhuiyan, Johana, Dean, Sam, and Hussain, Suhauna. 2020. "Black and Brown Tech Workers Share their Experiences of Racism on the Job." *Los Angeles Times*, June 24. https://www.latimes.com/business/technology/story/2020-06-24/diversity-in-tech-tech-workers-tell-their-story.

Bishop, Jonathan. 2014. "Representations of 'Trolls' in Mass Media Communication: A Review of Media-Texts and Moral Panics Relating to 'Internet Trolling'." *International Journal of Web Based Communities* 10(1): 7–24.

Black, Liza. 2020. *Picturing Indians: Native Americans in Film, 1941–1960*. Lincoln, NE: University of Nebraska Press.

Bloom, Paul. 2017. "It's Ridiculous to Use Virtual Reality to Empathize With Refugees." *Atlantic*, February 3. https://www.theatlantic.com/technology/archive/2017/02/virtual-reality-wont-make-you-more-empathetic/515511/.

Blumenbach, Johann Friedrich. 1865 (1775). "On the Natural Varieties of Mankind," in *The Anthropological Treatises of Johann Friedrich Blumenbach*. London: Longman, Green, Longman, Roberts and Green.

Boffone, Trevor. 2021. *Renegades*. Oxford: Oxford University Press.

Bonilla, Yarimar and Rosa, Jonathan. 2015. "#Ferguson: Digital Protest, Hashatag Ethnography, and the Racial Politics of Social Media in the United States." *American Ethnologist* 42(1): 4–17.

Bonilla-Silva, Eduardo. 2017. *Racism without Racists: Color-Blind Racism and the Persistence of Racial Inequality in America*. Lanham, MD: Rowman and Littlefield.

boyd, danah. 2012. "White Flight in Networked Publics: How Race and Class Shaped American Teen Engagement with MySpace and Facebook," in Lisa Nakamura and Peter Chow-White (eds), *Race after the Internet*. New York: Routledge, 203–22.

Brock, André. 2009. "Life on the Wire: Deconstructing Race on the Internet." *Information, Communication and Society* 12(3): 344–63.

Brock, André. 2012. "From the Blackhand Side: Twitter as a Cultural Conversation." *Journal of Broadcasting and Electronic Media* 56(4): 529–49.

Brock, André. 2018. "Critical Technocultural Discourse Analysis." *New Media and Society* 20(3): 1012–30.

Brock, André. 2020. *Distributed Blackness: African American Cybercultures*. New York: New York University Press.

Broussard, Meredith. 2018. *Artificial Unintelligence: How Computers Misunderstand the World*. Cambridge, MA: MIT Press.

Browne, Simone. 2015. *Dark Matters: On the Surveillance of Blackness*. Durham: Duke University Press.

Buchanan, Larry, Bui, Quoctrung, and Patel, Jugal. 2020. "Black Lives Matter May Be the Largest Movement in US History." *New York Times*, July 3. https://www.nytimes.com/interactive/2020/07/03/us/george-floyd-protests-crowd-size.html.

Buckley, Cara. 2016. "On Being a Black Female Math Whiz During the Space Race." *New York Times*, September 5. https://www.nytimes.com/2016/09/06/books/on-being-black-female-math-whizzes-during-the-space-race.html.

Burkhalter, Byron. 1999. "Reading Race Online: Discovering Racial Identity in Usenet Groups," in Marc A. Smith and Peter Kollock (eds), *Communities in Cyberspace*. New York: Routledge, 60–75.

Bynum, Terrell Ward. 2000. "A Very Short History of Computer Ethics." *American Philosophical Association Newsletter on Philosophy and Computing* 99(2).

Byrne, Dara N. 2008. "The Future of (the) 'Race': Identity, Discourse, and the Rise of Computer-mediated Public Spheres," in Anna Everett (ed.), *Learning Race and Ethnicity: Youth and Digital Media*. Cambridge, MA: MIT Press, 15–38.

Caplan, Robyn, Donovan, Joan, Hanson, Lauren, and Matthews, Jeanna. 2018. *Algorithmic Accountability: A Primer*. April 18. https://datasociety.net/library/algorithmic-accountability-a-primer/.

Carlsen, Audrey, et al. 2018. "#MeToo Brought Down 201 Powerful Men. Nearly Half of Their Replacements are Women." *New York Times*, October 29. nytimes.com/interactive/2018/10/23/us/metoo-replacements.html.

Carrigan, William and Webb, Clive. 2013. *Forgotten Dead: Mob Violence against Mexicans in the United States, 1848–1928.* Oxford: Oxford University Press.

CBS/AP. 2017. "More Than 12M 'Me Too' Facebook Posts, Comments, Reactions in 24 Hours." *CBS News*, October 17. https://www.cbsnews.com/news/metoo-more-than-12-million-facebook-posts-comments-reactions-24-hours/.

Ceuterick, Maud and Ingraham, Chris. 2021. "Immersive Storytelling and Affective Ethnography in Virtual Reality." *Review of Communication* 21(1): 9–22.

Chaar-López, Iván. 2019. "Sensing Intruders: Race and the Automation of Border Control." *American Quarterly* 71(2): 495–518.

Chan, Brian and Gray, Kishonna. 2020. "Microstreaming, Microcelebrity, and Marginalized Masculinity: Pathways to Visibility and Self-Definition for Black Men in Gaming." *Women's Studies in Communication* 43(4): 354–62.

Chander, Anupam. 2017. "The Racist Algorithm?" *Michigan Law Review* 115(6): 1023–46.

Chang, Emily. 2018. *Brotopia: Breaking Up the Boys' Club of Silicon Valley.* New York: Portfolio.

Chaudhry, Irfan. 2015. "#Hashtagging Hate: Using Twitter to Track Racism Online." *First Monday* 20(2). https://journals.uic.edu/ojs/index.php/fm/article/view/5450.

Chen, Adrian. 2014. "The Laborers Who Keep Dick Pics and Beheadings Out of Your Facebook Feed." *Wired*, October 23. https://www.wired.com/2014/10/content-moderation/.

Chen, Jiahao, Kallus, Nathan, Mao, Xiaojie, Svacha, Geoffrey, and Udell, Madeleine. 2019. "Fairness Under Unawareness: Assessing Disparity When Protected Class Is Unobserved." *Association for Computing Machinery.* Atlanta. 1–13. doi:https://doi.org/10.1145/3287560.3287594.

Chow-White, Peter and Duster, Troy. 2011. "Do Health and Forensic DNA Databases Increase Racial Disparities?" *PLOS Medicine* 8(10).

Christian, Aymar Jean. 2017. "The Value of Representation: Toward a Critique of Networked Television Performance." *International Journal of Communication* 11.

Christian, Aymar Jean. 2018. *Open TV: Innovation Beyond Hollywood and the Rise of Web Television.* New York: New York University Press.

Christian, Aymar Jean. 2020. "Intersectional Distribution," in Lori

Lopez (ed.), *Race and Media: Critical Approaches*. New York: New York University Press, 141–52.

Clark, Doris Hargrett. 1995. "Subject Access to African American Studies Resources in Online Catalogs: Issues and Answers." *Cataloging and Classification Quarterly* 19(2): 49–66.

Conger, Kate. 2020. "'Master,' 'Slave' and the Fight Over Offensive Terms in Computing." *New York Times*, April 13. https://www.nyti mes.com/2021/04/13/technology/racist-computer-engineering-terms-ietf.html.

Consalvo, Mia. 2012. "Confronting toxic gamer culture: A challenge for feminist game studies scholars." *Ada: Journal of Gender, New Media and Technology* 1(1).

Cook, Katy. 2020. *The Psychology of Silicon Valley*. London: Palgrave Macmillan.

Costanza-Chock, Sasha. 2014. *Out of the Shadows, Into the Streets! Transmedia Organizing and the Immigrant Rights Movement.* Cambridge, MA: MIT Press.

Cote, Amanda. 2018. "Curate Your Culture: A Call for Social Justice-Oriented Game Development and Community Management," in Kishonna Gray and David J. Leonard (eds), *Woke Gaming: Digital Challenges to Oppression and Social Injustice*. Seattle: University of Washington Press, 193–212.

Cottom, Tressie McMillan. 2020. "Where Platform Capitalism and Racial Capitalism Meet: the Sociology of Race and Racism in the Digital Society." *Sociology of Race and Ethnicity* 6(4): 441–9.

Cowie, Jefferson. 1999. *Capital Moves: RCA's Seventy-year Quest for Cheap Labor*. New York: Cornell University Press.

Crenshaw, Kimberlé. 1990. "Mapping the Margins: Intersectionality, Identity Politics, and Violence against Women of Color." *Stanford Law Review* 43: 1241–99.

Croes, Emmelyn A. and Antheunis, Marjolin L. 2021. "Can We be Friends with Mitsuku? A Longitudinal Study on the Process of Relationship Formation between Humans and a Social Chatbot." *Journal of Social and Personal Relationships* 38(1): 279–300.

Daniels, Jesse. 2009. *Cyber Racism: White Supremacy Online and the New Attack on Civil Rights*. Lanham, MD: Rowman and Littlefield.

Dawkins, Richard. 1976. *The Selfish Gene*. Oxford: Oxford University Press.

Davies, Harry. 2015. "Ted Cruz Using Firm that Harvested Data on Millions of Unwitting Facebook Users." *Guardian*, December 11.

https://www.theguardian.com/us-news/2015/dec/11/senator-ted-cruz-president-campaign-facebook-user-data.

De Leon, Jason. 2015. *The Land of Open Graves: Living and Dying on the Migrant Trail*. Berkeley: University of California Press.

DePass, Tanya. 2018. "#DiversifyStreaming Update – Official Stream Team is a Go!" *I Need Diverse Games*, April 11. https://ineeddiversegames.org/2018/04/11/diversifystreaming-update-official-stream-team-is-a-go/.

Dery, Mark. 1994. "Black to the Future: Interviews with Samuel R. Delany, Greg Tate, and Tricia Rose," in Mark Dery (ed.), *Flame Wars: The Discourse of Cyberculture*. Durham, NC: Duke University Press, 179–222.

Desmond, Matthew and Emirbayer, Mustafa. 2009. "What is Racial Domination?" *Du Bois Review* 6(2): 335–55.

Dewey, Caitlin. 2014. "The Only Guide to Gamergate You Will Ever Need to Read." *Washington Post*, October 14. https://www.washingtonpost.com/news/the-intersect/wp/2014/10/14/the-only-guide-to-gamergate-you-will-ever-need-to-read/.

Dillon, Grace. 2012. *Walking the Clouds: An Anthology of Indigenous Science Fiction*. Tucson, AZ: University of Arizona Press.

Duarte, Marisa. 2017a. "Connected Activism: Indigenous Uses of Social Media for Shaping Political Change." *Australasian Journal of Information Systems* 21: 1–12.

Duarte, Marisa. 2017b. *Network Sovereignty: Building the Internet Across Indian Country*. Seattle, WA: University of Washington Press.

Duggan, Maeve. 2015. "Who Plays Video Games in America?" in Maeve Duggan, *Gaming and Gamers*. Pew Research Center, December 15. https://www.pewresearch.org/internet/2015/12/15/gaming-and-gamers/.

Durr, Marlese. 2015. "What is the Difference between Slave Patrols and Modern Day Policing? Institutional Violence in a Community of Color." *Critical Sociology* 41(6): 873–9.

Dyer, Richard. 1997. *White: Essays on Race and Culture*. London: Routledge.

Edwards, Frank, Lee, Hedwig, and Esposito, Michael. 2019. "Risk of Being Killed by Police Use-of-Force in the US by Age, Race/Ethnicity, and Sex." *Proceedings of the National Academy of Sciences*. 1–12.

Eglash, Ron. 2007. "Broken Metaphor: The Master–Slave Analogy in Technical Literature." *Technology and Culture* 48(2): 360–9.

English, Daylanne K. and Kim, Alvin. 2013. "Now We Want Our Funk Cut: Janelle Monáe's Neo-Afrofuturism." *American Studies* 52(4): 217–30.

European Commission. 2016. "Code of Conduct on Countering Illegal Hate Speech Online." *European Commission.* June 30. https://ec.euro pa.eu/newsroom/just/document.cfm?doc_id=42985.

Evans, Sarah Beth and Janish, Elyse. 2015. "#INeedDiverseGames: HowtheQueer Backlash toGamerGateEnablesNonbinary Coalition." *QED: A Journal in GLBTQ Worldmaking* 2(2): 125–50.

Everett, Anna. 2002. "The Revolution will be Digitized: Afrocentricity and the Digital Public Sphere." *Social Text* 20(2): 125–46.

Federal Trade Commission. 2019. "FTC Imposes $5 Billion Penalty and SweepingNew PrivacyRestrictions on Facebook."July24. https://www. ftc.gov/news-events/press-releases/2019/07/ftc-imposes-5-billion-pen alty-sweeping-new-privacy-restrictions.

Florini, Sarah. 2014. "Tweets, Tweeps, and Signfiyin': Communication and Cultural Performance on 'Black Twitter.'" *Television and New Media* 15(3): 223–37.

Florini, Sarah. 2019a. *Beyond Hashtags: Racial Politics and Black Digital Networks.* New York: New York University Press.

Florini, Sarah. 2019b. "Enclaving and Cultural Resonance in Black Game of Thrones fandom." *Journal of Transformative Works and Cultures* (29). https://journal.transformativeworks.org/index.php/twc/ article/view/1498/2161.

Fojas, Camilla. 2021. *Border Optics: Surveillance Cultures on the US–Mexico Frontier.* New York: New York University Press.

Fordyce, Robbie, Neale, Timothy, and Apperley, Thomas. 2018. "Avatars: Addressing Racism and Racialized Address," in Kishonna L. Gray and David J. Leonard (eds), *Woke Gaming: Digital Challenges to Oppression and Social Injustice.* Seattle: University of Washington Press, 231–51.

Foucault, Michel. 1977. *Discipline and Punish: The Birth of the Prison.* New York: Vintage Books.

Fox, Jeremy C. 2019. "Brown University Student Mistakenly Identified as Sri Lanka Bombing Suspect." *Boston Globe*, April 28. https://www. bostonglobe.com/metro/2019/04/28/brown-student-mistaken-iden-tified-sri-lanka-bombings-suspect/0hP2YwyYi4qrCEdxKZCpZM/ story.html.

Frankel, Todd. 2016. "The Cobalt Pipeline: Tracing the Path from Deadly Hand-dug Mines in Congo to Consumers' Phones and Laptops." *Washington Post*, September 30. https://www.washingtonp

ost.com/graphics/business/batteries/congo-cobalt-mining-for-lithium-ion-battery/.

Fraser, Nancy. 1990. "Rethinking the Public Sphere: A Contribution to the Critique of Actually Existing Democracy." *Social Text* (25/26): 56–80.

Fredrickson, George M. 1989. *The Arrogance of Race: Historical Perspectives on Slavery, Racism, and Social Inequality.* Middleton, CT: Wesleyan University Press.

Gaboury, Jacob. 2013. "A Queer History of Computing." *Rhizome,* February 19. https://rhizome.org/editorial/2013/feb/19/queer-computing-1/.

Gaertner, David. 2015. "Indigenous in Cyberspace: CyberPowWow, God's Lake Narrows, and the Contours of Online Indigenous Territory." *American Indian Culture and Research Journal* 39(4): 55–78.

Garcia, Sandra E. 2017. "The Woman Who Created #MeToo Long Before Hashtags." *New York Times,* October 20. https://www.nytimes.com/2017/10/20/us/me-too-movement-tarana-burke.html.

Garvie, Clare, Bedoya, Alvaro, and Frankle, Jonathan. 2016. *The Perpetual Line-Up: Unregulated Police Face Recognition in America.* Georgetown Law Center on Privacy and Technology, October 18. https://www.perpetuallineup.org/.

Gee, Buck, Peck, Denise, and Wong, Janet. 2015. *Hidden in Plain Sight: Asian American Leaders in Silicon Valley.* New York: The Ascend Foundation.

Gillespie, Tarleton. 2010. "The Politics of 'Platforms.'" *New Media and Society* 12(3): 347–64.

Gladwell, Malcolm. 2010. "Small Change: Why the Revolution Will Not be Tweeted." *New Yorker,* September 27. https://www.newyorker.com/magazine/2010/10/04/small-change-malcolm-gladwell.

Glitsos, Laura and Hall, James. 2019. "The Pepe the Frog Meme: An Examination of Social, Political, and Cultural Implications through the Tradition of the Darwinian Absurd." *Journal for Cultural Research* 23(4): 381–95.

Gonzalez, Daniel. 2019. "Logistical Borderlands: Latinx Migrant Labor in the Information Age." *Society+Space.*

Gorski, Paul C. 2019. "Fighting Racism, Battling Burnout: Causes of Activist Burnout in US Racial Justice Activists." *Ethnic and Racial Studies* 42(5): 667–87.

Gorwa, Robert. 2019. "What is Platform Governance?" *Information, Communication and Society* 22(6): 854–71.

Grady, Constance. 2017. "How 'On Fleek' Went from a 16-year-old's Vine to the Denny's Twitter Account." *Vox*, March 28. https://www. vox.com/culture/2017/3/28/14777408/on-fleek-kayla-lewis-ihop-dennys-vine-twitter-cultural-appropriation.

Graham, Roderick and Smith, Shawn. 2016. "The Content of our #Characters: Black Twitter as Counterpublic." *Sociology of Race and Ethnicity* 2(4): 433–49.

Gramsci, Antonio. 1971. *Selections from Prison Notebooks*. London: Lawrence and Wishart.

Gray, Kishonna L. 2012. "Intersecting Oppressions and Online Communities: Examining the Experiences of Women of Color in Xbox Live." *Information, Communication and Society* 15(3): 411–28.

Gray, Kishonna. 2020a. *Intersectional Tech: Black Users in Digital Gaming*. Baton Rouge: Louisiana State University Press.

Gray, Kishonna L. 2020b. "Black Gamers' Resistance," in Lori Kido Lopez (ed.), *Race and Media: Critical Approaches*. New York: New York University Press, 241–51.

Green, Venus. 2012. "Flawed Remedies: EEOC, AT&T, and Sears Outcomes Reconsidered." *Black Women, Gender + Families* 6(1): 43–70.

Gross, Nora. 2017. "#IfTheyGunnedMeDown: The Double Consciousness of Black Youth in Response to Oppressive Media." *Souls* 19(4): 416–37.

Gunkel, David J. 2020. *Introduction to Communication and Artificial Intelligence*. Medford, MA: Polity.

Gutierrez, Arcelia. 2020. "Situating Representation as a Form of Erasure: #OscarsSoWhite, Black Twitter, and Latinx Twitter." *Television and New Media* 1–19.

Haas, Angela M. 2007. "Wampum as Hypertext: An American Indian Intellectual Tradition of Multimedia Theory and Practice." *Studies in American Indian Literatures* 19(4): 77–100.

Hadden, Sally E. 2001. *Slave Patrols: Law and Violence in Virginia and the Carolinas*. Cambridge, MA: Harvard University Press.

Hamilton, Mary. 2012. "#1reasonwhy: The Hashtag that Exposed Games Industry Sexism." *Guardian*, November 8. theguardian.com/technology/gamesblog/2012/nov/28/games-industry-sexism-on-twitter.

Hargittai, Eszter. 2012. "Open Doors, Closed Spaces? Differentiated Adoption of Social Network Sites by User Background," in Lisa Nakamura and Peter Chow-White (eds), *Race after the Internet*. New York: Routledge, 223–45.

Harmon, Amy. 2019. "Discussing Blackness on Reddit? Photograph Your Forearm First." *New York Times*, October 8. https://www.nytimes.com/2019/10/08/us/reddit-race-black-people-twitter.html.

Harrison, Sara. 2019. "Five Years of Tech Diversity Reports – and Little Progress." *Wired*, October 1. https://www.wired.com/story/five-years-tech-diversity-reports-little-progress/.

Heath, Alex. 2021. "Rise of the Super App." *Verge*, November 1. https://www.theverge.com/22738395/social-media-super-app-facebook-wechat-shopping.

Heaven, Will Douglas. 2020. "Predictive Policing Algorithms are Racist. They Need to be Dismantled." *MIT Technology Review*, July 17. https://www.technologyreview.com/2020/07/17/1005396/predictive-policing-algorithms-racist-dismantled-machine-learning-bias-criminal-justice/.

Hegde, Radha. 2014. "Food Blogs and the Digital Reimagination of South Asian Diasporic Publics." *South Asian Diaspora* 6(1): 89–103.

Hill, Kashmir. 2020a. "The Secretive Company That Might End Privacy as We Know It." *New York Times*, January 18. https://www.nytimes.com/2020/01/18/technology/clearview-privacy-facial-recognition.html.

Hill, Kashmir. 2020b. "Wrongfully Accused by an Algorithm." *New York Times*, June 24. https://www.nytimes.com/2020/06/24/technology/facial-recognition-arrest.html.

Hinzo, Angel M. and Clark, Lynn Schofield. 2019. "Digital Survivance and Trickster Humor: Exploring Visual and Digital Indigenous Epistemologies in the #NoDAPL Movement." *Information, Communication and Society* 22(6): 791–807.

Ho, Fred and Mullen, Bill V. 2008. *Afro Asia: Revolutionary Political and Cultural Connections between African Americans and Asian Americans*. Durham, NC: Duke University Press.

Hoffman, Kelly, Trawalter, Sophie, Axt, Jordan R., and Oliver, M. Norman. 2016. "Racial Bias in Pain Assessment and Treatment Recommendations, and False Beliefs about Biological Differences between Blacks and Whites." *Proceedings of the National Academy of Sciences of the US* 113(6): 4296–301.

Howard, Brian and Sundust, Mikhail. 2020. *COVID-19: The Impact of Limited Internet Access and Issues with Social Distancing for Native Students*. Phoenix: American Indian Policy Institute. https://aipi.asu.edu/sites/default/files/indigenous_digital_divide_policy_brief.pdf.

Hu, Jane. 2020. "The Second Act of Social-Media Activism." *New Yorker*, August 3. https://www.newyorker.com/culture/cultural-comment/the-second-act-of-social-media-activism.

Hu, Margaret. 2013. "Biometric ID Cybersurveillance." *Indiana Law Journal* 88(4): 1475–558.

Hu, Margaret. 2020. "Cambridge Analytica's Black Box." *Big Data and Society* 7(2): 1–6.

Hummel, Patrik, Braun, Matthias, Tretter, Max, and Dabrock, Peter. 2021. "Data Sovereignty: A Review." *Big Data and Society* 1–17.

Ince, Jelani, Rojas, Fabio, and Davis, Clayton A. 2017. "The Social Media Response to Black Lives Matter: How Twitter Users Interact with Black Lives Matter through Hashtag Use." *Ethnic and Racial Studies* 40(11): 1814–30.

Ireland, Danyelle T., Freeman, Kimberley Edelin, Winston-Proctor, Cynthia E., DeLaine, Kendra D., Lowe, Stacey McDonald, and Woodson, Kamilah M. 2018. "(Un)Hidden Figures: A Synthesis of Research Examining the Intersectional Experiences of Black Women and Girls in STEM Education." *Review of Research in Education* 42: 226–54.

Irom, Bimbisar. 2018. "Virtual Reality and the Syrian Refugee Camps: Humanitarian Communication and the Politics of Empathy." *International Journal of Communication* 12: 4269–91.

Iseke, Judy M. 2011. "Indigenous Digital Storytelling in Video: Witnessing with Alma Desjarlais." *Equity & Excellence in Education* 44(3): 311–29.

Jackson, Ronald L. 2006. *Scripting the Black Masculine Body: Identity, Discourse, and Racial Politics in Popular Media.* New York: State University of New York Press.

Jackson, Sarah J. and Welles, Brooke Foucault. 2015. "Hijacking #MYNYPD: Social Media Dissent and Networked Counterpublics." *Journal of Communication* 65(6): 932–52.

Jackson, Sarah J., Bailey, Moya, and Wells, Brooke Foucault. 2020. *#Hashtag Activism: Networks of Race and Gender Justice.* Cambridge, MA: MIT Press.

Johnson, Derek. 2014. "Figuring Identity: Media Licensing and the Facialization of LEGO Bodies." *International Journal of Cultural Studies* 17(4): 307–25.

Johnson-Jennings, Michelle, Jennings, Derek, and Little, Meg. 2019. "Indigenous Data Sovereignty in Action: The Indigenous Food Wisdom Repository." *Journal of Indigenous Wellbeing* 4(1): 26–38.

Jurkowitz, Mark and Vogt, Nancy. 2013. "On Twitter: Anger Greets the Zimmerman Verdict." *Pew Research Center*, July 17. https://www.pew research.org/fact-tank/2013/07/17/on-twitter-anger-greets-the-zimme rman-verdict/.

Kang, EunKyo, Lee, Jihye, Kim, Kyae Hyung, and Yun, Young Ho. 2020. "The Popularity of Eating Broadcast: Content Analysis of 'Mukbang' YouTube Videos, Media Coverage, and the Health Impact of 'Mukbang' on Public." *Health Informatics Journal* 26(3): 2237–48.

Kang, Jerry. 1999. "Cyber-Race." *Harvard Law Review* 113: 1130–208.

Katz, Yarden. 2020. *Artificial Whiteness: Politics and Ideology in Artificial Intelligence.* New York: Columbia University Press.

Kearney, Mary Celeste. 2015. "Sparkle: Luminosity and Post-girl Power Media." *Continuum: Journal of Media & Cultural Studies* 29(2): 263–73.

Kelly, Annie. 2016. "Children as Young as Seven Mining Cobalt Used in Smartphones, Says Amnesty." *Guardian*, January 18. https://www.theguardian.com/global-development/2016/jan/19/children-as-young-as-seven-mining-cobalt-for-use-in-smartphones-says-amnesty.

Keyes, Os, Stevens, Nikki, and Wernimont, Jacqueline. 2019. "The Government Is Using the Most Vulnerable People to Test Facial Recognition Software." *Slate*, March 17. https://slate.com/technology/2019/03/facial-recognition-nist-verification-testing-data-sets-children-immigrants-consent.html.

Koenecke, Allison, et al. 2020. "Racial Disparities in Automated Speech Recognition." *Proceedings of the National Academy of Sciences* 117(14): 7684–9.

Kreitz, Kelley. 2017. "Toward a Latinx Digital Humanities Pedagogy: Remixing, Reassembling, and Reimagining theArchive." *Educational Media International* 54(4): 304–16.

Kroeber, Karl. 2008. "Why It's a Good Thing Gerald Vizenor is Not an Indian." In Gerald Vizenor (ed.), *Survivance: Narratives of Native Presence.* Lincoln: University of Nebraska Press. 25–38.

Kukutai, Tahu and Taylor, John. 2016. *Indigenous Data Sovereignty: Toward an Agenda.* Canberra: Australian National University Press.

Kumanyika, Chenjerai. 2017. "Livestreaming in the Black Lives Matter Network," in Amber Day (ed.), *DIY Utopia: Cultural Imagination and the Remaking of the Possible.* Lanham: Lexington Books, 169–88.

Kuo, Rachel. 2016. "Racial Justice Activist Hashtags: Counterpublics and Discourse Circulation." *New Media and Society* 20(2): 495–514.

Kwok, Irene and Wang, Yuzhou. 2013. "Locate the Hate: Detecting Tweets against Blacks." *Proceedings of the Twenty-Seventh AAAI Conference on Artificial Intelligence.* Bellevue, WA.

Land, Jacqueline. 2021. "'Since Time Im-MEME-morial!': Indigenous Meme Networks and Fan-Activism." *Journal of Cinema and Media Studies* 60(2): 181–6.

Landau, Elizabeth. 2020. "Tech Confronts Its Use of the Labels 'Master' and 'Slave.'" *Wired*, July 6. https://www.wired.com/story/tech-confronts-use-labels-master-slave/.

LaPensée, Elizabeth A., Laiti, Ouiti, and Longboat, Maize. 2021. "Towards Sovereign Games." *Games and Culture* 17(3): 1–16.

Leavitt, Peter A., Covarrubias, Rebecca, Perez, Yvonne A., and Fryberg, Stephanie A. 2015. "'Frozen in Time': The Impact of Native American Media Representations on Identity and Self-Understanding." *Journal of Social Issues* 71(1): 39–53.

Lee, Nicol Turner, Resnick, Paul, and Barton, Genie. 2019. *Algorithmic Bias Detection and Mitigation: Best Practices and Policies to Reduce Consumer Harms.* May 22. https://www.brookings.edu/research/algorithmic-bias-detection-and-mitigation-best-practices-and-policies-to-reduce-consumer-harms/.

Leonard, David J. 2006. "Not a Hater, Just Keepin' It Real: The Importance of Race- and Gender-Based Game Studies." *Games and Culture* 1(1): 83–8.

Lidchi, Henrietta and Fricke, Suzanne Newman. 2019. "Future History: Indigenous Futurisms in North American Visual Arts." *World Art* 9(2): 99–102.

Light, Jennifer. 1999. "When Computers Were Women." *Technology and Culture* 40(3): 455–83.

Lindsey, Treva B. 2015. "Post-Ferguson: A 'Herstorical' Approach to Black Violability." *Feminist Studies* 41(1): 232–7.

Lips, Allison. 2018. "History of Hashtags: How a Symbol Changed the Way We Search & Share." *Social Media Week*, February 20. https://socialmediaweek.org/blog/2018/02/history-hashtags-symbol-changed-way-search-share/.

Lopez, Lori Kido. 2016. "Asian American Food Blogging as Racial Branding: Rewriting the Search for Authenticity," in Shilpa Dave, Tasha Oren and LeiLani Nishime (eds), *Global Asian American Popular Cultures*. New York: New York University Press, 151–64.

Lopez, Lori Kido. 2020. "Racism and Mainstream Media," in Lori Kido Lopez (ed.), *Race and Media: Critical Approaches*. New York: New York University Press, 13–26.

Lung-Amam, Willow. 2017. *Trespassers? Asian Americans and the Battle for Suburbia*. Berkeley: University of California Press.

MacCallum-Stewart, Esther. 2008. "Real Boys Carry Girly Epics: Normalising Gender Bending in Online Games." *Eludamos. Journal for Computer Game Culture* 2(1): 27–40.

Madsen, Deborah L. 2017. "The Mechanics of Survivance in Indigenously Determined Video-Games: Invaders and Never Alone." *Transmotion* 3(2): 79–110.

Maghbouleh, Neda. 2020. "From White to What? MENA and Iranian American Non-White Reflected Race." *Ethnic and Racial Studies* 43(4): 613–31.

Magnet, Shoshana Amielle. 2011. *When Biometrics Fail: Gender, Race, and the Technology of Identity*. Durham, NC: Duke University Press.

Mallapragada, Madhavi. 2014. *Virtual Homelands: Indian Immigrants and Online Cultures in the United States*. Urbana, IL: University of Illinois Press.

Maragh-Lloyd, Raven. 2020. "Black Twitter as Semi-Enclave," in Lori Kido Lopez (ed.), *Race and Media: Critical Approaches*. New York: New York University Press, 163–77.

Matamoros-Fernández, Ariadna. 2017. "Platformed Racism: The Mediation and Circulation of an Australian Race-based Controversy on Twitter, Facebook and YouTube." *Information, Communication & Society* 20(6): 930–46.

Mattoni, Alice. 2017. "A Situated Understanding of Digital Technologies in Social Movements: Media Ecology and Media Practice Approaches." *Social Movement Studies* 15(4): 494–505.

McCracken, Allison, Cho, Alexander, Stein, Louisa, and Hoch, Indira Neill (eds.).2020. *A Tumblr Book: Platform and Cultures*. Ann Arbor, MI: University of Michigan Press.

McGee, Ebony O. and Robinson, William H. 2019. "Introduction," in Ebony O. McGee and William H. Robinsonn (eds), *Diversifying STEM : Multidisciplinary Perspectives on Race and Gender*. New Brunswick: Rutgers University Press, 1–16.

McGinn, Conor. 2020. "Why Do Robots Need a Head? The Role of Social Interfaces on Service Robots." *International Journal of Social Robotics* 12: 281–95.

McIlwain, Charlton. 2017. "Racial Formation, Inequality, and the Political Economy of Web Traffic." *Information, Communication and Society* 20(7): 1073–89.

McIlwain, Charlton. 2019. *Black Software: The Internet and Racial Justice, from the AfroNet to Black Lives Matter*. Oxford: Oxford University Press.

McPherson, Tara. 2000. "I'll Take My Stand in Dixie-Net: White Guys, the South, and Cyberspace," in Beth E. Kolko, Lisa Nakamura and Gilbert B. Rodman (eds), *Race in Cyberspace*. New York: Routledge, 117–32.

Mejia, Robert. 2016. "The Epidemiology of Digital Infrastructure," in Safiya Umoja Noble and Brendesha Tynes (eds), *The Intersectional Internet: Race, Sex, Class, and Culture Online*. New York: Peter Lang, 229–42.

Menand, Louis. 2001. "Morton, Agassiz, and the Origins of Scientific Racism in the United States." *Journal of Blacks in Higher Education* 34: 110–13.

Mendes, Kaitlynn, Ringrose, Jessica, and Keller, Jessalynn. 2018. "#MeToo and the Promise and Pitfalls of Challenging Rape Culture through Digital Feminist Activism." *European Journal of Women's Studies* 25(2): 236–46.

Microsoft. 2016. "Learning from Tay's Introduction." *Official Microsoft Blog*. March 25. https://blogs.microsoft.com/blog/2016/03/25/learni ng-tays-introduction/.

Miner, Joshua D. 2021. "Ethnographic Photobomb: The Materiality of Decolonial Image Manipulation." *International Journal of Cultural Studies* 24(3): 414–433.

Monk-Payton, Brandy. 2017. "#LaughingWhileBlack: Gender and the Comedy of Social Media Blackness." *Feminist Media Histories* 3(2): 13–35.

Moreau, Sophia. 2010. "What is Discrimination?" *Philosophy and Public Affairs* 38(2): 143–79.

Nakamura, Lisa. 2002. *Cybertypes: Race, Ethnicity, and Identity on the Internet*. New York: Routledge.

Nakamura, Lisa. 2008. "Cyberrace." *Modern Language Association of America* 123(5): 1673–82.

Nakamura, Lisa. 2013a. "'It's a Nigger in Here! Kill the Nigger!' User-Generated Media Campaigns Against Racism, Sexism, and Homophobia in Digital Games," in Angharad Valdivia (ed.), *The International Encyclopedia of Media Studies*. Hoboken: Wiley, 1–15.

Nakamura, Lisa. 2013b. "Glitch Racism: Networks as Actors within Vernacular Internet Theory." *Culture Digitally*, December 10. https:// culturedigitally.org/2013/12/glitch-racism-networks-as-actors-within-vernacular-internet-theory/.

Nakamura, Lisa. 2014. "Indigenous Circuits: Navajo Women and the Racialization of Early Electronic Manufacture." *American Quarterly* 66(4): 919–41.

Nakamura, Lisa. 2019. "Gender and Race in the Gaming World," in Mark Graham, William H. Dutton and Manuel Castells (eds), *Society and the Internet: How Networks of Information and Communication are Changing Our Lives*. Oxford: Oxford University Press, 127–45.

Nakamura, Lisa, Stiverson, Hanah, and Lindsey, Kyle. 2021. *Racist Zoombombing*. New York: Routledge.

Nature Staff. 2020. "Henrietta Lacks: Science Must Right a Historical Wrong." *Nature Editorial*, September 1. https://www.nature.com/articles/d41586-020-02494-z.

Needhidasan, Santhanam, Samuel, Melvin, and Chidambaram, Ramalingam. 2014. "Electronic Waste – An Emerging Threat to the Environment of Urban India." *Journal of Environmental Health Science and Engineering* 12(36).

Neff, Gina and Nagy, Peter. 2016. "Talking to Bots: Symbiotic Agency and the Case of Tay." *International Journal of Communication* 10: 4915–31.

Nelsen, R. Arvid. 2017. "Race and Computing: The Problem of Sources, the Potential of Prosopography, and the Lesson of Ebony Magazine." *IEEE Annals of the History of Computing*, 29–51.

Nelson, Alondra (ed.). 2002. "Afrofuturism: An issue of Social Text." *Social Text* 20(2): 1–70.

Nelson, Alondra. 2016. *The Social Life of DNA: Race, Reparations, and Reconciliation After the Genome*. Boston: Beacon Press.

Nelson, Alondra, Tu, Thuy Linh N., and Hines, Alicia Hedlam (eds). 2001. *Technicolor: Race, Technology, and Everyday Life*. New York: New York University Press.

Nelson, Libby. 2016. "Why the Anti-Defamation League Just Put the Pepe the Frog Meme on its Hate Symbols List." *Vox*, September 28. https://www.vox.com/2016/9/21/12893656/pepe-frog-donald-trump.

Nielsen. 2020. *Engaging Asian American Consumers at the Dawn of a New Decade*. New York: Nielsen Company.

Nishi, Naomi W., Marias, Cheryl E., and Montoya, Roberto. 2015. "Exposing the White Avatar: Projections, Justifications, and the Ever-evolving American Racism." *Social Identities* 21(5): 459–73.

Nishime, LeiLani. 2017. "Whitewashing Yellow Futures in Ex Machina, Cloud Atlas, and Advantageous : Gender, Labor, and Technology in Sci-fi Film." *Journal of Asian American Studies* 20(1): 22–49.

Nixon, Lindsay. 2016. "Visual Cultures of Indigenous Futurisms." *GUTS Magazine*, May 22. http://gutsmagazine.ca/visual-cultures/.

Noble, Safiya Umoja. 2018a. *Algorithms of Oppression: How Search Engines Reinforce Racism*. New York: New York University Press.

Noble, Safiya Umoja. 2018b. "Close-Up: Black Images Matter: Critical Surveillance Literacy in Social Media: Interrogating Black Death and Dying Online." *Black Camera: An International Film Journal* 9(2): 147–60.

Noble, Safiya Umoja and Roberts, Sarah T. 2019. "Technological Elites, the Meritocracy, and Postracial Myths in Silicon Valley," in Sarah Banet-Weiser, Roopali Mukherjee and Herman Gray (eds), *Racism Postrace*. Durham, NC: Duke University Press, 113–34.

Noel, Urayoán. 2019. "The Queer Migrant Poetics of #Latinx Instagram." *New Literary History* 50(4): 531–57.

Norman, Natasha. 2020. "'Blackout Tuesday' on Instagram was a Teachable Moment for Allies Like Me." *NBC Think*, June 6. https://www.nbcnews.com/think/opinion/blackout-tuesday-instagram-was-teachable-moment-allies-me-ncna1225961.

Omi, Michael and Winant, Howard. 1986. *Racial Formation in the United States*. New York: Routledge.

Onwuamaegbu, Natachi. 2021. "TikTok's Black Dance Creators are on Strike." *Washington Post*, June 25. https://www.washingtonpost.com/lifestyle/2021/06/25/black-tiktok-strike/.

Panne, Valerie Vande. 2021. "Tribal Broadband as a Cyber Superhighway to Sovereignty." *Native News Online*, March 28. https://nativenewsonline.net/business/tribal-broadband-as-a-cyber-superhighway-to-sovereignty.

Pao, Ellen. 2017. *Reset: My Fight for Inclusion and Lasting Change*. New York: Spiegel and Grau.

Pardes, Arielle. 2018. "The Wired Guide to Emoji." *Wired*, February 1. https://www.wired.com/story/guide-emoji/.

Park, Lisa Sun-Hee and Pellow, David N. 2004. "Racial Formation, Environmental Racism, and the Emergence of Silicon Valley." *Ethnicities* 4(3): 403–24.

Parks, Lisa. 2015. "'Stuff You Can Kick': Toward a Theory of Media Infrastructures," in Patrik Svensson and David Theo Goldberg (eds), *Between Humanities and the Digital*. Cambridge, MA: MIT Press, 355–73.

Pasquale, Frank. 2015. *The Black Box Society: The Secret Algorithms That Contol Money and Information*. Cambridge: Harvard University Press.

Peckham, Matt. 2013. "The Geography of US Hate, Mapped Using Twitter." *Time*, May 20.

Perrin, Andrew and Duggan, Maeve. 2015. *Americans' Internet Access: 2000–2015*. *Pew Research Center*, June 26. https://www.pewresearch.org/internet/2015/06/26/americans-internet-access-2000-2015/.

Pitti, Stephen J. 2002. *The Devil in Silicon Valley: Northern California, Race, and Mexican Americans*. Princeton, NJ: Princeton University Press.

Plantin, Jean-Christophe and Punathambekar, Aswin. 2019. "Digital Media Infrastructures: Pipes, Platforms, and Politics." *Media, Culture and Society* 41(2): 163–74.

Qureshi, Sadiah. 2004. "Displaying Sara Baartman, the 'Hottentot Venus.'" *History of Science* 42(2): 233–57.

Ramirez, Catherine S. 2008. "Afrofuturism/Chicanafuturism: Fictive Kin." *Aztlan: A Journal of Chicano Studies* 33(1): 185–94.

Reges, Stuart. 2018. "Why Women Don't Code." *Quillette*, June 19. https://quillette.com/2018/06/19/why-women-dont-code/.

Richardson, Allissa V. 2020. *Bearing Witness While Black: African Americans, Smartphones, and the New Protest #Journalism*. Oxford: Oxford University Press.

Richardson, Rashida, Schultz, Jason M., and Southerland, Vincent M. 2019. *Litigating Algorithms 2019 US Report: New Challenges to Government Use of Algorithmic Decision Systems*. New York: AI Now Institute.

Ritterfield, Ute, Cody, Michael, and Vorderer, Peter. 2009. *Serious Games: Mechanisms and Effects*. New York: Routledge.

Rivera, Takeo. 2017. "Ordering a New World Orientalist Biopower in World of Warcraft: Mists of Pandaria," in Lori Lopez and Vincent T. Pham (eds), *The Routledge Companion to Asian American Media*. New York: Routledge, 195–208.

Roberts, Dorothy. 2011. *Fatal Invention: How Science, Politics, and Big Business Re-Create Race in the 21st Century*. New York: New Press.

Roberts, Sarah T. 2016. "Commercial Content Moderation: Digital Laborers' Dirty Work," in Safiya Umoja Noble and Brendesha M. Tynes (eds), *The Intersectional Internet: Race, Sex, Class and Culture Online*. New York: Peter Lang, 147–60.

Roberts, Sarah T. 2019. *Behind the Screen: Content Moderation in the Shadows of Social Media*. New Haven, CT: Yale University Press.

Rodriguez-Lonebear, Desi. 2016. "Building a Data Revolution in Indian Country," in Tahu Kukutai and John Taylor (eds), *Indigenous Data Sovereignty: Toward an Agenda*. Canberra: Australian National University Press, 253–72.

Roh, David S., Huang, Betsy, and Niu, Greta A. 2015. "Technologizing Orientalism: An Introduction," in David S. Roh, Betsy Huang, and Greta A. Niu (eds), *Techno-Orientalism: Imagining Asia in Speculative Fiction, History, and Media*. New Brunswick, NJ: Rutgers University Press, 1–22.

Rollefson, J. Griffith. 2008. "The 'Robot Voodoo Power' Thesis: Afrofuturism and Anti-Anti-Essentialism from Sun." *Black Music Research Journal* 28(1): 83–109.

Rose, Adam. 2010. "Are Face-Detection Cameras Racist?" *Time*, January 22. http://content.time.com/time/business/article/0,8599,195 4643,00.html.

Rosenblatt, Kalhan. 2019. "On Twitch, Women who Stream Say Their Biggest Obstacle is Harassment." *NBC News*, September 29. https://www.nbcnews.com/tech/internet/twitch-women-who-stream-say-their-biggest-obstacle-harassment-n1060016.

Ross, Aaron and Lewis, Barbara. 2019. "Congo Mine Deploys Digital Weapons in Fight against Conflict Minerals." *Reuters*, October 1. https://www.reuters.com/article/us-congo-mining-insight/congo-mine-deploys-digital-weapons-in-fight-against-conflict-minerals-idUSKBN1WG2W1.

Roth, Lorna. 2009. "Looking at Shirley, the Ultimate Norm: Colour Balance, Image Technologies, and Cognitive Equity." *Canadian Journal of Communication* 34(1): 111–36.

Rowe, Robyn K., Bull, Julie R., and Walker, Jennifer D. 2021. "Indigenous Self-Determination and Data Governance in the Canadian Policy Context," in Maggie Walter, Tahu Kukutai, Stephanie Russo Carroll and Desi Rodriguez-Lonebear (eds), *Indigenous Data Sovereignty and Policy*. London: Routledge, 81–98.

Russworm, TreaAndrea M. and Blackmon, Samantha. 2020. "Replaying Video Game History as a Mixtape of Black Feminist Thought." *Feminist Media Histories* 6(1): 93–118.

Saini, Angela. 2019. *Superior: The Return of Race Science*. Boston, MA: Beacon Press.

Saito, Natsu Taylor. 2020. *Settler Colonialism, Race, and the Law: Why Structural Racism Persists*. New York: New York University Press.

Salles, Arleen, Evers, Kathinka, and Farisco, Michele. 2020. "Anthropomorphism in AI." *AJOB Neuroscience* 11(2): 88–95.

Salminen, Joni, Almerekhi, Hind, Milenkovic, Milica, et al. 2019. "Anatomy of Online Hate: Developing a Taxonomy and Machine Learning Models for Identifying and Classifying Hate in Online News Media." *Proceedings of the Twelfth International AAAI Conference on Web and Social Media*. Stanford, CA.

Schlesinger, Ari, O'Hara, Kenton, and Taylor, Alex S. 2018. "Let's Talk about Race: Identity, Chatbots, and AI." *Conference on Human Factors in Computing Systems*. Montreal. 1–14.

Schultheiss, Sebastien and Lewandowski, Dirk. 2021. "How Users' Knowledge of Advertisements Influences their Viewing and Selection Behavior in Search Engines." *Journal of the Association for Information Science and Technology* 72: 285–301.

Scott, Mark. 2021. "Social Media Companies Remove Less Hate Speech in 2021." *Politico*, October 7. https://www.politico.eu/article/facebook-google-hate-speech-social-media-european-commission-transparency/.

Scully, Pamela and Crais, Clifton. 2008. "Race and Erasure: Sara Baartman and Hendrik Cesars in Cape Town and London." *Journal of British Studies* 47: 301–23.

Seetharaman, Deepa, Scheck, Justin, and Horwitz, Jeff. 2021. "Facebook Says AI Will Clean Up the Platform: Its Own Engineers Have Doubts." *Wall Street Journal*, October 17. https://www.wsj.com/articles/facebook-ai-enforce-rules-engineers-doubtful-artificial-intelligence-11634338184.

Shah, Niral. 2019. "'Asians Are Good at Math' Is Not a Compliment: STEM Success as a Threat to Personhood." *Harvard Educational Review* 89(4): 661–87.

Shaw, Adrienne. 2010. "What is Video Game Culture? Cultural Studies and Game Studies." *Games and Culture* 5(4): 403–24.

Shaw, Adrienne. 2014. *Gaming at the Edge: Sexuality and Gender at the Margins of Gamer Culture.* Minneapolis, MN: University of Minnesota Press.

Shiri, Ali, Howard, Deanna, and Farnel, Sharon. 2021. "Indigenous Digital Storytelling: Digital Interfaces Supporting Cultural Heritage Preservation and Access." *International Information and Library Review.* doi:https://doi.org/10.1080/10572317.2021.1946748.

Siapera, Eugenia and Viejo-Otero, Paloma. 2020. "Governing Hate: Facebook and Digital Racism." *Television and New Media* 22(2): 112–30.

Skardzius, Karen. 2018. "Playing with Pride: Claiming Space through Community Building in World of Warcraft," in Kishonna L. Gray and David J. Leonard (eds), *Woke Gaming: Digital Challenges to Oppression and Social Injustice.* Seattle: University of Washington Press, 175–92.

Skawennati. n.d. "A Chatroom is Worth a Thousand Words." *CPW2K,* http://www.cyberpowwow.net/STFwork.html.

Skloot, Rebecca. 2010. *The Immortal Life of Henrietta Lacks.* New York: Crown.

Smith, Diane E. 2016. "Governing Data and Data for Governance: The Everyday Practice of Indigenous Sovereignty," in Tahu Kukutai and John Taylor (eds), *Indigenous Data Sovereignty: Toward an Agenda.* Canberra: Australian National University Press, 117–35.

Spangler, Todd. 2021. "GoFundMe Teams With Director Bao Nguyen for '#StopAsianHate Together' Film With Olivia Munn, Ken Jeong and More." *Variety,* April 14. https://variety.com/2021/digital/news/gofundme-stopasianhate-together-olivia-munn-ken-jeong-bao-nguyen-1234951186/#!

Squires, Catherine R. 2002. "Rethinking the Black Public Sphere: An Alternative Vocabulary for Multiple Public Spheres." *Communication Theory* 12(4): 446–68.

Squires, Catherine R. 2014. *The Post-Racial Mystique: Media and Race in the Twenty-First Century.* New York: New York University Press.

Srauy, Sam and Cheney-Lippold, John. 2019. "Realism in FIFA? How Social Realism Enabled Platformed Racism in a Video Game." *First Monday* 24(6).

St Felix, Doreen. 2015. "Black Teens Are Breaking the Internet and Seeing None of the Profits." *Fader*, December 3. https://www.thefader.com/2015/12/03/on-fleek-peaches-monroee-meechie-viral-vines.

StatCounter Global Stats. 2021. *Search Engine Market Share Worldwide.* May. https://gs.statcounter.com/search-engine-market-share#monthly-200901-202105.

Steele, Catherine Knight. 2022. *Digital Black Feminism.* New York: New York University Press.

Stephens, Monica. 2013. *The Geography of Hate.* May 10. http://www.floatingsheep.org/2013/05/hatemap.html.

Strong, Myron T. and Chaplin, Sean. 2019. "Afrofuturism and Black Panther." *Contexts* 18(2): 58–9.

Sutherland, Tonia. 2017. "Making a Killing: On Race, Ritual, and (Re) Membering in Digital Culture." *Preservation, Digital Technology, and Culture* 46(1): 32–40.

Sweeney, Miriam E. 2016. "The Intersectional Interface," in Safiya Emoja Noble and Brendehsa M. Tynes (eds), *The Intersection Internet: Race, Sex, Class, and Culture Online.* New York: Peter Lang, 215–28.

Sweeney, Miriam E. 2017. "The Ms. Dewey 'Experience': Technoculture, Gender, and Race," in Jesse Daniels, Karen Gregory, and Tressie McMillan Cottom (eds), *Digital Sociologies.* Bristol: Policy Press, 401–20.

Sweeney, Miriam and Whaley, Kelsey. 2019. "Technically White: Emoji Skin-Tone Modifiers as American Technoculture." *First Monday* 24(7). doi:http://dx.doi.org/10.5210/fm.v24i7.10060.

Takasaki, Karen. 2020. "Stop AAPI Hate Reporting Center: A Model of Collective Leadership and Community Advocacy." *Journal of Asian American Studies* 23(3): 341–51.

TallBear, Kim. 2013. *Native American DNA: Tribal Belonging and the False Promise of Genetic Science.* Minneapolis: University of Minnesota Press.

Taylor, Taryne Jade. 2020. "Latinxs Unidos: Futurism and Latinidad in United States Latinx Hip-Hop." *Extrapolation* 61(1–2): 29–51.

The Sentencing Project. 2018. *Report to the United Nations on Racial Disparities in the US Criminal Justice System.* Washington, DC.

TikTok. 2021. "One Year Later: Our Commitment to Diversity and Inclusion." *TikTok*, June 23. https://newsroom.tiktok.com/en-us/one-year-later-our-commitment-to-diversity-and-inclusion.

Tiku, Nitasha. 2020. "Tech Companies are Asking their Black Employee Groups to Fix Silicon Valley's Race Problem – Often for Free." *Washington Post*, June 26. https://www.washingtonpost.com/technolo gy/2020/06/26/black-ergs-tech/.

Time Staff. 2015. "Here's Donald Trump's Presidential Announcement Speech." *Time*, June 16. https://time.com/3923128/donald-trump-announcement-speech/.

Trawalter, Sophie, Hoffman, Kelly M., and Waytz, Adam. 2012. "Racial Bias in Perceptions of Others' Pain." *PLOS* 7(11): 1–8.

Tsosie, Rebecca. 2021. "The Legal and Policy Dimensions of Indigenous Data Sovereignty," in Maggie Walter, Tahu Kukutai, Stephanie Russo Carroll, and Desi Rodriguez-Lonebear (eds), *Indigenous Data Sovereignty and Policy*. London: Routledge, pp. 205–24.

Tu, Fangjing. 2016. "WeChat and Civil Society in China." *Communication and the Public* 1(3): 343–50.

Turner, K. B., Giacopassi, David, and Vandiver, Margaret. 2006. "Ignoring the Past: Coverage of Slavery and Slave Patrols in Criminal Justice Texts." *Journal of Criminal Justice Education* 17(1): 181–95.

Twine, France Winddance. 2018. "Technology's Invisible Women: Black Geek Girls in Silicon Valley and the Failure of Diversity Initiatives." *International Journal of Critical Diversity Studies* 1(1): 58–79.

United States Census Bureau. 2018. "Five-Year Trends Available for Median Household Income, Poverty Rates and Computer and Internet Use." December 6. https://www.census.gov/newsroom/press-releases/2018/2013-2017-acs-5year.html/.

US Equal Employment Opportunity Commission. 2014. *Diversity in Tech*. Washington, DC: Special Report. https://www.eeoc.gov/special-report/diversity-high-tech.

Van Dijk, Jan. 2020. *The Digital Divide*. Cambridge, UK: Polity.

Van Noorden, Richard. 2020. "The Ethical Questions that Haunt Facial-Recognition Research." *Nature*, November 18. https://www.nature.com/articles/d41586-020-03187-3.

Varma, Roli. 2002. "High-Tech Coolies: Asian Immigrants in the US Science and Engineering Workforce." *Science as Culture* 11(3): 337–61.

Varma, Roli. 2007. *Harbingers of Global Change: India's Techno-Immigrants in the United States*. Minneapolis: Lexington Books.

Vassallo, Trae, Levy, Ellen, Madansky, Michele, et al. 2017. *Elephant in the Valley*. Palo Alto, CA: Women in Tech.

Villa-Nicholas, Melissa. 2016. "The Invisible Information Worker: Latinas in Telecommunications," in Safiya Umoja Noble and

Brendesha M. Tynes (eds), *The Intersectional Internet: Race, Sex, Class, and Culture Online*. New York: Peter Lang, 195–214.

Villa-Nicholas, Melissa. 2019. "Latinx Digital Memory: Identity Making in Real Time." *Social Media and Society* 5(4): 1–11.

Villa-Nicholas, Melissa. 2020. "Data Body Milieu: The Latinx Immigrant at the Center of Technological Development." *Feminist Media Studies* 20(2): 300–4.

Vincent, James. 2016. "UN Condemns Internet Access Disruption as a Human Rights Violation." *Verge*, July 4. https://www.theverge.com/2016/7/4/12092740/un-resolution-condemns-disrupting-internet-access.

Vizenor, Gerald. 2008. *Survivance: Narratives of Native Presence*. Lincoln, NE: University of Nebraska Press.

Wakabayashi, Daisuke and Conger, Kate. 2021. "Google Wants to Work with the Pentagon Again, Despite Employee Concerns." *New York Times*, November 3. nytimes.com/2021/11/03/technology/google-pentagon-artificial-intelligence.html.

Walter, Maggie. 2016. "Data Politics and Indigenous Representation in Australian Statistics," in Tahu Kukutai and John Taylor (eds), *Indigenous Data Sovereignty: Toward an Agenda*. Canberra: Australian National University Press, 79–97.

Warner, Kristen. 2015. "ABC's Scandal and Black Women's Fandom," in Elana Levine (ed.), *Cupcakes, Pinterest, and Ladyporn: Feminized Popular Culture in the Early Twenty-First Century*. Champaign, IL: University of Illinois Press, 32–50.

Warwick, Kevin, and Huma Shah. 2016. "Can Machines Think? A Report on Turing Test Experiments at the Royal Society." *Journal of Experimental and Theoretical Artificial Intelligence* 28(6): 989–1007.

Washington, Anne and Kuo, Rachel. 2020. "Whose Side are Ethics Codes On?" *Proceedings of ACM Fairness Accountability Transparency Conference*. Barcelona: ACM. 1–10.

Washington, Harriet A. 2006. *Medical Apartheid: The Dark History of Medical Experimentation on Black Americans from Colonial Times to the Present*. New York: Doubleday.

Watkins, S. Craig. 2018. "How Black and Latino Youth are Remaking the Digital Divide," in S. Craig Watkins, Andres Lombana-Bermudez, Alexander Cho, et al. (eds), *The Digital Edge: How Black and Latino Youth Navigate Digital Inequality*. New York: New York University Press, 19–49.

Williams, Dmitri, Martins, Nicole, Consalvo, Mia, and Ivory, James D. 2009. "The Virtual Census: Representations of Gender, Race and Age in Video Games." *New Media and Society* 11(5): 815–34.

Williams, Jennifer. 2019. "The Erasure of Virtual Blackness: An Ideation About Authentic Black Hairstyles in Speculative Digital Environments." *Journal of Future Studies* 24(2): 37–46.

Williams, Stacie M. and Drake, Jarrett M. 2017. "Power to the People: Documenting Police Violence in Cleveland." *Journal of Critical Library and Information Studies* 1(2): 1–27.

Witkowski, Wallace. 2021. "Videogames are a Bigger Industry than Movies and North American Sports Combined, Thanks to the Pandemic." *MarketWatch*, January 2. https://www.marketwatch.com/story/videogames-are-a-bigger-industry-than-sports-and-movies-combined-thanks-to-the-pandemic-11608654990.

Woodhouse, Taylore. 2021. "Live Streaming and Archiving the Hegemony of Play." *Popular Culture Studies Journal* 9(2): 20–38.

Wu, Ellen. 2016. "The Invention of the Model Minority," in Cindy I-Feng Cheng (ed.), *The Routledge Handbook of Asian American Studies*. New York: Routledge, 285–301.

Yeung, Karen and Lodge, Martin (eds). 2019. *Algorithmic Regulation*. Oxford: Oxford University Press.

Yu, Ning, Chen, Feng-Chi, Ota, Satoshi, et al. 2002. "Larger Genetic Differences Within Africans Than Between Africans and Eurasians." *Genetics* 161(1): 269–74.

Zamalin, Alex. 2019. *Antiracism: An Introduction*. New York: New York University Press.

Zimmerman, Arely. 2016. "Transmedia Testimonio: Examining Undocumented Youth's Political Activism in the Digital Age." *International Journal of Communication* 10: 1886–906.

Index